Who Stole My India?

Amit Reddy grew up and (as his dad bemoans) grew rotten in the no-longer-Bangalore of the eighties and nineties. His first, and only, paying job was that of a copywriter for an advertising firm in Hyderabad, where at the end of four years he'd become quite adept at lying and living it up. He's spent the last decade trying to distance himself from the two unfortunate talents by alternately traveling off the beaten track and gaining an education. Armed with a master's in literary nonfiction from the Royal Melbourne Institute of Technology, a master's in public policy from Georgetown University, and a year's worth of travel stories, *Who Stole My India?* is his maiden attempt at writing something Real.

Who Stole My India?

Revelations, Humiliations, and Hallucinations on Two Wheels

Amit Reddy

KARMA YATRI PUBLISHING

KARMA YATRI
:: www.karmayatri.com ::

Published by Amit Reddy
MLA Colony, Banjara Hills,
Hyderabad, India
www.amitreddy.com

Maps by Karma Yatri Publishing

Printed in Hyderabad at Pragati Offset Pvt. Ltd.
First Printing: 2014

Trade paperback ISBN 978-93-5156-823-0

For further information, or to purchase this book, please visit:
www.whostolemyindia.com

For Those Who Made the Journey Possible

Chapters

Amit's Terrible Drawing of Kaya's Route

How can you wonder your travels do you no good, when you carry yourself around with you? You are saddled with the very thing that drove you out.

Socrates

A change of character, not a change of air, is what you need.

Seneca

What On Earth Is My India?

THE ROAD NEVER ENDS, only our vision does.

The road, unfortunately, isn't aware of this profound observation. This morning I set out on a 40,075 kilometer motorcycle journey around India. Having completed 287 of them, the highway I'm following suddenly goes AWOL. The road didn't unexpectedly turn unpaved – it already was. It didn't get any worse – there's no way it possibly could. It simply isn't there anymore.

If I didn't know roads better I'd suggest this one went for a swim. How else do you explain a trail leading right up to the river bank, and . . . well, that's when it appears to have gone amphibious. One instant I'm bouncing along an unfriendly road, and the next, I'm standing at the edge of an unfriendly river. I glare at the turbulent waters and gesticulate with outstretched hands like in the movies. No, the waters don't part for me.

'Any suggestions, TT?' I sigh at the end of a ponderous minute.

'How about some coconut water, machaa?' he replies promptly. 'I saw a vendor a few meters back.'

The coconut shop is a patch of shade under the tree from which the coconuts come. In the shade sits a young man, all lean muscle, his skin dark and weathered. His eyes gleam under a turbaned head. A farmer with no machinery, a tree climber with no rope, a salesman without a store. He is the multi-tasking citizen of rural India.

'Where are you going?' he questions, deftly hacking into the coconuts with a heavy blade.

'Chhattisgarh,' I reply, 'we must have taken a wrong turn somewhere.'

'No, no, this is the correct route.'

'But there's no road ahead.'

'Nothing to worry about, it continues on the other side.'

'*Ah!* But it looks like there's a river in between,' I scoff. 'And bikes have the tendency to head downwards in water, rather than forwards.'

'No, no,' he insists, ignoring my sarcasm. 'A boat shuttles across to Sironcha town few times a day, carrying people, two wheelers and sometimes cattle.'

'What about bigger vehicles?' I ask, not entirely convinced.

'There is a road, but you have to head back along the path you just came and take the long way round. Take the boat. Really, there's nothing to worry about.'

Machaa, if you're painting a mental picture of docks and ferries I suggest reining in your imagination. Please remember that this story is set in India. Before us is a sandy river bank, which post monsoons will be a sandy river bed. The boat is . . . a boat, as depicted in the drawings of an untalented four-year-old; a bunch of planks held together by a few rusty nails and a whole lot of wishful thinking. To get Kaya aboard, we need to lift her over our shoulders, step into thigh-high water, and then haul her onto the boat.

'*Arre saab*, nothing to worry about,' the captain assures me. 'We'll lift it like *this*,' he snaps his fingers to indicate how simple an endeavor it is.

As it turns out, there's a lot to worry about. And though I do hear a few snaps during the procedure, none emanate from his reassuring fingers. Kaya is a deceptively heavy bike, all the more so with the extra racks and baggage. TT, el capitano, his first mate, and I are standing in the water attempting to heave Kaya over the boat edge when her weight shifts to one side. We manage to get her under control before she topples over, but from the pained expressions around me I can tell we won't be able to hold her up for long. Magically, four extra arms make an appearance, and then four more, like one of our multi-armed Hindu deities. It's our co-passengers coming to the rescue. With the extra help we lift Kaya vertically and hook the front tire over the edge, then those of us in the river push the rear end while others on board drag her up.

A roar of approval sweeps through the boat when both her tires rest firmly on the deck. Those who helped us slap each other's backs and grin triumphantly. Onlookers tease and congratulate them. They joke about how much more difficult the unloading is going to be. None seem to care that they are splattered with mud and water, all on account of two silly strangers and one fat motorcycle. I smile sheepishly at them, grateful for the help.

I cling tightly to a precariously swaying Kaya while the boat putters slowly to the other side of the river. As we make our way across, the sun disappears in shades of orange and pink; hues mirrored by the murky water. The faces around me are animated and radiant. They look at us – half amused, half curious. A warm sense of satisfaction courses through me. For the first time that day I feel real exhilaration. I'm crossing my Rubicon and from here there can be no turning back.

I'm no Hero. I'm no Rebel. Nor am I trying to be either. All I want is to belong. Well, I also think it will help knowing what exact it is that I belong to. Along with an irrepressible horde of dysfunctional genes, my parents have bequeathed me two other equally dysfunctional influences – nationality and religion – which apparently are more important than my genes. Tell me, has anyone ever come up to you and said, 'Hey there, if you're a XXX chromosomal, we'll provide you with an AK-47 and the opportunity to die for our cause.' So from what I've gathered, where we're from and who we pray to pretty much defines who we are.

I was born an Indian. I was born a Hindu. I haven't a clue what it means to be either. I'm a stranger in a familiar land. I've got a lot of belief, but no faith to put it in. I've got a lot of questions, but no answers to fit them. If we are a nation of farmers, why are we driving them to collective suicide? If we think motherhood is divine, then why has womanhood become a curse? Why is killing a cow reprehensible, but burning alive the cow-eater an acceptable way to spend Sunday? Why are all our patriots queuing up at the American Consulate? And why does my mum think I should join the line?

'You should go away to America,' mummy dear keeps insisting. 'You are nothing like an Indian.'

It's all so frightfully confusing, but I intend to rectify this situation. The plan is ingenious, and quite simple. I'm going to explore India like few people ever have, by taking an inordinately long journey around the country; 40,075 kilometers long, to be precise. Just Kaya – my soul on two wheels – and me, and anyone who wants to hop on for a ride, like my pal TT here. If everything goes accordingly, by the end of this journey I hope to be the complete Indian.

To begin with, though, not only do I have to mud-wrestle my own fears and doubts, I have to appease those of my family as well. This family includes my parents, my cousins, my parents' cousins, uncles, aunts, an aunt's uncle, mom's friends, the neighbors, and the neighbor's sister in Toronto. None of them come close to comprehending my motivations, but they unanimously agree that I'm throwing my life away, regardless of whether I survive the journey or not.

Proximately, they fear for my life. Bandits roam the countryside of Bihar. The highways of Bengal are pot-holed death traps. Kashmir is full of terrorists. Tamil Nadu is full of Tamils. Shimla is petrifyingly cold, Gujaratis are nauseatingly sweet, as is their food, and nobody can understand those Malayalis, not even with the assistance of a Babel fish.

'This is our country you're talking about,' I repeatedly pointed out. 'There are foreigners, young men and women, backpacking all over the place.'

'Yes, but they are foreigners,' my mum stressed. 'Indians will never hurt foreigners,' she continued with what sounded oddly like pride.

Ostensibly, we Indians only treat our own kind badly.

Ultimately, the well-wishers fear for my future. What kind of a career move is this? Who quits a good job, unless it's for a better paying one? You can't put 'traveled around the country' on a CV, and it most definitely doesn't belong in a marriage proposal.

'What is wrong with this boy?' an exasperated uncle spluttered. 'Why can't he behave more like an Indian?'

So, even before the journey had begun, I'd learnt my first lesson about India: travel does not fit into our way of life. Nor did the irony of the situation escape me. My very path to Indianness had deemed me un-Indian.

'Machaa,' TT interrupts my thoughts, 'we're almost there.'

The boat slows down, and as it approaches the opposite bank I catch sight of the path again.

See, the road never ends . . . only our vision does.

LEG ONE

I Don't Like Tourists

KAYA HEADED OUT from Sironcha at dawn, having spent the night at this small town on the opposite bank of our river crossing. A wretched gravel trap led us through a dry, unhealthy forest. The trees were bare and lifeless. Kaya's tires crunched over the gravel. Dust bellowed in our wake. It was no man's land. There were no men around. There were no women, animals or birds either. Silence, except for the rhythmic beat of Kaya's heart. Occasionally her rear tire thumped into the mudguard. A stone zinged off the path.

'Are you sure this is the right route, machaa?' TT shouted.

'Why don't you look at the map?' I replied, eating dirt.

The rustle of paper. Curses. A moment of thoughtful silence. 'Fuck me, machaa. According to this piece-of-shit map we should have reached Jagdalpur thirty fucked-up kilometers ago. It shows a thick black line all the way from fucking Hyderabad, which even goes over the fucking rivers.'

Quite early in the game I learned not to trust mapmakers and weathermen; 'cartographer' and 'meteorologist' are just pretentious names for a gang of incompetent monkeys who pretend that make-it-up-as-you-go-along is an exact science. If you ask me, the metaphorical monkey producing the complete works of Shakespeare almost surely has a greater probability of success.

'Maps: Don't use them,' TT pronounces gravely, 'but always carry one, even if it's of the wrong country. They make you look professional.'

We were mostly at the mercy of locals, who being fortunate enough to have never seen a map were essentially more competent. But this only increased the chance of finding the correct route by an infinitesimally small margin. While asking for directions in India, it is always preferable to get second opinions. Thirds aren't a bad idea either. When all of them provided conflicting information, I just smiled, and continued riding in whatever direction Kaya was pointing.

After hours of nothingness we came upon an old man tilling a parched field. TT asked him of our whereabouts. He waved a stick at us, indicating he didn't care about our whereabouts as long as it was somewhere else. Well, at least we knew we were back in the real world. Gravel gave way to tar, and night replaced day. The moon and stars watched over us as we rode into Jagdalpur, twenty-four hours later than calculated.

Kaya came to a halt before Narayan Reddy's house.

We are greeted by the loud cackle of hens. Narayan, a poultry farmer, is an obscure relation of mine that someone dug out of the weighty family directory. I've never heard of him before, but that's okay, because he's never heard of me either.

'What took you so long?' he asks, as we settle down to dinner.

Momentarily it is ascertained that we have strayed from the ordained path, by a substantially large margin of error.

'But . . . but we followed the thickest line on the map,' I mutter in defense.

'You should be glad you made it at all.' Narayan shakes his head disapprovingly. 'The route you came through is notorious for robberies and abductions. Occasionally people are even blown up by land mines. The forest is full of Naxalites and—'

'Enough talk. Let the boys eat,' Mrs. Reddy interrupts what is clearly a touchy subject. 'Try the *rasagollas*. They are the best in India.'

'Everyone says the Bengali *rasagollas* are the best,' I observe.

'Hah, that's just lies, all marketing. Try our *rasagollas* and see.'

An hour and many *rasagollas* later we take a tour of their poultry. Holding one of the helplessly cheeping chicks in my palm, I can't help wonder at the absurdity of the ongoing bird flu scare. Every time one of these delicate little chaps coughs, the powers that be start to shit. The United Nations System Coordinator for Avian and Human Influenza warns the world that an outbreak of avian influenza could kill anywhere between 5 and 150 million people. The hen as an apocalyptic force. And all this time I was foolishly worrying about meteor strikes, global warming, and George W. Bush.

'What do you think about the bird flu?' I ask Narayan.

'I think nothing of it,' he replies, disdainfully brushing the notion aside. 'These are all problems created by foreigners. Chickens have been with us for thousands of years and we've never had trouble with them. Did you know the chicken comes from India?'

'Say how.'

'We were the first people to domesticate it,' he nods with proprietary pride. 'This bird-flu shird-flu will not affect us in India.'

Kilometer 591

The cackle of hens escorted Kaya as she rode out of Narayan's house the next morning. Less than a year later, an outbreak of the bird-flu virus was discovered in these parts. More than a million birds were culled within weeks. If it's any consolation to Narayan, he was right on one count. Indians really were the first people to cohabit with the fowl.

A clear and radiant sky. A sun-baked world, with rolling hills and green forests. Kaya wandered deep into Bastar, deep into Central India's tribal belt, still home to a larger tribal population than anywhere else in the world – the Bhil, Gond, Oraon, Santhal, Birhor. People with ancient rituals, bedecked in animal parts, performing bizarre dances, who think the television is magic and prefer to exist in nature. Sounds remarkably similar to everyone else I know, except for the existing in nature part.

Sixty years ago the tribes were much larger, but they had no place in the vision of the future. Mainstream India's view of its tribal subjects is personified by how the politically incorrect, and predictably insensitive, Ministry of Tribal Affairs characterizes them: people of '*primitive* traits' who are 'economically *backward*'. Since independence we've regularly provided them the opportunity to sacrifice their communities and their customs on the altar of development. Our dams, a.k.a. the temples of modern India, have become the tombs of their traditional worlds, submerging their past and their future. To extract 'our natural resources' we have usurped their natural homes, rending their forests and their lands from under them.

Between 1951 and 1991 more than 85 lakh tribals have been forcibly removed from their ancestral homelands to join the ranks of a new-age tribe: Internally Displaced People. It's remarkable how the land required for the 'greater common good' just happened to be occupied by the least common people. So, despite being only eight percent of the population, the Scheduled Tribes account for nearly half of all displacement, and less than one in four of those displaced have received proper resettlement or rehabilitation. Since 1991, economic liberalization has involved the further liberation of STs from their lands, only this time it's in support of the greater corporate good.

Having destroyed their world in the name of national growth, we've done little to help them grow in ours. A cursory glance at NFHS data reveals that national development has left the scheduled tribes languishing at the bottom of every human development indicator.* We've replaced their traditional resources with modern poverty. We've stolen their forests and handed them slums. We've taken away their freedom and shackled them with democracy – the tyranny of the majority.

The river Indravati emerged from the forest, shimmering white in the midday sun, intermittently running alongside us before disappearing into the thicket. Back in 1966, supported by Pravir Chandra Bhanj Deo, the last Maharaja of Bastar, the tribals had risen in revolt against the Congress government. In response, the Maharaja and a number of protesters were killed by the police, outside his Jagdalpur palace, in a shootout – though by all appearances only one side did the shooting. The government claims that the Maharaja was hit by mistake. But seeing that he died from multiple bullet wounds, it begs the question: what exactly did they mistake him for so many times?† The official report states that 12 tribals were killed during the 'incident', but locals insist hundreds died that day. The bodies were supposedly dumped into the river beside us.

---

* That glance will also show trends of deteriorating health and socio-economic status of tribal populations compared to national figures. Infant mortality among tribal populations is 50 percent higher than the national average; under five mortality, 30 percent higher. Almost 80 percent of ST children suffer from malnutrition, and they are twice as likely to have no access to drinking water. While one in four Indians fall below our miserly national poverty line, in tribal regions like Bastar, the number is closer to one in two.

† Before declaring him a people's martyr, it should be noted that the Maharaja had his own axe to grind with the Congress, having been deposed by the government. He also suffered from a distinct case of megalomania, as discerned from the title of his biography: 'I Pravir – The Adivasi God'.

Forty-five kilometers beyond Jagdalpur, Kaya came to a grinding halt.

Here the Indravati plummets down a wide crescent moon gorge as the Chitrakoot Falls. Owing to its width, it has earned the sobriquet 'Niagara of India', which is like comparing me to Superman because I wear red jocks and never get laid. That aside, Chitrakoot offers a human element that no Niagara can. And I'm not talking about busloads of tourists.

Surrounded by dense jungles, the red rock face rises 96 feet above a churning green pool, marked by ragged ledges. Hidden behind a shimmering curtain of water, nature has sculpted a series of yawning caves. For reasons known only to them, sages have found peace on these ledges and prayer in these caves. Over time we've turned men into magicians, legends into myth, and caves into temples.

We follow the locals, as they gingerly climb down the precarious cliff face, the waterfall thundering beside us – one slip and we plunge down with it. Crouching on the ledges or disappearing into caves, people pray to a bunch of odd-shaped rocks. The stones are marked by sacred vermillion, adorned with flowers, offered fruit and coin. They are imbued with faith.

Some of the caves are occupied by sadhus. Now where there's a sadhu, there's a *chillum* waiting to be lit. We find a suitably cheerful candidate and sit down beside him to share his herbal wisdom. He has a well-used *chillum* with him. We have unused marijuana with us. We are well met. I proffer the sacred plant and he starts the sacred ritual. Meanwhile, two other devotees of

Mary Jane join our circle. One of them is middle-aged, the other much older.

'Hello. Where are you from?' I ask.

'Where are you from?' the older man throws right back at me.

'Uh . . . Hyderabad.'

'Are you tourists?' his tone suggests the answer better be to his liking.

'Nooo!'

'I don't like tourists.' He appraises me purposefully, probably concluding that I'm harmless. 'We aren't animals in a zoo for you to stare at,' he adds finally.

Boom Bholenath!

Boom Shankar! The *chillum* burns red.

Kaya rumbled through the tribal circuit, the wind whipping against my face, glimpses of our artifice searing my mind. With the tourist industry's discovery of the tribes of India, quite suddenly, these long disparaged communities had become glamorous; descriptive words like 'uncivilized' and 'anti-development' were replaced by 'exotic' and 'sustainable'. We had embraced the global phenomenon of tribal tourism, and just like that, the most marginalized societies in the country were pushed into the limelight. Did it occur to anyone to ask the tribes for their opinion on the matter?

The signs were everywhere – Chhattisgarh, Orissa, Gujarat – always advertising the same lie: 'a real tribal experience'. Joining the action, at first I struggled to understand tribal tourism. Then I wished I hadn't. Age-old tribal rituals were now being ritualized for my viewing. The dances once performed for gods were performed for me. Celebrations that once had to be earned were now a means of earning. A real experience of staying with the tribes came with mineral water, a choice of cuisine, and luxury tents, if you so please. Settlements had taken on the appearance of tourist camps, and over the weekend we tourists could play being-a-tribal. I'd wanted to observe a way of life as these people lived it, instead they were leading a way of life so that I could observe it.

We'd turned life into theatre. What was natural had become an act, as real as reality television, and the tribals had become actors, playing roles they needed to. I saw a lot of them, and fortunately, got to know a few: like the bare-chested youth at the Bonda market who laughed that he'd rather be wearing a shirt like me, but then 'nobody wants to buy stuff from a fully-clothed tribal'; like the tattooed woman in the Kondh village who didn't like being photographed, but was told it was good for the local economy; like the old man in Araku who was distressed that his modernized – brick and plaster – home was considered an eye sore by tour operators.

And where are the economic benefits that tourism was supposedly bringing? Why do the tribal regions encompassed by the tourism circuits continue to be the most neglected, lacking basic amenities like drinking water, healthcare centers, and sanitation? Am I a cynic in believing it behooves the powers-that-be to maintain the status quo; after all, why would we visit the tribes if they lived like us? How much of the 4,347 crores generated by tourism in Orissa in 2011 has made its way to these parts? By commoditizing their culture, mainstream India has simply found a new way to exploit its tribes.

It has been pointed out that the Bonda who poses for a photograph or the Kondh who let you into their homes have done so out of choice. And what of those who've chosen not to participate? Do they have the power to prevent camera-happy tourists from flooding their markets? Will they get justice against the forest officer who forces them to dance for visitors? Can they stop the tourist road from passing through their lands? How do they resist an economic order that has relentlessly encroached on their world? Let me point out that leaving a person with no alternative is not the same as giving him a choice.

What we've done is turn them into objects of display. Perhaps it's apt that these tours are called 'tribal safaris', animals in a zoo as the old man said. The old man and his companion were from the tribe of Gonds (a disappointing revelation, really, seeing how they were dressed like my neighbors). Popular for the Ghotul system of marriage, wherein adolescent boys and girls live together in dormitories until they pick their partners, the Gonds attracted droves of gawking visitors, myself included.

It's not surprising he didn't like tourists.

Kilometer 825

The road was lonely. It was moody. Mostly unkind, it led Kaya through tangled wilderness, sometimes green, otherwise dry. The hills rippled upward, occasionally domed, intermittently craggy. Though I didn't realize it then, this was the topography of revolution. The paths of red earth before me branched like arteries into India's heart of darkness.

A lone khaki-clad cop stood to the side of the road, leaning against a motorcycle. Kaya drew to a halt.

'*Sab kuch theek hain*, sir,' TT enquires as we approach him. That's when I notice a second cop, peeing in the bush.

'Yes, yes, and how about you?'

'Oh, we just needed a break, my entire body is aching. This road has destroyed me.'

'Ha, ha! Where are you boys coming from?'

'Bastar.'

'And you're tired already! Where do you have to go?'

'We're trying to get to Kanger,' TT replies, going on to enthusiastically describe the adventure we're on. In the meantime the pissing cop, his job completed, joins our little circle.

'Why do you want to go to Kanger, it is unsafe,' he advises us gravely. 'Besides there's nothing there, nothing other than adivasis and Naxals, not even a decent road.'

Kaya kicked up the earth as she sped onwards. The two cops waved from behind the red veil of dust. And as they grew smaller in the rear-view mirror I recollected a similar conversation with Narayan Reddy. 'There's no development happening in the area,' he'd groaned angrily, 'not even roads, because every time the government takes an initiative, the tribals oppose it. Chhattisgarh would be one of the richest states if the tribals weren't supporting the Naxalites.'

The line between tribal and Naxal had become blurred.

If tribals have become the lifeblood of a resurgent Naxal movement, let's acknowledge our role in this. To do otherwise is to go for a swim and blame the water for getting you wet. For forty years the region existed in the blind spot of our national conscience, a forgotten population braving it out against venal forest officials, repressive security forces, and abusive landlords. Though their motives are debatable, during this period it was the Naxalites who provided the tribes recourse, mobilizing them to claim rightful access to the forests, to demand higher wages, to fight their oppressors. Every time our democracy failed the tribals, which was predictably often, we further legitimized Naxalism.

Having barely survived the socialist decades, the tribals are now being devastated by capitalism in the form of MoU-toting industrialists. The tragedy of the poorest people in the country is that they just happen to own its richest land. The mining industry has displaced two million tribals since 1991, but when they protest this forced impoverishment, they are branded as anti-development and confronted by state-sanctioned intimidation. Mainstream India seems to think it rather inconsiderate of the tribals to be prioritizing homes and lives ahead of GDP figures.

Rather than ideological belief in the 'little red book', it is this new age of exploitation that has driven the region to violence; more people died from insurgency-related incidents in the first four years of this century than in the preceding fifteen.* And it would only get worse. Within weeks of our passing through, Salwa

* 2,571 people were killed between 2001 and 2005 as opposed to the 2,485 people between 1985 and 2000.

Judum – a government-sanctioned, private militia funded by the mining industry – would lead Chhattisgarh down a path of brutality usually restricted to nightmares and African nations. A path marked by scorched villages, rape, pillage, and the use of child soldiers. An estimated 1,50,000 tribals have been forced into refugee camps, and with more than 6,500 casualties, the years since 2005 have been the bloodiest yet. Justifying our acts by arguing that 'the other side has also committed atrocities' is to condemn ourselves.

Today most Indians are aware of Rani Bodi, Dantewada, and Darbha – associating them with carnage and terrorism – but the names meant little to us when TT and I passed through these places. We didn't get kidnapped or shot at. We most definitely didn't hit a landmine. We didn't come across any insurgents, not that we would have known any different if we had. What we came across were people going about life, as best as they could in these remote parts. If there was anger towards us, we didn't feel it. If we were meant to experience fear, we missed it. Mostly we experienced indifference; occasionally, kindness.

Our war against Naxalism has become a war against these people, an opportunity to suppress the tribal struggle for their forests, water, and mountains, and a pretext to grab their lands. Despite the best efforts of the media, the pundits, and our leaders, I cannot bring myself to hate a people fighting for self-preservation.

Kilometer 987

Kaya kept riding. Hills parted to form valleys, forests gave way to farmland. Red mud huts with thatched roofs, small, dark. Windows outlined in white chalk. Fields on either side of the road, the plots mainly dry, a rare few flooded. Bare-chest men, mud running up their legs. Churning the soil. Barefoot women, hands caked in mud. Sowing the soil. The air smelled rich, of earth and toil.

Kaya pulled off the highway and rolled to a halt beside a couple of tea stalls.

I park Kaya and look up. Every head in the vicinity is turned to us. They stare goggle-eyed, jaws dropping to the ground – an expression I'd wear if I ever spotted TT in a library. Before I can register the fact, a bunch of people have gathered around us, and are inching ever closer. It frightens the crap out of me. Not surprising, seeing how it's the first time I've been mobbed.

My fears dissipate as I find myself staring at a dozen yellow-toothed grins. But I'm not the center of their attention. Kaya is. She's the one who's intrigued them. They gather around her at arm's length and begin an animated discussion. I understand so little of what they are saying, they might as well be speaking Elvish. From what I gather by their gestures, they are debating what kind of a creature Kaya is.

'*Yein gaadi Pulsar hain,*' I interrupt hopefully. This causes their jaws to drop even lower.

'You know Hindi,' one of them gasps.

'Yes, I speak Hindi, but what language are you speaking in?'

'Oriya. But most of us can talk Hindi as well. Where are you from?'

'Hyderabad.'

'You are Indians?'

'Of course, do we look otherwise?'

'No, no . . . just asking. So, where are you going?'

'Today up to Vizianagaram.'

'What's there in Vizianagaram?'

'It's only a stopover. Our intention is to travel around the country.'

'By bike???'

'Yes.'

'Till Dilli!'

'Yes, even Delhi.'

'It will take you a whole month.'

'It will take us a whole year.'

At this point they reach the conclusion that we are either mad or deliriously dehydrated and start to funnel liquids down our throat. They offer us water, tea, and the ubiquitous coconut water. In return, we regale them with a summary of our intended expedition. They find the idea extremely intriguing and absolutely pointless.

I could just sit here and chat forever, but the farmers are losing interest in us. It's time to leave, but not without making a suitable impression first. After all, I now have a reputation to protect. I sit astride Kaya and push the electric start button, still a relatively new concept. Her engine roars to life. P.C. Sorcar would kill to elicit the reaction I get. It's sheer magic, machaa.

The road was beautiful. The world continued to be rural. For me 40,000 kilometers represented an experience. For them, it probably symbolized a lifetime. I dreamed of travelling the country because I struggled to understand my place in it. They knew the country only as far as the horizon, but they seemed sure of their place in it. My plans and reasons made little sense to them, and yet they were keen on knowing. What did we have to share with each other? Our differences perhaps, or simply the joy of encountering the unknown.

LEG TWO

Non Hindus Not Allowed

KAYA RODE PAST Lake Chilika in a dreamy blur, turquoise waters dissolving into the distant blue sky. Waves lapped gently against a wooden pier, swaying the bright-hued boats tied to it. Tree-covered islands peeked over the sparkling surface, and palms rose from the green shores. Kaya didn't skip a beat, she cruised, until forced to pull over for a procession on the road.

A group of about seventy men are . . . well, I think they're trying to dance. To me they seem to be enjoying a collective epileptic fit. Indian men and dancing: the two have never actually met. It looks like we're pounding something into the ground, while simultaneously attempting to take off into the sky, resulting in an involuntary pelvic spasm, all of this while biting our lips in a grimace of severe constipation. The ones more Bollywood-inclined perform calisthenics mixed in with a few pelvic thrusts. Neither group follows a beat or rhythm.

The chaps in front of us are the former kind, and they look suitably constipated. At the rear end of the procession a few men shoulder a tacky throne. A man is seated on it, dressed in fine white robes, garlands of fresh flowers, and a princely turban.

'TT, I think it's a wedding procession.'

'That's weird, machaa. It looks like the groom is sleeping.'

I step into the quivering crowd to get a better look. The turbaned head rests limply on its owner's shoulder. Only a man with no sense of survival can fall asleep at his wedding. I inch closer. *What the!* The groom isn't just asleep, he's also tied up. I've heard of forced weddings, but this is ridiculous. As I'm staring, his head rolls off the shoulder and hangs limply from the neck. Machaa, it's a funeral procession. Suddenly, my sympathies went out to him. Being dead must be troubling enough without having to be ridiculed for it.

We run past them and find a discrete position atop a railway bridge to capture the moment on camera without intruding or causing offense. As the mourners approach the bridge, the men dancing at the front of the procession come to a sudden halt. One of them frantically points in our direction and an instant later all of them are staring at us. Seems like our camouflaging skills suck. I hold my breath, expecting indignation, a flurry of abuses, and maybe even aggressive fist waving. Instead we are greeted with a loud cheer, followed by a bout of extra-frenzied gyrations. They are now performing for the cameras. There's an actor hiding within every Indian. Show him a camera, and he can't help acting silly.

I was glad to be back on Kaya and in the process of being somewhere else. They had danced for us till our arms ached from holding the camera, before finally heading on to the cremation grounds. In all that excitement the ropes holding the corpse had come loose and the body half hung off the seat. It didn't seem to trouble people one bit. I learned a valuable lesson that day: there are some things in life worse than death. Like your funeral for one.

Kaya rode hard. She rode long, late into the night, all the way to the shores of Konark.

Kilometer 1938

Dawn had brought with it not only the sun but also his temple at Konark, conceived as the chariot of Surya. Astride our own chariot, we headed to Puri, along forty kilometers of road that hugged the coast. Tall pines grew in dark clumps on one side. Soft white dunes of sand spilled onto it from the other. When the dunes hit a trough, we caught glimpses of bewitchingly blue seas. The wind blew across my face. It carried the scent of great open spaces.

As we entered Puri, from open spaces we were squeezed into crowded streets. The wind carried with it bits of litter and the scent of garam masala. The beach exuded life. Children gaped at the sand sculptures of the Little Mermaid, Ganesha, and King Kong. Pilgrims and hawkers added color to the beach, along with a whole lot of rubbish. Sadhus and locals sat by the sea. Assisted by narcotic substances, they communicated with the gods. The weed burned openly, unapologetically. It burned in the name of religion.

Boom Bholenath! Boom!

Puri is amongst the most sacred places in the country – the trouble with this statement is that over the next few months I was going to come across an endless litany of 'most sacred' places – and the religious fervor of Puri is centered on the ancient Jagannath 'Lord of the Universe' Temple. Conceived between the 11th and 12th centuries, the 4,00,000-square-foot temple complex is dominated by a curvilinear stone tower rising 214 feet over the inner sanctum and protected by 20-foot-high fortified walls. As much a homage to the gods, the temple stands as a celebration of empire.

Kaya came to a halt at the temple's scared entrance, the Lion's Gate.

Relinquishing our bags and shoes at the storage counter, we permit our barefooted selves to be swept along a steady stream of devotees. Just as I am about to pass under the main gateway of the temple, a hand reaches across my chest, bringing me to an abrupt halt. I follow the stray arm to its owner. It belongs to a uniformed security guard, and though I can't see it, I am quite sure the other hand wields a wooden baton.

'Are you Hindu?' he asks me brusquely. While it doesn't surprise me that I'm being singled out for special treatment – with my flowing locks and long beard, I bear a remarkable resemblance to those chaps playing with AK-47s in Taliban training videos – it's the question I resent.

'Yes, I am Hindu, but what does that have to do with anything?'

'Only Hindus are allowed inside.'

'What rubbish are you talking!'

'Go look at the board,' he says, pushing me to the side so the pilgrims behind me can pass through.

Contrary to the general assumption about inanimate objects, signboards frequently unnerve me by how expressive they are. The one I'm staring at right now especially so, looking all smug and purposeful, and a tad sinister I might add. It seems terribly proud to be hanging around here. 'Non Hindus Not Allowed' it announces in stiff no-nonsense letters. Other cultures have put up similarly authoritative signs. Plenty of them were aimed at Jews, and they called it anti-Semitism. Many were targeted at blacks, and they called it apartheid. I wonder what we call this.

'TT, have you seen one of these before?'

'Can't say I have, machaa. I've heard of them, though.'

'They can't be—'

'Where are you from?' a sugary voice interrupts. It belongs to a short, rotund man with glowing cheeks and a shiny pate. He is dressed like a panda – the local priests, not the Chinese bear. A white hand-spun lungi embraces his substantial waist, the knot disappearing behind rolls of flesh. He wears no shirt, a sacred thread runs briefly over the shoulders before getting lost in the thick curls of chest hair. The forehead is marked by vermillion powder. The mouth is stained red from chewing *paan*. His grin is crooked.

'Where are you from?' he repeats.

'Hyderabad,' TT replies.

'I have been there myself. Charminar, very beautiful,' he gushes, casually falling into step with us. 'Come this way with me,' he continues eagerly.

'Where to?'

'The main shrine is this way.'

'We're in no hurry to get there. I want to look around the place.'

'Yes, yes. You see everything, but first you must have *darshan* of the gods and take their blessings. Very, very quickly I will take you to all places and explain important things.'

'Thank you, but I'd much rather be by myself.'

'No, no, it will not be good to be on your own. If they see you alone, some other panda will approach you. You can pay me how much you feel like. I'm an old man. Please.'

The trap has swung shut. His threat of someone else making the pitch isn't a lie either. They are everywhere, his brethren, priests who also serve as escorts. I want to tell him to back off, but I don't. I can try to ignore all of them. I don't do that either. I'm not bold enough. The truth is, I don't know how to deal with these priestly types. I haven't rung too many temple bells in the last decade, but a voice deep within, the voice of childhood parental guidance, tells me I have to respect these men of god. The fear of inappropriate conduct, of causing religious offense, overwhelms me. My eyes drop in resignation, and the panda-guide starts to lead us down the ordained path.

'You must buy flowers.'

'I don't want to.'

'But you must. It is ritual. And you have to get a *tambolam* for the *aarti*.'

'I don't want to participate in any rituals.'

'No, no, listen to my words, son,' he gasps. 'How can you go in front of the God with empty hands?'

I find myself holding a box of greasy sweets as we make our way to the primary sanctum. But first we have to walk past a series of subsidiary shrines, each dedicated to a different god, each with a dedicated priest. In these small, dimly-lit, single-cell chambers, I witness my first miracles. As I step up to them, the chambers magically transform into toll booths. Non-payment meant we wouldn't be able to access the smooth path to salvation. My 'voluntary' donation is never sufficiently generous and it earns a withering look, followed by a curt rebuke. And it isn't just me with a come-rob-me-I-don't-have-a-clue look on my face. It's happening to everyone. If our government learns to extract taxes with such efficiency, we'll soon be threatening American hegemony.

At the entrance to the main sanctum the panda-guide comes to a satisfied halt. 'My job is done. From here you are his responsibility,' he says, handing us over to a senior-panda. Hands folded, he bows at the waist, his head tilting up to gaze at the senior-panda with suitable reverence. 'Only he can take you inside.'

'I don't want anybody to show me inside,' I say in annoyance. 'I can very well see the way.'

'You cannot go inside without me,' senior-panda growls. His voice belongs to dark alleyways, police stations, and the principal's office. Physically he resembles a nightclub bouncer.

'This is ridiculous,' I fight back with false bravado. 'Why do I need a guide to go inside the sanctum?'

'I am not a guide. I am a temple priest.'

'Yes, then why are you . . .' I surrender once again, timidly. Meanwhile, off to the side a loud fight has broken out between two other pandas. They scream into each other's faces, spittle raining off their thick lips. It's harsh and obscene. They sound like bad rappers. Shuffling past, I look at them furtively, disgusted. If this is Orissa's priesthood, what are its politics like?

The sanctum is chaotic. Disturbed as I am, the super-sacred idols are a blur. There is no *hundi* in front of the idol, instead a brass plate beckons us. All offerings are being made in the open. They belong to god for about fifteen seconds and then they disappear. The woman beside me makes an offering of a hundred rupees. Her panda doesn't look pleased.

'What, is that all? You should give more,' he orders. 'This is the holiest of holies, whatever you give here is blessed. How much you give is how much you will be rewarded.'

'B . . . but that's all I have.'

'It's up to you, but if you want to please god . . .' he leaves the threat hanging ominously.

'HOW DARE YOU,' my mouth yells, taking the rest of me by surprise. It also startles the priest it was aimed at and everybody else around us. 'If there is a god, it is you who will be punished. Why, you—'

'Oye, *madhar chodh*,' my panda-guide roars, looming menacingly over me, one fist raised in threat.

'*Kya kar lega be*,' I snap. 'If you are a priest, try behaving like one. Every time you open your mouth you reveal more of your—'

'Shut up, you—' His eyes blaze with murder.

'Let's go,' TT says, stepping in between and pushing me back.

'Yes, take him away,' the priest smirks, waving us aside with a disdainful flick of the wrist. The smile on his face is fuel to my rage. Fortunately, TT's hold on me is strong, and he willfully drags me out. My outburst had brought an awkward pause to the proceedings, but everything is already back to normal. The pilgrims return their attention to the priests. The woman is still there. The pillaging goes on.

'What's gotten into you, machaa?' TT snaps, still holding my arms. His grip is tight. 'You can't talk to a priest like that! You think that woman appreciates what you did? The pilgrims in there would have been the first to maul you, in case of a fight. It's a good thing your Hindi sucks, they probably didn't understand any of it.'

I say nothing in my defense. Everything he said is true, including the slander about my Hindi. I walk out the gate, past the obnoxious sign. The street on which the temple stands is wide and busy. Old cluttered shops cram the opposite side, all of them conducting brisk business. People drone in and out of the temple like bees, faceless and dedicated. Voices come together in seamless discord, then broken by a shrill bicycle bell. A long line of flat-topped carts wait along the side of the road, piled with tropical fruits and global vegetables. Street children scurry about selling flowers with pleading faces. The air carries a hint of jasmine, but mostly it smells of humanity and rot. The road is stained by gobs of saliva and red splats of *paan*.

I walk to where Kaya is resting and get her engine started. I hunker down in the narrow space between Kaya and a red Yamaha, and I listen to her steady beat. Everything else turns into white noise. I listen to her for a long time. I pull out my Leatherman and make a minor adjustment to the fuel intake. I listen to her some more. I tweak her occasionally, but mainly I listen. I need something I can control. I am there for a brief eternity, till I touch a rhythm that feels right.

Kaya rode fast, hoping to outrun the anger. But the dragons chased us; the words on the sign so rich in bigotry, the eyes of the priest so filled with greed. It's not that I wasn't aware of money's influence in a temple. I'd seen it all my life, especially at Tirupati. But what I'd experienced just then was something else. Puri exposed me not only to my own cowardice but also my naivety, and with the latter I lost the very ideals I set out to find. In the months ahead, I faced this bigotry and greed repeatedly. I learned that these were not aberrations; they were the norm. It is one thing to be aware that the corrupt have usurped an idea, but it is shattering to realize that the idea itself is corrupt.

The thievery of priests is in essence viler than that of dacoits. Being robbed by the priesthood leaves you feeling deeply violated, for what they've taken away is not just the material. When a dacoit robs someone with a gun, he targets the person's weakness. But when a priest robs someone with his words, he is targeting what that person believes is his strength: god. After an encounter with a *daaku*, you look to the skies and thank god that you've survived. After a run-in with a priest, you drop your eyes and question this god person. Those meant to be the trustees of faith were robbing the faithful of all trust.

But more than anything, for me, it is the board-sign that caused the greatest disillusion. While the corrupt priest can be viewed as betrayal of religion, the board-sign is betrayal by religion. Non Hindus Not Allowed. It struck at the core of all the prejudices we should be putting behind us. Before I'd set out on this journey, when asked what I'd do in case I found myself in a dire situation, my reply had always been that I'd look for the first temple or mosque or gurdwara or church, or whatever else you might call it, and seek sanctuary behind its sacrosanct walls. It never once occurred to me that it mattered whether I'm circumcised or wear a thread. That sign did not belong in a liberal world. It is hard to respect the institution that put it up. It is even harder to accept that I belong to such an institution.

And this prejudice is not restricted to Hinduism alone. In Lucknow, my entry into the city's famed Jama Masjid would be blocked by a similarly obnoxious sign, only this one said, 'Non Muslims Not Allowed'. Nor was that the last, for the sign would show up often, in all corners of the nation. What remains a mystery to me is why all of them insist on pointing out who isn't welcome, rather than who is. Maybe it's written in some manual that the entire country follows, and we should be pleased that Muslims are showing solidarity by adhering to the same rules of discrimination as Hindus. At least we are united in segregation.

LEG THREE

It's Good Fortune to Die from a Snake Bite

KAYA WENT BOLDLY where no map had been before. At least not the one that we were referring to. There must be more traces of uranium in India than trustworthy maps of the country, though you're quite liable to trip over an excellent one of France. Most of the foreigners I'd come across were travelling with maps of India that made mine look like free-hand drawings. Obviously, they had smuggled theirs in. Still, it was embarrassing to be me. It got so bad I tried stealing one from an Israeli traveler in Vashist but got caught. With my luck, I must have picked a Mossad agent to rob.

Apparently not many roads have been here either. Once we were off the highway, everybody had a different opinion on where Bhitarkanika lay. There were a few who even questioned its very existence, but I chose to ignore them. The road became narrow. No more tar. Just rain-eroded mud, potholed and gutted. The road got narrower still. Kaya took a pounding. We left the villages behind, replaced by a haphazard scattering of meager huts.

Children frolicked in small ponds of chocolaty water adjoining the huts, while young men and women waddled through them, dredging the muddy floor for fish. The only signs that 'civilization' had not completely passed them by were the electricity pylons. The purpose of the pylons, though, escapes me, since of electricity we saw no signs. We saw no signs of squalor and ugliness either. Beauty and poverty. A confusion of emotions.

We were greeted by alternately amazed and amused faces. Each time we stopped for directions, entire families gathered around us, poking, prodding, and laughing. But Bhitarkanika never seemed to get any closer. It was always *bas thoda aage* and *agle gaaon ke baad*. Kilometers did not belong here. The road pounding continued.

And then Kaya reached the gates of Bhitarkanika.

A rusty and peeling sign board confirms our accomplishment. The sign seems lonely, uncared for. The gate itself looks like it hasn't been exercised in a while. There isn't a soul in the forest officer's cottage, so we walk into the dense mangrove, crisscrossed by numerous creeks and contoured mud flats. This hot, humid, and fly-infested swamp is where crocodiles feel at home and Olive Ridley turtles migrate to lay their eggs. When we return to the gate an hour later, soaked like we've walked through a car wash, there is thankfully someone at the office.

'Do you have permission to enter the sanctuary?' the uniformed man asks us.

'Permission? What permission?'

'Have you made a prior reservation?'

'I didn't know about any reservation!'

'Have you made arrangements for the boat ride?' he continues unperturbed.

'What boat are you talking about, sir???'

'You have to make arrangements through an agent before arriving here,' he says, looking at us like we are dangerously stupid. 'Please wait till the senior officer arrives.'

It turns out to be a long wait. Meanwhile, I make another startling discovery. From Bhitarkanika to our next destination we will have to make a boat crossing. Boats! Again! Where the fuck have all the roads gone?

When we finally meet the chief officer, he is all smiles and very hospitable. I tell him about my great adventure and how important it is. He listens attentively.

'So, you really wish to visit the park,' he asks with a courteous smile.

'Yes sir,' I nod eagerly.

'What's the point, there's really no need to.'

'Er . . . excuse me?'

'The season isn't right. It isn't much fun to visit the park now.'

'Oh! I . . . eh, we would still like to.'

'Yes, excellent! But there are no boats now. Maybe tomorrow.'

'Is there any place to stay here?'

'There are some cottages, but very uncomfortable. And there's no food. I tell you, it's not worth the effort.'

'So, what do you suggest we do, sir?' I manage, the conversation having turned surreal.

'I think it's better to keep riding.' He is still smiling.

We decide to follow his suggestion, but first we need to get Kaya on the boat. We wait, squeezed onto a narrow pile of rocks that are trying real hard to look like a jetty. And what should flow before us? Not just another river but the tides of the Bay of Bengal. Once again, my imagination has failed me.

While we wait, an assorted crowd gathers around us. I'm getting more comfortable with it now, beginning to enjoy the attention Kaya draws. Once people recover from the initial surprise of finding regular Indians under the helmets, she becomes the ice breaker. She makes me approachable, and more importantly, worth approaching. Kaya opens the doors to their thoughts, drawing me closer into the circle.

Someone from the crowd offers us bananas, but I barely have the chance to peel back the ripened skin when the now-familiar interrogation commences.

'Which bike is this?'

'Must be going very fast?'

'How much did it cost?'

'Where are you from?'

'Is it same as Allahabad?'

'Where are you going?'

'What??? Are you mad?'

I'm mulling over this accusation when we are interrupted by a commotion behind us. I turn around to see a group of men moving towards us in a tight huddle. As they brush past us on their way down the pretentious rocks, I notice they are carrying a man between them. Within seconds, a larger, more voluble group arrives at the scene. The men seem agitated. The women are in hysterics.

'Arre, what happened?' someone from our group yells out. A flurry of replies fly back at us. 'He is possessed.' 'Something bit him.' 'His wife bit him.' Once the initial excitement subsides, a few calm answers reveal that the man has indeed been bitten, only by a snake. Everyone gathers beside the now-overwhelmed rocks, and that's it, nothing really happens. The victim's body lies limp on a thin cloth spread over the ground. He's bitten in the neck and the puncture is covered with a towel. A thick trail of drool is crusted on the side of his mouth. The men grow more restless. The women start to wail. The body continues to lie as is.

'Is it possible to take him to a hospital by road?' I offer, concerned by the apparent lack of urgency, the inaction. 'We can use my bike.'

'No, there's no doctor nearby. It won't be possible to make it all the way on a bike.'

'What to do then? We can't just sit here waiting,' TT insists.

'Whatever god wills.'

Just then a small boat comes coughing out of nowhere and stops at the rocks. Little is asked. Nothing is said. The body is carefully carried onto the boat and two of the men stay on board. Then the boat turns around and coughs away. No fuss at all. What I'd misunderstood as helplessness is in reality stoic patience. Life can be fragile here, but they give it strength by supporting each other. It is the victim's neighbors that have gone with him on the boat. His wife sits by the rocks, crying. A group of women stand over her watchfully.

'I hope he'll be okay.'

'He's been blessed,' the man standing beside me sighs philosophically. 'He must be dear to the gods.'

'What do you mean?'

'If you must die, it is good fortune to die from a snake bite,' he states simply, like it's the most obvious thing.

It was far into the night before Kaya hit the highway. The boat had dropped us off somewhere on the other side of the watery interruption. This place wasn't on my map either. We rode blindly, my mind pondering over the snake bite theory. Allegedly, for a Hindu an agonizingly venomous death is a good way to meet our maker. Seen as a mark of Shiva, to die from a snake bite is to be purified of all sins; hence, a route to salvation. I considered this for a moment before concluding that I'm happier without attaining salvation, and I most definitely don't want to be favored by any of our gods.*

Kilometer 2991

Kaya didn't sound too good as we continued along the lesser paths. She had taken a beating over the last few days and was

* A recent project — 'The Million Death Study' — has discovered that more than a million Indians suffer from snake bites every year, and around 50 thousand succumb to them; the highest in the world.

starting to show wear. The right thing would have been to stop and have her looked at, but I was fatigued as well, more mentally than physically, and caught up in my own uncertainties, I ignored the signs. The wind screamed in my ear as it whipped by. A trail of dust chased us. The road got ugly, and still I kept pushing.

Kerrrraaang! Screeeech! Kaya's chain has snapped with a violence that sends it tearing through the chain guard. Her rear locks up completely, sending her into a wild slide to the right. She comes to a shuddering halt in the middle of the empty road. Fortunately, moments before the chain let go, we'd slowed down on approaching a T-junction. A minute earlier and we'd have turned into roadspread.

'What the fuck is wrong with you?' TT spits, giving me a push in the back as he jumps off Kaya. 'I've been fucking yelling for you to go easy on her. What were you trying to prove just then?'

I can't look him in the face. What do I tell him? That the adventurer might already have run out of steam. That I'd stayed up all night troubled by doubts, wondering if there was any real purpose to this journey. What if it actually meant nothing, and made no difference? I had given up on a good job and, judging from a recent phone conversation with my girlfriend, on a three year relationship as well. All for nothing? In the end I don't say a word to him. I get off Kaya and lift her onto the center stand. The highway rolls on, uninterrupted by my unraveling. Behind me lay a charted path. Ahead, a world unknown. A small lane shoots off to the west, leading to some insignificant town. The road less taken. A couple of beaten-down tea stalls stand on either side of it. Nothing more. I turn to Kaya. She stands helplessly at the junction, going nowhere. I've let her down.

TT refuses to help, and I'm left dragging Kaya to the side of the road by myself. I have all the tools to fix her, or convert her into a submarine if I so choose, but none of the necessary skills. Getting down on my knees, I unroll the tool bag. It holds spanners in an extravagant array of sizes. I pick up a suitably large one and start to hammer the ground with it. Whack. Whack. Whack. Feeling better, I pick up a size 12 and unscrew the chain guard. I sense someone approach and turn my head. It's a man in crisp grey pants, pastel shirt, and leather slippers. He looks mighty pleased.

'Hello,' he waves enthusiastically.

I ignore him, hoping he'll take the hint and go away. No such luck.

'Is there something wrong with the bike?'

'Yes, the chain is broken,' TT replies.

'Ooh, very bad, very bad. This is a Pulsar, isn't it? I have Pulsar myself. A brand new one. DTS-I technology, very latest.'

'That's nice.'

'You want mechanic. My friend Baiju, he is the very best. He has a Bajaj Service Centre three kilometers from here. He will fix it easily.'

'You're telling me there's a service center nearby!' I gasp, showing a sudden interest. It's beyond belief that there could be one *here*, in the middle of nowhere.

'Yes, there is a big town if you go down this other road.'

'Do you think your mechanic will be able to come here?' I ask hopefully.

'Ah! Let me just check,' my new best friend says, pulling out a shiny new Motorola Slim. It is gold colored.

Baiju the Mechanic doesn't answer the phone. My friend insists this is not a problem. Asking us to wait, he disappears behind the tea stall and returns a minute later riding a pristine new Pulsar. Leaving TT with Kaya, we take the lesser road to Baiju's small town garage. He isn't in. My friend shrugs casually and we proceed to Baiju's house. Baiju's wife answers the door. She wants to know where he is as well.

This doesn't deter my friend one bit. He rides up to another house and starts screaming Baiju's name. Someone replies. It isn't Baiju, but he gets on a scooter and joins in the search. We move on to a different road and a different house. On our fourth attempt, we find Baiju. He has closed shop to sit at a friend's place and watch the live telecast of the India versus Pakistan test series.

'*Bhaiyya, mera gaadi kharab hain, madad chahiye*,' I plead.

'Sorry, I is very busy,' Baiju explains in English.

'Please, you must help me. I am on a journey around the country . . .' I go on to describe the journey we are on, trying to give it a sense of importance I'm not even sure of myself. The speech is frequently interrupted by the usual questions, and some new ones.

'Wow, this really is a special journey,' the television owner exclaims. 'Tell me this, is Bajaj sponsoring your ride?'

'No, they aren't,' I reply. 'We tried, but they said it was against company policy to get involved with outsiders.'

'Arre, very bad they no help,' Baiju shakes his head in disapproval. 'Coming, let's go look you bike.'

And with that, Baiju puts aside the best interests of the Indian batting line-up and comes to Kaya's rescue. Over the next hour he tinkers and tampers with Kaya, tut-tuting at regular intervals. In tandem with his working fingers, he keeps up a constant chatter, curious about every aspect of our journey. At one point he disappears for a brief while, claiming to need a few spares – it is suspiciously close to the final minutes of the day's play. He comes back and tinkers around for another hour. The sun is sinking.

'Is done,' Baiju announces with an air of satisfaction.

'Are you sure everything is alright?'

'Yes, yes, is no problem. But is only temporary.'

'What do you mean temporary?'

'The chain tearing the guard and fully damaged. Gear sprocket also bad. I no have all spares.'

'So, when you say there's no problem . . .'

'Is no problem now,' he smiles reassuringly. 'Some far it will go, but not say surely how much far. Get full check-up in Kolkata.'

Kaya rode slowly, but unerringly.

I listened to her carefully, seeking out any phantom sounds. The night was cold. The wind had a bite. Lightning streaked over our heads, and the night sky rumbled. Traffic was scarce. Reality existed only as far as Kaya's headlight. On both sides the jungle converged on us. It made me realize how kind fate had been to us. For more than a hundred kilometers we saw no town of significance, none that might have a mechanic. In all this available nothingness, Kaya had chosen to break down at the one crossroad where I would meet a Motorola-toting, Pulsar-riding benefactor whose name I never thought to ask, and a carefree, Tendulkar-loving mechanic who refused to charge me for the two hours of his time.

'Is my donation for yous bike ride,' he assured me. 'Is good for mechanic karma.'

LEG FOUR

You Must Try Our Siliguri Weed

KAYA WANDERED AIMLESSLY through the deserted streets of Kolkata, the traffic most noticeable by its absence. The metropolitan of chaos stood still, and silent, like a city under curfew. Shops stayed shut, the shutters rolled down and firmly padlocked. Engines slept, and the city air detoxed. Eighteen million people and not a trace of this swollen population – not even of the city's much-advertised beggars. Kolkata was holding its breath in anticipation of an epic battle.

All eyes were trained on Eden Gardens, feverishly watching their 'Prince', Sourav Ganguly, lead the Indian cricket team onto the field for the final day's play of the India-Pakistan Test. When you think about it, it's not surprising that of all the influences that Colonial Britain brought to India, cricket was the one that we took to heart. Perhaps less applicable today, but historically speaking, sports can reveal a lot about the society that plays them. Some games were never meant to be played by certain people. Take rugby, for example: 170 centimeter tall, non-beef-eating, ahimsa-spouting people have no business, or hope, in a scrimmage. Football doesn't have much scope either, not in a culture that believes touching someone with your feet is sacrilegious. Test cricket, on the other hand, is a sport tailor-made for us.

Test cricket is the truest 'sport' in that it lives up to the definition of the term: leisure, pastime, diversion. It's hard to find a sport that was more leisurely, taking 5 eight-hour days for both teams to amicably conclude that neither of them is good enough to win, or that both of them are too good to lose, depending on how you like to look at things.* Test cricket is singularly suited for populations with high unemployment rates; a forty-hour pastime to replace a forty-hour work week. What better diversion to escape the realities confronting us? Bollywood is just too short.

Test cricket in its heyday required little athleticism and minimal expenditure of energy; once again, ideal in this country where temperatures hover in the forties. It's also convenient that test cricket didn't involve any diving or sliding, which meant it could be played in a dust bowl. Considering we are a nation of chronic water shortages and poorly irrigated farmland, creating lush playing fields is difficult and unseemly. Besides, this is a nation where people are passionate about adhering to job descriptions – what do you think the caste system is all about – where going beyond the call of duty is a disease that can destroy the social fabric. A thoughtful cricketer can perform as required

---

* This includes a 40-minute lunch, 20-minute tea, and 30-minute extra to complete required overs.

and still go five whole days without having to do anything, quite like an employee with the Indian public services.

For a nation obsessed with purity and not coming into contact with the impure, cricket is a wonderfully safe game. There's none of this vulgar sweating on each other that is so fashionable in other popular sports. You could play for five days and not have to come within five feet of anybody the entire time. I also suspect that cricket is so popular in the subcontinent because it appeals to our sensibility that grown men should wear full-length pants. It wasn't all that long ago when my uncle caught me heading out to play basketball, dressed in what I presumed was the appropriate attire, i.e. shorts and a T-shirt. 'Tsk, tsk,' he grimaced. 'Are you going out to play in your knickers? Why can't you behave your age, what will people think if they see you running around in shorts?'

And I love test cricket as much as the next Indian. This is the ultimate test of one's passion for a sport, demanding real dedication. How many Brazilians are willing to watch forty hours of football so that the rival captains can congratulate each other on a well-fought draw? We, meanwhile, cheerfully dedicate five entire days to watch nothing happen. In test cricket, you went into a game with the intention of not losing: a draw was excellent, while a win, an unexpected windfall. It suited a nation of low expectations.

Unfortunately, this has become a thing of the past. That today we expect test matches to produce results – preferably with our team on the winning end – is indicative of our changing attitude as a people. We view ourselves as a successful nation – assertive on the global front – a young nation that has growing aspirations and seeks instant gratification. And so too with cricket. It's all very sad, really, next thing you know we're going to expect our public services to produce results as well.

The roads became more active as we neared Eden Gardens, with all traffic leading to the stadium. Normally I'd enjoy the game from the isolated comforts of my sofa, watching multiple replays of how something more interesting could have happened, letting the commentators numb me with a deluge of opiate statistics. But this was different. We're talking about a game between India and Pakistan here, at the most volatile sporting venue in the country. Eden Gardens is like the Ozzfest of cricket. Squeeze 120 thousand usually-disappointed fans into a stadium intended for 90 thousand happy ones, and before long the angst has to break through in grand fashion. Twice in recent memory matches were halted to protect the opposition team from the crowd. Eden Gardens is the essence of modern Calcutta, like the Coliseum was of ancient Rome – a place where heroes are born, and more frequently, die. The epicenter of a phenomenon where mob is king.

Kaya squeezed to a halt in between thousands of other motorcycles.

Eden Gardens is guarded like a fortress. But the war rages within, behind its circular walls. Police vans idle by the road. Their occupants sit in clusters, none too active themselves. A ring of not-so-lucky cops cordon the perimeter. The gates are a hive of uniforms. We are late and the lines have thinned out. Inside, a second ring of policemen guard the field. None stand amidst the supporters. Technically the cops should be facing the crowd, but they are fans as well. Besides, they have nothing to worry about. Unlike in some cricketing nations where the grounds are open to the viewers, our stands run head long into a high mesh fence, separating us from the pitch. Along with technical innovations like hawk-eye and snickometer, a new development in some stadiums is the wire net, hanging from the rafters and covering the entire stands to prevent disgruntled fans from hurling unpleasant objects onto the field.

The general stands are packed to the rafters, and the rafters are where some excitable chaps are perched, getting a gargoyle's eye view of the game. We only got in by making a few desperate calls, which landed us a couple of complimentary tickets that the complimented person wasn't using. In a country that runs on doling out favors, it's only natural that it is easier to get a complimentary ticket than buy a regular one. The fans are screaming themselves hoarse. They wave flags and run around. I think they're trying to make up for the lack of activity on the field. We are looking for a convenient place to sit when everyone and everything around us defy gravity. We've just missed Kumble's fifth wicket. We also miss the sixth. India is closing in on a historic victory. I see the seventh batsman get out, but fail to understand how it happened. Batsmen eight and nine, come, see, and leave.

The air of expectancy hangs heavy, and the stadium waits with bated breath. Harbhajan Singh to Danish Kaneria, and he's bowled him through and through. With the fall of that last wicket, India has won the game. There's a moment of pregnant silence, and then the stadium erupts. Crazed, beastly, our primal instincts pour forth in roars and screeches. The youngsters beside us are performing the epileptic dance. TT joins in. A moment later, caught up in the passion, so do I. At this point I notice the fires have started. Not arson or anything, just little bonfires of joy. Sparks go off all around us. The flames glow pink and blue. Dark clouds of smoke fill our sights. The stadium takes on the appearance of a war zone. Oh, how we are loving it!

Kilometer 3213

From Gosaba, on the muddy brown banks of the Gangetic Delta, Kaya headed north to the peaks of the Lesser Himalayas. Having cooled her wheels for a couple of days while we unsuccessfully hunted for the royal Bengal tiger, she ate up the miles with relish. The road, meanwhile, discarding its usual somber-black garb, was wearing splashes of vibrant color. As did the local cows and stray dogs, and people, of course. It was Holi and, whether you liked it or not, it was going to bring color into your life. For most of the morning I felt like Neo, dodging water balloons and squirts of color in freeze frame. By the end of the morning I could have camouflaged myself as a rainbow.

For a conservative culture, I'm always surprised by Holi's atmosphere, more scandalous than sacred. Fathers known to kill men for looking at their daughters laugh as the colony boys grope their precious girls. Women who only go swimming during 'ladies timings' nonchalantly splash about with strangers. Grandparents that spend all year despairing our party ways are found swinging at the local rain dance. A conservative middle class permits its women and children to indulge in narcotics. Holi is a nation stoned out of its repressed little mind and indulging in no-holds-barred paintball wars.

By the side of the road, as casually as he might be selling sugarcane juice, a young man had set up a *thandai* counter. The ground-level counter was all of a steel utensil covered with a towel and two steel glasses. The young man appeared to have broken the dealer's only rule: don't be your own best customer. TT insisted that it was his religious duty to quaff down a glass, and having done so, he spent most of the day in unusually reserved contemplation. As for me, my first time with *bhang* involved two hours of rolling on the road in laughter, and the next eight trying to get an imaginary rock off my head. Since then I've had the good sense to stay away, preferring my cannabis smoked, not stirred.

Kaya was riding with the first summer showers. Red rivulets flowed along the road, laden with rich topsoil. Leaves, twigs, and plastic wrappers drifted by. Fields stood flooded, and the potholes, dangerously covered. Lorries splashed by us. We rode into the evening, and the light turned dim. We rode on into darkness. At the end of a long, rain-soaked ride it was blessed relief when Kaya finally stopped at a dhaba on the outskirts of Raiganj.

The dhaba is dark and dingy, lit by a single 60-watt tungsten bulb dangling from the rafter supporting the thatched roof. The walls sweat in the humidity, the stains dark and alive. In the shadows I sense lizards and spiders. There is nothing gloomy about the owner, though. His glowing white shirt is straight out of a detergent advertisement, and the smile belongs in a Colgate commercial. TT and I order two teas, find ourselves a suitably shady corner and start a discussion on the niceties of smoking a joint in here.

Normally we'd simply step out while dinner is being prepared, but I am too tired and the outside is too wet. Not sure how tolerant our host will be towards disreputable substances, I'm in the process of getting up to ask him when I catch a glimpse of the dhaba's only other patron: a disheveled middle-aged man in a crumpled orange shirt and frayed blue lungi, a thin towel wrapped around his head like a turban. He is intently studying a small pile of weed sitting on the table before him.

'Is that good weed?' I ask walking over to his table.

'Would you like to smoke some?' the dhaba owner calls out from behind us.

'Er . . . if you don't mind, sure.'

'*Bandhu*, make a nice one for them,' the dhaba owner instructs Orange Shirt before returning his attention to me. 'Why would I mind? I sell the stuff.'

Whoa! We've discovered a ganja bar. The owner walks over to his desk and returns with the goods. The weed is in the form of small balls, wrapped tightly in gold and silver foil to denote quality. They look like Hershey's Kisses, only these are more fun, and a lot cheaper. The silver is five rupees and the gold is ten, each with enough stuff to roll two joints. We buy a gold Hershey and join Orange Shirt at his table.

'I come here every evening, smoke one and carry one home,' he informs us. 'I pull a cycle rickshaw for a living, and at the end of a tiring day I need something to relax. Ganja works out cheaper than alcohol. It also causes fewer problems with the wife, ha, ha.'

'You have no problems if people smoke so openly?' I ask the owner.

'Not really. Almost all the dhabas sell weed and most truck drivers smoke a bit.'

'And the police don't say anything?'

'They know, and pay me an occasional visit for donations,' he shrugs. 'I think they prefer smokers to drinkers anyway. It's better than dealing with drunken brawls on the street and drunken wife-beating at home. Some of the police even sit down for a smoke.'

Orange Shirt hands me the *chillum* he's prepared.

Boom Bholenath!

Boom! The smoke rises to the heavens.

In a country beset with contradictions, India's relationship with cannabis is schizophrenic to the point of making all else seem harmonious. The bond between Hindu and cannabis dates as far back as the 2nd millennium BC; its virtues extolled in the Atharvaveda, which was 'directly revealed' by divine powers. The gods, in fact, were so enamored of cannabis, Lord Shiva declared it a holy plant that required tender loving care. Our ancestors have been tripping on it from the day these transcendental secrets were shared with them. Some historical interpretations of Hindu mythology identify the divine nectar *soma* as an intoxicating mixture of poppy and cannabis; the constant reference to *soma* in the sacred texts is probably reflective of the nostalgic yearnings the first Gangetic settlers felt for the intoxicants, which didn't naturally grow there.*

Ancient history aside, cannabis is an integral part of Indian culture; as manifest, for instance, in the casual consumption of *bhang* on Holi. On Shivaratri, *chillums* everywhere in India are raised in salutation to the Lord, and on any given day the air around Shiva temples is imbued with the redolence of cannabis freshly smoked. Across the country, devotees prostrate before the sacred lingam with offerings of marigold and coconuts, and marijuana. At the Lingaraj temple, along with oil, yogurt, and sandalwood baths, the lingam also receives a nice cannabis scrub. On the ghats of Varanasi, by the shores of Somnath, along the trail to Kedarnath, I'd see men huddled in circles, a *chillum* passing from hand to hand. As for the few million dreadlocked sadhus, the *chillum* an appendage, these 'holy men' spend their lives behind a plume of smoke.

Yet, cannabis is rather incongruently classified as an illegal narcotic by Indian law, and the urban middle class pretends like no such thing exists in our culture. 'It's more like a fringe element' the story goes, and while looking up to Shiva, they look down upon his favored offering. And so, while my mother is devoted to the Lord, she breaks down in tears every time she finds a baggie

---

* Alternately, some have identified ephedra plants and hallucinogenic mushrooms as sources for *soma*.

in my drawer. A sadhu can smoke in the open, in front of a police station if he so wishes, but I have to smoke in the dark and hand out a bribe each time I'm caught. Drinking *thandai* is being part of a social event, but smoking cannabis is being anti-social. The government declares cannabis illegal, but sells it all year round, with shops cheerfully advertising 'Government Notified Bhang Shop'. I hear, in Allahabad, there's even a government ration shop that sells weed. Matter of fact, our colonial masters might just have had a better understanding about our relationship with cannabis.

Observing the prevalence of cannabis use, it was here in Bengal, in 1894, that the British commissioned the Indian Hemp Drugs Report. Undertaken with typical British thoroughness, the 3,700-page, 9-volume document is the most complete and systematic study on cannabis undertaken to date. On the cultural front, the report notes: For the Indian, the guardian angel of mankind lives in the cannabis bud. Using it deters evil, destroys all sickness, and cleanses one of all sins. To meet someone carrying *bhang* is a sure sign of success. Longing for hemp foretells happiness, and to dream about it is to gain power over the goddess of wealth. To tread on *bhang* is a terrible sin. Hemp is the spirit of freedom and knowledge, a joy-giver and liberator. He who uses no cannabis shall lose all happiness in this life and the lives after, and he who scandalizes a *bhang* user shall suffer torment as long as the sun endures – the government and my mother, beware. No man is as good as the devout *bhang* user.

Regarding other aspects, the commission found that: Physically, moderate use produces practically no harmful results, nor does it have any injurious effects on the mind. Even the excessive consumer of hemp drugs is ordinarily inoffensive and, for all purposes, it can be stated that there is no connection between the use of hemp and crime. On the other hand, cannabis drugs are believed to assuage fatigue, and for laborers involved in heavy physical work, it helps their endurance while reducing stress. At the end of a hard day, using hemp produces a sense of wellbeing, without causing the social harm of alcohol. *Bhang* also alleviates hunger, and the supporting power of hemp has brought many a family safe through the miseries of famine.

From this, the commission concluded that suppressing the use of cannabis would be completely unjustified; total prohibition was neither necessary nor expedient, and to seriously restrict the use of hemp would cause widespread suffering and rob people of a solace in discomfort. Furthermore, the commission realized, because of the religious implications of hemp use, it would be impossible to enforce any kind of prohibition. Instead, seeing that there was a profit to be made, the commission advocated a policy of licensing and taxation. Sad that a century later we are still incapable of such enlightened policy to decriminalize cannabis. Meanwhile, our government continues to be the nation's biggest drug peddler.

Kilometer 3946

Sitting on a shining white porcelain throne, I gaze out a picture window, the pine-carpeted hills of the Shiwalik Range looming before me. A dense fog rolls in, the mountainscape slowly disappearing in its milky wake. Golden pagodas peek through the mists. The guest house we're in grows on the side of a steep hill, the rooms floating amidst the clouds. Below me, the hill station of Darjeeling continues its erratic flow down the slope.

I step out of the bathroom to find TT sitting on the bed, a burning joint between his fingers.

KNOCK! KNOCK! KNOCK! Someone raps loudly at the door, startling us.

'Shit! Put that joint off, TT.' I leap off the bed and flap my hands in a pointless attempt to disperse the smoke. Tiptoeing to the door, I open it a crack, only for the hotel manager to fill the space immediately.

'I just . . .' he starts, but pulls up in mid-sentence. His brows rise up a notch, while his nose sniffs at the air suspiciously. 'Are you smoking marijuana?'

'Uh . . . no.'

'Don't lie to me, I can smell it – it's terrible. Where did you get this stuff from?'

'We . . . from Raiganj, ' I confess, resignedly.

'No wonder it's so bad. You must try out our Siliguri weed, it's the best in these parts. Before you leave just come and ask me. I'll give you directions to the peddler.'

LEG FIVE

You Are an Inspiration to Me

KAYA CUT THROUGH the floating clouds, a dark angel. The skies remained grey, occasionally pissing down on us. Despite the cold and the wet, the ride was invigorating, narrow roads coiling alongside emerald green tea gardens and forests of silver fir. Delicate fingers picked at the Darjeeling leaves in a synchronized dance. The world smelled like a cup of English Twinings, crisp and refreshing.

Replacing the temple towers of the plains, Buddhist pagodas emerged from the pine forests to crown the hills in a burst of gold. Radiant white monastery walls climbed the slopes, the large windows framed by bright motifs. The air reverberated to the meditative rattle of prayer wheels. Shimmering, the waters of the Teesta meandered through the narrow confines of the valley floor. Old wooden bridges spanned across it, the loose planks rumbling under the weight of Kaya like the roll of thunder. Prayer flags fluttered from the bridge rafters, holding them up with faith. We crossed the river, into Sikkim.

On reaching Gangtok, Kaya pulled up at the headquarters of Sikkim Tourism.

As part of the journey, I've tied up with the Tourism Ministry to promote biking adventures in whatever way I can, and Sikkim Tourism has invited me to their offices.* Having had the misfortune of visiting government offices earlier – experiences that have invariably led to a sense of futility and an unhealthy urge to blow the place up – I am dreading this meeting. Taking in a deep breath of cold, damp mountain air to steel my resolve, TT and I step dripping wet into the building. It is like stepping through the looking glass.

Instead of gloomy surliness, we find ourselves in a space of airy chirpiness. A smile on her face, the secretary to the director of tourism shows us to a sparkling clean washroom so that we can change out of our wet clothes. On stepping out, we are greeted by another lady, this one holding out two cups of piping tea for us to warm ourselves. And she's smiling too. Voices float around, courteous but casual. I hear laughter at the enquiry desk, it carries a hint of flirtation. People shuffle in and out, busy without being hectic. Is this possible? Government employees who enjoy working . . . what a disconcerting notion. I'm about to

---

* The tourism department of each state received a letter from the Tourism Ministry about my journey, and it was left to them to decide if and how they would like to use my help. Most states chose not to have anything to do with me, a rare few did.

finish my tea when Mr. Dong, the director for tourism, joins us in the waiting room. He welcomes us like long-lost friends.

Informing us that he's organized an informal press meet, Mr. Dong leads us to the conference room. Our interrogators are already there, consisting of four young men – Subash Rai of *Now Daily*, Ravi Pradhan of *The Mail*, Prasant Rasaily a television reporter, and Norji the cameraman – and one grand old lady who everybody in the room seems to revere, Santosh Nirash, editor of *Zamana Sadabahar*. Grey tresses flow down her creased face. Frail but larger than life, she is the nucleus of our little gathering, and her energy is infectious. She speaks of Gangtok like it's her child. I get the impression the entire town knows her; the kind of person everyone loves, but also knows not to rub the wrong way.

I'm taken unawares by the enthusiasm with which we are greeted. The atmosphere in the room is one of camaraderie, immediately putting us at ease. They are overjoyed that we're here, in their state, and more than us trying to impress them, it's them making sure we're impressed with Sikkim. The questions they pose are ones I've heard before, the difference being the keenness with which the answers are received. Why did I decide to do this journey on a bike, they want to know, and what are my first impressions of Sikkim. Having prepared for this line of questioning, I am more than happy to launch into a speech.

'Animals travel on all fours. Mankind on two,' I pronounce sagely. 'Motorcycling is not a means of transport, but an ideology, a nomadic way of life. If we think of life as a journey, and not a destination, it's odd that we don't give more thought to how we travel. It never crossed my mind to do head out on this expedition by car because I want to be a part of the world I travel through, not apart from it. While a motorcycle opens up the world, cars cut us off from it. Cars have become shields against the outdoors, self-contained bubbles that take us from Madras to Delhi without once exposing us to real air. Drive, and we don't so much travel through space, as carry our space everywhere with us: air that comes through vents, sounds belonging to record companies, and scents from a plastic box. With Kaya, I feel the sun on my back and the insect in my eye. I smell the forest and the exhaust fumes. I listen to the song of birds and the blare of traffic. Reality isn't mine to create. As for Sikkim, this is a motorcyclist's dreamscape, underlining the essence of riding. Here, Kaya and I become one. She is an extension of my body, my heart racing to the beat of her engine. When she hugs the roads, I hug it with her. When she knifes through the wind, I cut it with her.'

My speech isn't met with the applause I'm expecting. Seeing that nobody is sniggering, or throwing up, I'm going to conclude that they are too awestruck to respond. The interview is drawing to a close when Mr. Dong's secretary steps into the conference room bearing a tray of cupcakes, each of them sporting a burning candle. The room breaks out in a spontaneous rendition of 'Happy Birthday'. Everybody is singing, including Mr. Dong. Instinctively, TT and I join in, wondering whose birthday we are celebrating. It is mine. I'd turned 26 at midnight, but had forgotten the momentous event.

'This is . . . thank you,' I manage through my joy and embarrassment, 'but how did you know?'

'We are journalists after all, aren't we?' the grand dame grins.

'I don't know how to thank you. I . . . I find myself at a loss for words.'

'Don't be silly. You have nothing to thank us for. It's my pleasure to meet young people like you who are willing to take on life differently,' she brushes aside my emotionally choked mutterings and hands me a birthday present. It is a Reynolds ballpoint pen. 'From one writer to another, always pen only what you believe in,' she smiles.

'Sikkim Tourism would like to present you with two nights stay at the Mt. Pandim Resort in Pelling,' Mr. Dong offers.

'I love biking, and you are an inspiration to me,' Ravi says in parting.

Happy birthday indeed.

Kilometer 4204

I can't say I've had a revelation about the populace of Sikkim, but they are amongst the friendliest people I've come across. They are also excellent judges of character. They recognize a hero when they see one – and don't mind telling me about it either.

We're sitting at a cafe, waiting for breakfast to be served, when a teenager comes over to our table with an open copy of *The Mail*. 'Two Thunder into Sikkim', the headline roars above a photograph of TT and me sitting on Kaya.

'You guys are cool,' the young chap informs us.

A trio waylay us at the parking lot waving a copy of *Now Daily*, which calls us 'The New Heroes'. They praise our daring and wish us luck. Unsure how to deal with this new found stardom, I take a cue from other celebrities. I raise an eyebrow and grin like an Idiot.

From Gangtok, Kaya headed north, deep into the belly of the mountain range. The road swept along the cliff edge, teetering high over the gushing river. Bare blue peaks, the lower slopes blanketed by green forest, sparkly waterfalls crashing down on them. Clear emerald streams of glacial melt crossed by fragile pontoons and rope bridges. Our first glimpse of snowcapped peaks. We climbed higher. The ride turned more breath taking, literally. In time the mountains were swallowed by cloud, and soon enough we were as well.

Behind these misty veils we encountered a culture singularly disparate from anything on the plains. Though the Gangetic Plain is the birth place of Buddhism, the religion as it exists in our country today is not Indian but Tibetan in tradition. By the 12th century classical Buddhism had disappeared from India, turned into ash and rubble by Islamic and Hindu persecution. The great centers of art and learning at Nalanda and Ajanta, the temples and relics of Sanchi and Somnath, stand now as purely archeological wonders. Classical Buddhism left India to spread eastwards, and centuries later, from across the Himalayas, it returned to the land of its origin. Only it came back in a new avatar.

The Buddhist monasteries were everything the Hindu temples hadn't been. The doors stood unguarded, open and receiving. No boards questioned my origins or my beliefs. No priests waited at the altar, hands outstretched. No ceremonies were forced upon me, nor were any votive offerings. Bald monks draped in maroon, bereft of footwear they shuffled by in thoughtful silence. Soft light diffused through the shadowy interiors of the prayer halls. Giant tapestries and *thangka* paintings hung from lofty beams. Kaleidoscopic *mandalas* and mythical visions adorned the plastered walls, faded and peeling. Smoky wisps of incense mingled with the musty scent of age. The prayer hall formed a womb of spiritual energy, and within its confines there was only me and my musings. I felt at peace. I felt welcome.

Kaya rode past Pelling, abandoning the soft bed and hot shower gifted to us by Mr. Dong in order to camp in the shadow of Kanchenjunga. I belong to the school of thought that travelers should do everything to make travel uncomfortable. Character building happens while you toss about on the uneven ground beneath your leaky tent, cold and damp, cursing yourself for not staying in a hotel. Suffering is the essence of real travel, and we were about to get a large dose of it. With only forty kilometers separating Yuksom from Pelling, we expected to be there in a couple of hours at the outside, well in time to find a suitable camping site. We learned that forty kilometers in the mountains is a lot longer than forty kilometers anywhere else.

Tarred road gave way to a dirt path cut into the mountain side. Littered with sharp gravel and loose sand, it was just wide enough for a car to plunge to its crushing misfortune. Streams cut across our trail, the mossy pebbles offering no purchase to Kaya as she rolled over them. She slipped on the pebbles and skidded in the dirt, the stones ricocheting sharply off the cliff walls. Evening turned to dusk, and dusk into night. The bends leapt out of the darkness with unnerving suddenness, Kaya's headlight abruptly pointing into emptiness. Strong winds swept into us. And then the rain came, stinging our exposed hands and face. Numb fingers clenched Kaya's handle stiffly, unresponsive to my needs. My chest caved in, leaving me gasping for air. Tears coursed down my face, into my chattering mouth. I had never been colder in my life. The agony was ecstatic, similar to flagellation.

Yuksom is far more removed from civilization than I had expected, a tiny huddle on the very edge of the inhabitable world, the last settlement beyond which rise the snow dusted massifs of the Himalayas. The settlement, with all of ten permanent structures, was cloaked in an impenetrable darkness, only accentuated by the meek candle light from the one cafe/shop that was still open. Like a fly drawn to light, Kaya headed straight for it.

On entering the place we bump into Phillipe and Viola, a French couple in their fifties, sitting at one of the tables, a steaming cup of tea in his hand, a smoking joint in hers.

'Your mozer must be so woeied avout you,' Viola gasps when I tell her about our journey.

'Yup. I have to call her every night. And when I can't, like today, she will probably have a sleepless night.'

'Same same, all mozer. I ave to talk to my childzen evezyday. And my mozer too, she want to talk to me evezyday.'

'So, where are you staying tonight?' Philippe asks.

'Don't know. We'll have to wait for the rain to stop first, I guess.'

'You ave sleeping bags. You sleep on floor of our room if you like.'

'We wouldn't want to impose—'

'Poo! Poo!' Viola cuts me off. 'We contzibute to you jowerney, ya.'

With that we are deprived of our personality development exercise.

Kilometer 4461

Dawn is a revelation. Orange light creeps through the dark, striking the summit of Kanchenjunga up in the heavens. The light overflows the sky, rushing down the mountains like an avalanche, flooding the lush green valley below. Kanchenjunga translates from the local language to 'five treasures of high snow', and – as the name so eloquently suggests – it consists of five peaks, four of which rise above 27,500 feet. The hike to Dzongri, the base camp for scaling Kanchenjunga, begins from Yuksom, and most of the travelers here are the kind who want to relive the Ice Age migration. Preferring not to trouble our legs unnecessarily, we get back astride Kaya.

Returning to Pelling, Kaya pulls up in front of the Pemayangtse 'Sublime Lotus' Monastery. Hypnotic reverberations of the monastic rituals carry through the soft morning air – the muffled boom of drums, the murmur of chants, the rattle of prayer wheels.

A group of excitable child monks gather around us, posing for the camera. I pull out a bag of cookies from my backpack and offer it to them. They giggle, and throw glances at each other, hoping someone will make the first move. A tiny hand reaches out hesitantly. Zip! Zip! Zip! . . . The packet is empty.

Meanwhile, an elderly monk has come over to see what the commotion is all about. His body is frail and the skin wizened. But his face glows like a fresh bloom; the radiant aura of infants, and newly discovered celebrities. His voice is soft, soothing, each word seems to be uttered with deliberate care.

'I would like to join you on your travels,' he says. 'Will you take me with you?'

'Sure, we can leave as soon as you pack your bags.'

'I am a monk. I have no possessions to take with me.'

'Well, then let's go.'

'What about your friend? Shall we leave him in charge of the children?'

'Hmm, I'm sure TT will be able to teach them a lot of valuable lessons, but I doubt any of it will be good for their karma.'

'Ha, ha. I am too old to travel anyway,' he smiles, 'but my spirit will go with you.'

LEG SIX

These Are Dangerous Times in Assam

KAYA SLAMMED INTO another pothole with a jarring thud, questioning our decision to turn east towards guerilla-troubled Assam, instead of west into plain-old-troubled Bihar. During a road trip around a country like India, which is geographically all-over-the-damn-place, the 'when' is as critical as the 'where'; in winter the Himalayas are impassable, summers in the Thar are murderous, and Tamil Nadu migrates underwater for the monsoons. Keen on reaching the Himalayan passes as they open, I'd initially chosen to skip the North East. Instead, following a sudden burst of inspiration, we squeezed through the 'Chicken's Neck' into the land of the Seven Sisters.

The road was torn by neglect, an uninterrupted procession of elephant traps and meteor craters. Kaya absorbed the brunt of the vicious beating, but my arms were sore and my nerves unnerved. Fifty years of fighting, a few thousand dead, billions spent on security, and we still haven't built a decent road. Every time they use this 'highway' the insurgents are probably motivated to fight harder. The ruling class, on the other hand, should simply surrender in shame. The people of the region, meanwhile, have come to terms with a sore prostate.

I cursed and ranted, saving the choicest expletives for whoever was responsible for these roads. I was conjuring up some unusually cruel punishments to subject this imaginary person to, when a Honda Splendor rode up beside us, unmindful of the potholes. It carried two men, both wearing thickset moustaches. The rest of their face was hidden behind menacingly dark glasses. Neither wore helmets, and despite the breeze their hair sat neatly oiled down. The pillion waved his hand at us to stop, a little too aggressively for my comfort.

'PULL OVER! PULL OVER!' he shouted.

'I don't like this, machaa, don't stop, don't stop,' TT shouted back.

Kaya, foolishly taking TT's side, picked up the pace, pulling away from the strangers. Within seconds they were abreast of us again. The pillion's left hand dropped to his waist. He raised the lapel of his shirt with menacing intent . . . to reveal a walkie-talkie??? It seemed like an odd choice of weapon to threaten someone with. Kaya ran faster. But it was an unequal chase. They weren't weighed down, and they knew the terrain. After crashing hard into a couple of potholes, I decided we were better off taking a chance with these guys than the road.

Kaya pulled over to the side.

They stop a few feet ahead of us and purposefully walk over to where we are standing. The pillion – obviously senior in ranking; his Ray-Ban aviators outshine the plastic junk the rider is wearing – waves his walkie-talkie menacingly in my face. I think it is supposed to mean something, but I'm just not getting it.

'Why didn't you stop when we asked you to?' he yells at me.

'We didn't know who you were.' I still don't actually, and the fact is worrying me.

'Can't you recognize the police?'

'But you're in plainclothes . . . sir. How was I supposed to know?'

'What do you mean by that, I showed you the walkie-talkie, didn't I?'

'Oh! But . . .' I'm not sure what the appropriate response is. Since when did a walkie-talkie become a form of identification? Hell, I'm still not sure these guys are who they claim to be. 'How– '

'Let's not have too much talk,' he interrupts, patting our bags. 'That's a lot of luggage to be carrying on a bike. *Chalo*, unhook them, I need to take a look inside.'

'Sir, we are on an all India journey,' I stall him, not wanting to go through the painful process of unstrapping and re-strapping all our bags. More crucially, I don't want him to discover our bag of critically acclaimed Siliguri weed. 'I even have papers from the Tourism Ministry to confirm it.'

'Oh, I see. But we still have to check, okay,' Mr. Ray-Ban shrugs, his demeanor softening.

Resigned, I start to unhook the bungees.

'What are you looking for, sir?' TT asks.

'Explosives,' Junior replies with an air of drama.

'*Ah explosives!* Please, go ahead and look.'

TT and I are comforted in knowing an Indian's single-minded focus to what his job description entails. A traffic cop can't care to interfere in a roadside brawl, and a riot cop won't stoop so low. Even if Mr. Ray-Ban's searching hands were to stumble wrist deep into a bag of illegal herbage, he won't care as long as it doesn't explode. Irrespective, they rummage only through the main compartment of the backpacks, ignoring the side pockets, which contain our weed. At this point I'm more concerned about the training our police receive. Does it not occur to them that if we had bombs hidden in our bags, we might also have guns tucked in our pants? Come to think of it, the Leatherman in my pocket has more firepower than that walkie-talkie. These guys must truly believe words are mightier than swords.

'It's all good, you can go now,' Mr. Ray-Ban nods. 'We're only doing our duty, and it's for your own safety. These are dangerous times in Assam.'

And we apparently looked like dangerous people to the Assam Police. Kaya had barely traveled another forty kilometers when we were pulled over again. And then once more on the outskirts of Guwahati. With their founding day, April 7th, less than 96 hours away, the United Liberation Front of Asom (ULFA) had stepped up terror bombings to remind the government that they were still around. In the previous three days, Assam had witnessed ten separate explosions. One of the bombs blew up in Guwahati, injuring twelve innocent civilians, and liberating none.

'What's with this ULFA?' TT mused at one point. 'Why can't they celebrate their birthday like the rest of us, by blowing candles?'

The insurgency in Assam arose from the fear of becoming an outsider, a secondary citizen within one's homeland; a fear driven by the changing demography of the state through immigration. After independence, Assam witnessed a steady influx of 'foreigners', starting with more than five lakh refugees from East Pakistan during Partition, followed by another ten lakh 'illegal immigrants' over the next two decades. In addition to the primary concern of Bengalification of the state, by the mid-seventies many Assamese began to perceive the central government as colonial exploiters, with a disproportionate portion of revenues generated from natural resources flowing into federal coffers.

In 1979, Assam finally erupted in the most potent and sustained mass-agitation in the country since the freedom struggle, involving curfews, street protests, civil disobedience, oil blockades, intimidation, boycott of non-Assamese businesses, and eventually, massacre.* It was against this backdrop that ULFA emerged, growing in strength after the farcical elections of 1983, which left 130 dead at the hands of police firing and the Congress victorious. A revolutionary political organization, whose aim is 'the liberation of Assam from the illegal Indian

* Following soon after the 1983 assembly elections, 2,191 Bangladeshi Muslims, mostly women and children, were killed over a six hour period in Nagaon district.

occupation, through armed struggle', the ULFA has fought the state through extortion, assassination of prominent businessmen and government officials, and terror bombings. Mostly killing Assamese.

The Indian army stepped into Assam in 1990. It hasn't left since.

Kaya crossed the Brahmaputra River and entered Guwahati as the sun descended over it. It was a city under siege, with the police out in full force. And every time they spotted us, their paranoia went into overdrive. Two young men on a motorcycle, with big bags – have to be terrorists! We were flagged down four times in as many kilometers, and as much as I understood the circumstances, if I'd come across a bomb just then, I might have gleefully detonated it.

Kilometer 5214

Kaya followed the path of the Brahmaputra, riding upstream in the direction of its source. The sun stayed muted behind grey cloud. Once beyond Guwahati, the army replaced the police. The road formed a corridor between rich green paddy fields, the tranquility punctuated by razor-wired gun posts, the purposeful guns trained at passersby, at us. A rhino ambled beside the highway, daisy in mouth. Armored convoys prowled the route. The skies rumbled, the guns remained silent. A disturbing confluence of serenity and violence.

At Jorhat, Kaya drew to a stop. Spread out around us, in roughly horseshoe formation, are the states of Arunachal,

Nagaland, Manipur, Mizoram, and Tripura. Since the fifties the latter four have habitually witnessed internal conflict, with nearly ten thousand dead between 1990 and 2005. Arunachal, meanwhile, is threatened from the outside. With an alphabet soup of more than fifty militant groups operating in the region, the conflict is a confusion of secessionist movements, autonomy struggles, and ethnic warfare; pitting tribal against state, tribal against tribal, tribal against non-tribal. And the state against everybody. Kaya no longer had the right to travel freely, requiring Inner Line Permits to cross into Arunachal, Nagaland, and Mizoram. We turned around, heading back the way we'd come.

That mainland India inherently views the people of the North East as 'not like us' is articulated by the condescending, and extremely casual, use of the word 'chinkie'. I have witnessed the distrust and disconnect we feel towards them in the classroom, within my family, and in my social circle, the so-called educated liberals. Mostly though, they are invisible people, barely featuring in our daily consciousness. The region has produced no pretentious Bollywood hero and no darling cricketer. It has no holiest temple to visit and no history to share. Where we think they belong is in Chinese restaurants. While the Inner Line Permit ostensibly protects the region from immigrants and infiltrators, unfortunately, it also reiterates our otherness.

For many, the North East is about an outline on a map. We want the land that it encompasses, but we reject the people. After all, nationalism is not about the welfare of the citizen but rather the integrity of 'our borders'. So, with ample moral conviction we subject the North East to the AFSPA (Armed Forces Special Power Act), as draconian an act as any thought up by the likes of Mugabe, Gadhafi, or Assad. Introduced in 1958, as a temporary measure to keep Nagaland in check, today the AFSPA covers the entire region and is celebrating 50 years of subjugation.* Through this act we gift our occupying forces exceptional powers, providing them the right to shoot on sight, arrest arbitrarily, search without warrant, and detain without trial. As a perk, they also get to indulge in torture, rape, and extrajudicial killing. The army is immune from prosecution. The citizen has no right to redress. And we proudly call ourselves the world's largest democracy.

When will we awake to the fact that we can't win the hearts and minds of a people through the barrel of a gun? Decades of repression have left indelible scars on the population, with reports of collective post-traumatic stress disorder, and of communities inured to violence. Instead of resolving the problem, we have radicalized and militarized the region. On July 10th, 2004, a group of soldiers stormed into the house of Manorama Devi in Imphal, Manipur. Dragging the 32-year-old woman out of the cottage, they violently assaulted her before taking her into custody. A few hours later, her abandoned body was discovered by villagers, battered, raped, and riddled by bullets. Rage against the military and an indifferent Center, so long simmering, erupted in a wave of protests and strikes. In response, the Prime Minister set up

---

* The AFSPA also covers Kashmir. A question that has been asked of the government, but never answered, is: why the act has never been in the 'disturbed' areas of central India? Is it because of the 'otherness' of Kashmiris and North East Indians?

the Jeevan Reddy Commission to review the AFSPA, promising to replace it with a 'more humane act'. Two months after our visit to the North East, the commission submitted a damning report, favoring the repeal of the AFSPA. A far cry from doing so, an unfeeling and cowardly government refuses to even publish the report. A leaked copy languishes on the website of *The Hindu*.

Kilometer 5853

'Rising Day' found Kaya heading out of Assam. It was just me and her now, with TT headed back to Hyderabad from Guwahati. The time spent in the state is best remembered for the number of check-posts we were pulled over at. On this revolutionary day, we saw no sign of the rebels, and we saw little of the public. The only people who appeared to be in a celebratory mood were the police. Well, they were the ones out on the streets, dressed in dapper uniforms and waving shiny new batons.

When night fell, we were still in Assam, riding through Kokrajhar district, land of the Bodo people. The road had beaten the joy out of my soul, and darkness tore at my frayed mind. Little has changed since I passed through. We have neither solved the demographical pressures of immigration, nor have we assuaged the bitterness of military occupation. And the economic discrimination has only gathered momentum, with resources flowing out and nothing going in, other than the military, of course. In 2008, and then again in 2012, Bodoland was wrecked by violence, indigenous Bodos clashing with migrant Muslims.* The two incidents left hundreds dead and nearly five lakh people, mostly Muslim, driven from their homes. As for mainland India, the chinkie remains the 'other', as evidenced by the mass exodus of thousands from Bangalore, Pune, and Chennai in August 2012. That they fled to the North East to escape the 'atmosphere of fear' shows this has never been home. It shows how little faith they have in 'us' standing up for 'them'.

Close to the state border, Kaya stopped at a dhaba.

I park Kaya by the side of the highway, on the gravel strip that all our asphalt roads peter down to. We are in the dhaba for a couple of minutes, when a distinctly South Indian man approaches us, a tentative smile peeking from under his bushy moustache.

'Andhra Pradesh?' he asks.

'Yes.'

'*Telugu ochha*?'

'Yes, I speak Telugu,' I reply in my native tongue.

'*Balle!* I saw your motorcycle registration. Have you come all the way from Andhra by motorcycle?'

'Yes.'

'What kind of madness is that?' he exclaims in genuine shock. This comes from a man who tells me he drives all the way from Andhra to the mountain kingdom of Bhutan and the hills of

* I pointedly choose the word migrant because, despite the mainstream's intention of painting the issue as a problem of illegal immigration, much of the demographic change is being effected by the movement of people from within the country.

Arunachal. 'I've never run into people from home in these parts, and you've come here on a bike.'

'Well, it is a long way, and it's taken me a more than a month to get here,' I laugh. 'How long does it usually take you to complete your trip?'

'That is completely dependent on the political situation here. We have to go through hundreds of check-posts, and now with these bombings it will be slow going. If not that, there is always some strike or road blockade. They are forever protesting something or the other here, I think there were fifty or sixty days of strike last year,' he shakes his head in disapproval. 'Forget all that. Come join our table and tell us about your journey, it sounds a lot more interesting.'

I can't recollect how it has led to this, but I find myself arbitrating a disagreement between him and another lorry driver on the merits of having Yuvraj Singh in the batting lineup. The Yuvraj supporter is putting forth a well-animated case for his idol's straight drive when we are distracted by the squeal of tires, followed by a sharp clash of metal. I turn around in time to see Kaya fall on her side and slip down the embankment.

'*Bewda madhar chodh*,' someone screams at the fast disappearing lorry, which had veered off the two-lane highway and bumped into Kaya as it flew past. I run to where she is lying and bend to pick her up. By now a crowd of excited onlookers has gathered around to watch the *tamasha*. The Yuvraj fan approaches me and stretches out a hand to help lift Kaya up.

'I don't need your assistance,' I hiss viciously, brushing his hand aside. 'Why do you lorry chaps drive like this?'

I stop short and look around. Every face I meet belongs to a lorry driver. These are giant men with hairy arms, and they can use me like a toothpick, but they don't. Without a word they raise Kaya to her tires. Other than a dent to her tank and broken indicators, she has suffered little damage. We return to dinner and tentatively pick up the conversation where it left off. Shamed by my outburst, I find it hard to relax and regain the earlier sense of camaraderie. All I want is to finish eating and skulk away.

'*Chotu*, bill,' I call out to the boy who has served me.

'Don't worry about the bill,' Andhra driver says, waving his hand. 'We will take care of it.'

'Please, there's no need for you to—'

'What's the question of need in this? It's only a gesture of friendship,' laughs the Yuvraj fan, interrupting my feeble protestations.

'But I feel bad about making you pay for my dinner.'

'Come on, little brother,' says the Andhra driver, 'think of it as our contribution to your trip.'

LEG SEVEN

We Can't Enter Because We Are Chamars

I MIGHT HAVE TO spend the night in a police station, and like any upright member of society, the possibility fills me with disquiet. Kaya and I are outside Siliguri railway station, contemplating the road ahead, which for all practical purposes is going to transport us to the Dark Ages. At least that's the media portrayal of Bihar – a lawless land of thieves, murderers, and horse-mounted dacoits waving their guns like untalented extras from a Wild West movie. That dacoits still thrive in the present day is thanks mainly to the short arm of the Indian law. As a generally unexcitable professor of mine spluttered between paroxysms of indignation, 'Bihar is the asshole of the universe'.

Considering that this is a place where even electricity cables and railway tracks are not safe from the hands of enterprising criminals; cameras, motorcycles, wallets, and other unfixed objects, like people, are all too easy targets for carrying off. Not surprisingly, Bihar sees few visitors, and then not unless they are desperate delinquents or Buddhists with much to atone for. Instances of armed gangs intercepting and robbing vehicles along the highway are common. The occasional tale tells of people who've just been robbed being waylaid by a second gang of thieves a few kilometers down the road, and finding nothing to steal, the thugs proceed to thrash the unfortunate bastards for inconsiderately wasting their time.

Unfortunately for me, my mum has heard these stories as well. Every call home is greeted by hysterics, and she insists that I load Kaya on a train to Varanasi. This isn't an especially comforting solution either. Ever so often, drawing inspiration from *Sholay*, bandits have successfully intercepted trains and pillaged their entire contents. Besides, there's no guarantee that someone won't just ride away with Kaya at one of the stations. Rather, my intention is cowardly simple, or simply cowardly, depending on your viewpoint – make a dash for Kishanganj just over the eastern border of Bihar today, spend a watchful night there, wake up early, and race across the state to Patna on the western end.

Before heading out, though, it occurs to me to conduct a few enquires and get some feedback on my plan from people in the know. Just to be sure, you see.

'Kishanganj! Bah! Not safe at all,' a hotel owner swears. 'Everybody is a crook there.'

'*Bike pe? Kya pagalpan hain*,' the STD-booth owner scolds.*

Taking into consideration their unsupportive reactions, I try to think up an alternate strategy. After a period of unsuccessful mulling, I decide the easier solution is to assume these people don't know what they are talking about. Decision made, I call home to tell them I'm going to go ahead as planned. Thankfully, my more resourceful mother has made her own arrangements. Through someone who knows someone who's heard of someone else, she's communicated with the Kishanganj Police.

'Go straight to the police station,' she orders me.

'What! But why?'

'I've spoken with the inspector and he says you can stay the night there.'

The day quickly grew older as Kaya raced towards Bihar, and the last thing we needed was to find ourselves on these roads after nightfall. The seat that had so far belonged to TT was now occupied by Dwain, a 26-year-old Canadian we met in Kaziranga, who, on hearing that TT was returning home, had jumped on the idea of traveling with Kaya for a few days. Dwain had showed up at Siliguri station as promised, which, in all honesty, surprised me, considering that the *Lonely Planet* he was toting had a highlighted column on the dangers of Bihar, unambiguously suggesting that travelers should arrange for a police escort when traveling through the state. Besides, to put your life in the hands

* For any confused foreigner reading this, the STD here stands for Subscriber Trunk Dialing, and not Sexually Transmitted Diseases.

of an unknown motorcyclist on Indian roads, well, that simply indicates a serious lack of judgment.

The sun had mostly burned out, and darkness slowly crept over the town as we rode in. In the eerie grip of twilight, Kishanganj seemed a sinister place. The streets stood silent. My imagination stalked the highway. Shadows flittered across like ghosts. Evil lurked in the corners waiting for the last traces of light to die out. I smelled wickedness in the air. I felt demons breathing down my neck. With an audible purr of relief, Kaya came to a halt inside the station compound.

Our triumphant entry is met by stunned silence. I'm guessing the police aren't used to people showing up voluntarily, what when as many crimes are said to be committed within the stations as outside them. The officer we are to meet isn't at his desk, and no one knows what to do with us, including ourselves. As police stations go, it isn't particularly worse than the others I've had the pleasure of visiting. A large room with peeling yellow plaster, a few cluttered desks and closets pushed to the side, two old ceiling fans producing more noise than comfort, the stifling smell of sweat and stale onions. And fear.

Off to one side is the lockup. I spot a couple of unsavory types, separated from us by bars. My glances are furtive, fueled by cheap curiosity. Dwain and I are whispering, discussing the technicalities of spending the night here, when a constable walks over and tells us to get into the police jeep.

'What about my motorcycle?'

'It is safer here,' he says.

That's not very reassuring. It seems to imply that we are going somewhere 'less safe'. The jeep wanders down the dark confines of a small lane and pulls up in front of a rundown hotel. Two policemen escort us to a grimy little room and make sure we are settled in. One of the cops stands at the door and speaks to the room-boy. I don't follow the conversation, but the cop's tone suggests an unfriendly visit if everything isn't handled according to expectations.

'The jeep will come and pick you up at five thirty in the morning,' the constable informs me before leaving. 'Anything you need will be taken care of by the boy. There is no reason for you to leave the hotel.'

I can't tell if it's a suggestion or an order, and I have no intention of finding out.

Next morning, when I try to settle the bill, the hotel staff refuses to take money from me, not even for dinner. I get the distinct feeling they are fearful of us. I feel like a dictator. Of a cheap little country.

Kilometer 6377

Kaya had barely gone ten kilometers past Kishanganj when a profound realization dawned on me. All this time spent worrying about Biharis – my real concern should have been their roads. If the route through purgatory was anywhere as bad, Dante would have surrendered after the first mile. NH31 through Bihar should be declared a violation of human rights, and the entire government executed for crimes against humanity.

In an era long gone by, the surface had been tarmacked. We could tell from the trace remains of pitch and tar, precious relics that need to be come under the protection of the Archeological Survey. For the most part, it resembled the epicenter of a nuclear explosion. And it wasn't just the road. Even the world turned ugly. Leaving behind green landscapes and cold winds, we had entered a parched wasteland. Dust filled the air, our eyes, and our lungs. The heat bored into me, sapping every ounce of energy. The towns were arid, forlorn in the baking heat. We saw little color and sensed no joy.

Bihar's infrastructure lagged a generation behind the rest of the country, weighed down by a level of corruption that makes leprosy seem like a mildly annoying rash. While every state in the country showcases a crop of politicians who are criminals by profession, Bihar's Legislative Assembly makes all the others look like a gathering of Buddhist monks. In fifty years, it has replaced thirty chief ministers, and declared a state of emergency as habitually. As we passed through, Rabri Devi ostensibly held the reins of power without even standing for elections, having replaced her discredited husband. In Bihar, democracy has met a slow, undignified, and well-ridiculed death.

The pounding was relentless, kilometer after kilometer after kilometer. Pain replaced frustration replaced pain. Broken-down lorries marked the road at regular intervals, replacing the missing milestones. Other than truckers, only bullock carts and the occasional motorcycle braved the road, and then only for short distances. Of a car I have absolutely no recollection. When someone complained about the roads to then Chief Minister Lalu Prasad Yadav, his Laluesque reply was that 'this is a state of peasants with bullock carts, repairing the roads will only help the rich in their fancy cars to run over the children of the poor'.

Kaya came to a groaning halt under the shade of a Banyan tree on the outskirts of Barauni.

I get off her and take a deep breath. We've been riding past tanneries, and I appreciate the pleasure of inhaling without retching. Dwain, meanwhile, is performing random stretching exercises; I guess he's trying to get some blood flowing through his numbed behind. I hunker down to examine Kaya, making sure she hasn't shed a few parts along the way. Reassured that she'll survive, I look up to notice we've caught the attention of three men. They are standing at an unobtrusive distance, smoking *beedis* and gawking openly at Dwain. In these parts, a white man is as rare as an honest politician.

Flashing a smile to put them at ease, I walk over to where they stand.

'*Bhaiyya*, can I borrow one your *beedis*?' I request, and then turning around to Dwain, 'Hey, would you like try one of these?' I call him over.

He nods yes, and hails the trio with a nasal *namaste*. They break out in big grins and offer him one of the foul-smelling tobacco-wraps. The youngest of them eagerly strikes a match and holds it up for Dwain, a good foot taller. The *beedi* lit, he takes a long satisfied pull, endearing himself to them forever.

They ask about our journey; mostly, they are interested in Dwain.

'Where are you from?'

'Canada.'

'America! America!'

'*Nooo*. Canada.'

'In America, yes.'

'Why don't we continue this conversation over a cup of tea?' I invite them, pointing to the tea stall next to where Kaya is parked. My suggestion is met by an immediate shift in atmosphere. They go silent and look at each other uncomfortably.

'. . . eh . . . no, that's alright, you boys can carry on,' the eldest says.

'Come on, it's my treat,' I offer, presuming it's about the money. 'We'd really like to have the pleasure of your company for a while longer.'

'No . . . it's not that . . . you see we can't enter this place.'

'Why not?'

'It is owned by a Brahman.'

'Yes.'

'We work in the tannery see.'

'No, really I don't see,' I reply with complete honesty. I can think of no logical connection between a Brahman, a tannery, and a cup of Brooke Bond Red Roses.

'We can't enter because we are *Chamars*,' he says looking me in the eye, 'Dalits.'

Still, it takes what seems like an eternity for the meaning to sink in. And when it finally does, I break away from his stare, consumed by guilt I do not understand.

The first time I dealt with the word 'caste' was on my high school application form, and it stumped me. It made little sense, this word 'caste' with a bunch of boxed options for me to tick, one of which said SC/ST. It could have said Φ/Ψ and not made a difference. From my parents, I learned that SC stands for Scheduled Caste. Later that same day, I also learned that two of my closest friends belonged to Scheduled Castes. There was nothing downtrodden about them, though, or their privileged lifestyle. Ultimately, we all got into the same school, and that's all I'd cared about. The reality is, the caste system doesn't exist for me. But I've made the mistake of assuming it doesn't exist at all. Therein lies my guilt, my shame.

'I . . . surely . . . there must be somewhere else that we can go,' I ask, struggling for words.

'Yes, why not. There is another tea stall close by.'

'Very good,' I smile tentatively, 'shall we go there then?'

Sitting down at a table in the non-discriminatory chai shop, the conversation is initially awkward. But as the tea goes down, the words pour out. The eldest man is Subo. His father had worked with leather, as had his father's father. About the fathers who came before, he isn't sure.

'But I am a free man,' he says with calm confidence, 'as are my sons.'

'What do they do?'

'My elder son works with me in the tannery. But not my younger son, Saakar. He is in school now, in the eleventh class,' he says, his voice rich with pride. 'Nowadays it is possible for him to get into college also, some of the boys from our community already have. Maybe he will become an engineer like you, ha, ha.'

There are a million questions swirling around in my head. About what it means to be a Dalit. I want to ask if this kind of discrimination is common. I want to know if he has any recourse against it. I want to find out what his feelings are about the upper classes, about people like me. I am too scared to ask. We stick to family topics.

Kaya coursed a subdued path towards Patna. A bleak world rolled past us, unseen. The dry air singed our exposed arms. It carried the stench of desolation. The ride remained painful, only the hurt was no longer physical. Subo's family consisted of him, a wife, four children, a daughter-in-law, and a granddaughter. Between him and his eldest son, they worked more than sixteen hours a day in the tannery and took home a hundred rupees. Along with these generously meager wages, they also earned grand titles to go with the job. Impure. Impious.

By Hindu logic, working with leather is a profanity. The *Chamars* are outcastes because they handle the hides of cows. Meanwhile, we, the pious, strut about in the slippers and belts made from the sacred animal. Other inconsiderate workers who 'pollute' the rest of society are cleaners, cremators, and barbers. Why don't we simply oulaw these barbaric professions and see how efficiently our society functions. 'Work shall set you free,'

Nazism promised falsely. 'Work shall enslave you,' the caste system promises honestly.

Dwain had questions about the caste system, and he wasn't the first foreigner to ask me if it still existed. I never had a satisfying answer at hand. Only because it's a question I never asked myself. It didn't belong in the circles I grew up in, so I'd ignored it as a thing of a past. Come on now, this is a progressive country with a constitution that informs us that all are equal. Every now and then stories of caste-related violence make the paper, but I'd brushed them aside as a rare, shocking event, like Air India turning a profit or Rahul Gandhi being intelligible. The reality was only a Google search away. But I'd chosen to be blind.

Many lakhs of Dalits still live as bonded laborers or unpaid slaves paying off the one-bag-of-rice loan their great-great-grandfather took. Fifteen lakh Dalits work in sewers and dry-pit lavatories, clearing out our society's shit. Your shit and my shit. Many die in these cesspools. According to Human Rights Watch, caste-motivated killings, rapes, and abuses are a daily occurrence. In fact, a crime is committed against Dalits every 20 minutes. Of the hundreds of thousands of cases registered under the SC/ST Prevention of Atrocities Act, few ever reach the courts, and 90 percent of the ones that do make it end in acquittals. Did I mention that the constitution has declared all are equal?

While the greedy attention-seeking white man has grabbed all the credit for instituting racial policies, the glory rightfully belongs to us. We are the model supremacists, founding a claustrophobic and oppressive system of segregation many centuries before it became fashionable elsewhere. We are such virulent racists; we hate our own kind. Only, we call it the caste system, and claim it was ordained by the gods. And it's an Indian thing, not merely Hindu. When Islam and Christianity marched into the subcontinent, instead of destroying the social stratification, they embraced it. Suddenly, you had Harijan John and Dalit Ali.

With the lower castes gaining a powerful voice over the last two decades, albeit through corrosive vote-bank politics, the upper castes have risen up to reclaim their 'rights'. Nowhere in the country has this taken a more violent form than in Bihar. Since 1995, the Ranvir Sena, a landlord army, has terrorized the countryside. Indulging in hit-and-run tactics that went out of style with the Vikings, they are responsible for killing more than four hundred people. On December 1st, 1997, they massacred 62 lower caste peasants, including 19 children and 20 women. In April two years on, 20 landlords were killed in retaliation. Which led to a counter-retaliation. Another 33 people dead. The blood-letting continues.

A world in which Subo's son can go to college and escape all this can only be a better place. And if reservation, despite all its drawbacks, is his ticket out, then so be it. If nothing else, courtesy of reservation we get to witness the exquisite irony of upper caste youth trying to procure fake backward caste identities. Some of my fellow caste members argue that fifty years of reservation is long enough to uplift the condition of the lower castes. After three thousand years of screwing them over, we could show a tad more patience. Others fear that soon we will be the exploited, victims of reverse discrimination. A good Hindu should appreciate that it might rightfully be our turn now. After all, it's just karma, machaa. Just karma.

Kilometer 6762

We stand on the Mahatma Gandhi Setu, looking down at the muddy brown dregs of a near dry Ganga. Completed in 1982, this is the longest river bridge in India. We are only half-joking about the possibility of it collapsing, when Dwain's pale face attracts the attention of a middle-aged man, dressed in a smart safari suit. He introduces himself as the engineer working on the renovations that the bridge is undergoing.

'We should be proud of this bridge. It shows that when we put out our mind to it, Indians are capable of anything the West can do,' he insists. 'But look at it now,' he sighs, growing suddenly wistful. 'It's in a dangerous state of disrepair, but nobody seems to sense the urgency.'

'You are repairing it now,' I indicate the work going on. 'So obviously they realize it, no?'

'This! This . . . it's just patchwork,' he spits. 'If we can finish this by the time the rains come, it will be a miracle. On top of that, the materials we have been given are both insufficient and substandard. Even that little is sometimes stolen from the work site. By this time next year it will return to the same condition.'

Kaya battled her way through the anarchy of Patna's traffic. We had nearly made it out of the city when a motorcyclist under the influence of a mugful of over-optimism attempted to overtake a bus, squeeze between two cyclists and edge past a scooter, all in one smooth maneuver, while riding on the wrong side of the road. He overtook the bus, squeezed between the cyclists, but then kissed Kaya on the side and promptly crashed to the ground. I pulled up a couple of meters ahead filled with dread, expecting an immediate and violent reaction from the mob.

A large crowd had already gathered around the prone man, but no one seems to have noticed our involvement. Few moments later, we saw the crowd part as two men helped the dazed and grazed motorcyclist to the side of the street. Damn! The stupid bastard had survived. Before he could regain enough sense to point an accusatory finger in our direction, we disappeared from the scene, knowing very well it didn't matter if I was to blame or not. Our system of people's justice is actually quite egalitarian. The one who isn't injured in the accident is the one that gets thrashed by the public; this way both involved parties end up equally dead or dying.

Beyond Patna, Kaya retraced the path of the Buddha and the origins of India's earliest empires. Sixth-century-BC Vaishali, the land of Mahavira and site of the Gautama's final sermon. Rajgir, capital of the mighty Magadha, where the ruins of Ajatashatru Fort stand forlorn. The World Heritage ruins of Nalanda, which between the 4th and 12th centuries was amongst the world's foremost sites of learning. And Bodh Gaya, the ancient Mahabodhi Temple, a delicate pyramidal tower soaring over the town. Adjacent to the temple, grows the giant Bodhi Tree, casting a leafy shadow over the hallowed ground where the Buddha attained nirvana.

This glorious legacy is a scathing witness to the paradox of Bihar's present, whose relics stand mocking, condemning, mournful. The seat of India's greatest and wealthiest empires, today Bihar is the poorest state in the country; with more than a third of the state's residents lying crushed under the poverty line and a per capita income that's a quarter of the national average. Home to Nalanda University, once the embodiment of knowledge, Bihar is currently the least literate place in India. Birthplace of Buddhism and Jainism, symbols of peace and harmony, Bihar has become symbolic of violence, second only to U.P. in absolute number of murders, attempted murders, and abductions. The past has been relegated to dusty museums and fading memories.

Kilometer 7023

It's our last night in Bihar. Following an early dinner, Dwain and I are sitting on the porch of our room when suddenly I feel an irresistible urge to head into town and interact with the much-maligned Bihari. Since entering Bihar, my fears have held me on a tight leash, to the point of avoiding the night with the same desperation that parliament eschews lawmaking. We've even taken to leaving the lights on when we go to sleep in order to deter any would-be thief. What the hell am I thinking – these guys are criminals, not zombies. I am disappointed with myself. A real traveler never wastes a perfectly fine opportunity to get into trouble. With that thought, purposefully slinging the camera around my neck, I step out into the night in search of excitement. A momentary hesitation and Dwain follows.

It is late, but the market is still relatively busy. I'm immediately aware of the eyes following our every move. Excited whisperings follow in our wake. But nobody approaches us. Nobody troubles us. And nobody attacks us. They seem curious, but maintain their distance. These people are better behaved than everybody else I've come across in the country. Emboldened, I decide to initiate contact.

In front of a local sweetshop two enormous woks bubbled with sizzling oil, waiting for the sweet-maker to paint the golden circles of dough. Walking over to the shop, I ask for '*ek plate garma garam jalebi*'. I am greeted by looks of utter disbelief, and then the smiles break out. The questions begin tentatively, but soon they are pouring out in a flood. However, my role is purely that of an interpreter. With a white man around, I am no more than a voice.

'Which country? America?'

'No, Canada.'

'Ooh! In America!'

'Alright then, America.' I shrug.

'You try hot-hot *samosa*, very tasty,' someone is offering us a plate.

'No, no, Americans don't like spicy food,' someone else pushes away the plate. 'Here, you try the *jalebi*. Very sweet,' he says, offering a different plate.

'You take photo with us,' a young man holds up an old-school Kodak film camera.

This is my introduction to 'white celebrityism', a wonderful Indian tradition, wherein anybody with white skin becomes an instant superstar and is hounded for photographs. An hour and entire roll of film goes by, as one after the other they pose with Dwain. The food keeps coming right through the photo shoot. Before leaving, we stop at a fruit cart to purchase apples. The fruit vendor throws in an extra apple. 'Because you are a guest from far away.'

I'm extremely disappointed. All that hype, and we've come across nothing but a bunch of warm and generous people. It's tragic how you can't depend on anyone these days. What's the world coming to if you can't find decent violence even when you go looking for it?

'It's odd how we spend most of our time fearing each other, when the world is mainly made of good and honest people,' I declare to Dwain as we head back to our room. 'All the violence is just media hype.'

'You've nailed it spot on,' Dwain concurs. 'Bihar is as peaceful as the Buddha.'

While we lay asleep in the Bhutanese Monastery, around four kilometers away the town of Gaya is forced wide awake. At midnight, a gang of armed dacoits cordon off an entire section of the town, and then proceed to loot the place at their own leisure. The police, reacting with exemplary enthusiasm, arrive only after the last thug had taken his pickings and lumbered away. Exactly as depicted by Bollywood. And the media.

LEG EIGHT

You Are the Worst Kind of Indian

BY NOON KAYA was across the River Son and Bihar's border. Not that entering Uttar Pradesh made a celebratory difference. The road showed little improvement and the towns remained rundown and dusty. Then suddenly, our eyes fell upon Varanasi. Mystical, mythical Varanasi. The city burned under the gaze of the sun, engulfed in a cloud of dust, a crush of buildings spilling over the banks of the sacred Ganges. All was still, except the flowing waters of the most worshipped river in the world.

Crossing the bridge into Varanasi, Kaya was overwhelmed by a sea of humanity and a crush of metal. She swerved, I swore, and together we knifed through improbable spaces. Accelerating hard. Braking harder. Traffic stood at a tangled standstill. Dust and fumes permeated the air. Thoughts were numbed by the din of blaring horns and screaming lungs. The place smelled like it was dying a poor death. What myth and mystique? It damn well felt like every other Indian city.

But then we crossed an unseen threshold, beyond which we were instantly transported into an older world, an unaltered map of the past. The crowds vanished. Gone was any sense of urgency. Time slowed down and time-worn walls closed in. The sun only broke through in dark shadows. Sounds became earthy and muffled. The air smelled of the ages, and fresh cow dung. Narrow lanes branched out erratically, into still narrower gullies and blind alleys, forming a bewildering maze. With barely sufficient space for a well-fed buffalo to meander through, I worried that Kaya's wide bottom would put us in a fix.

For three millennia Varanasi drew the devout. For the last three decades it has seduced the traveler; backpackers and hippies, excited by its aura of exoticism, profound spiritualism, and readily available narcotics. Catering to the needs of this new-age pilgrim, little enclaves have sprouted up along the ghats, where traditional homes have transformed into rustic hotels and cafes. We found a suitably atmospheric guesthouse. It was a place that writers write about, the kind where struggling authors – and the rare famous one – disappear to, to live in gloom and seek inspiration.

Leaving Dwain to rest his stiff back, I step out into the streets alone. A few meters forward, one turn, a few more meters, a second turn, another turn, a . . . where the hell am I? That I've already misplaced myself is not surprising. I have the ability to lose my way in a closet. I look around to regain my bearings and see a young boy walking towards me. Five feet tall, he is wearing a precisely ironed shirt and trousers, his oil-soaked hair pressed flat against his scalp, a thin wisp of pubescent growth foretelling his manhood.

'Hello brother, where from are you?' he throws at me in English.

'Hyderabad.'

'You're an Indian?'

'Why, don't I look like one?

'*Kya hain ki* we don't run into too many desi tourists around this area . . . Let it be brother, my name is Lucky and I'm very lucky for tourists.' He holds his hand out and I shake it.

'My name is Amit, and . . . well, I don't think I've brought much luck to anybody.'

'Do you smoke?' he asks nonchalantly, ignoring my poor attempt at humor.

'Smoke what?'

'I am selling very good hashish.'

'*Lucky* indeed.'

He leads me deeper into the maze. Uniformly yellow houses spill onto the road, no walls to separate the two. No sidewalks. Buildings merge into one another, a single structure running the length of the lane. Shops crouch at knee level, half underground and half over, tiny cupboard-sized niches-in-the-wall that require me to crouch if I want something. Occasionally, corridors extend low over our heads, connecting buildings on opposite sides of the street. Markets spill onto the cramped lanes, gleaming silverware, colorful vegetables, sooty blacksmiths, and smelly cattle sheds. The sharp scent of spices hangs in the air, mixed with the heady smell of sweets and the pervasive stench of dung.

Finally we pull up in front of a blue door, framed against a *paan*-stained wall. Above the door hangs a faded, hand-painted board, unconvincingly stating that this is a musical instruments store. Pasted on the wall beside it, a frayed poster offers flute, sitar and tabla classes. Lucky knocks on the blue door. It opens a crack and he squeezes through, gesturing for me to wait outside. I stand beside the door nonchalantly and pretend to show a keen interest in the town planning. My scanning eyes fall upon a pretty girl standing in the opposite doorway. She is in a blue dress, her hair pulled back in two plaits. She must be twelve. I wave to her. She smiles shyly and steps back into the darkness of the house.

'Do you like her?' Lucky asks, his head poking through the half-open blue door.

'She is re . . . what are you talking about?'

'This is Varanasi. You can have anything you desire,' he laughs wickedly, opening the door for me.

I step into a small room, and through the dense opium cloud I discern three people sitting on the floor. One is the Indian master and the other two his white disciples. I squat on the carpet and a Janis Joplin types hands me the pipe. I thank her, but refuse the offering. My mind is sufficiently exercised by marijuana. Two shelves contain an array of well-abused classical Indian instruments. Two glossy, color-ridden posters of Lord Shiva grace the wall in front of me. A pouty lipped Aishwarya Rai looks at me coyly from the right.

Once the couple has staggered out of the room, Lucky introduces me to his *Ustaad*. Forty-year-old Dhanur hails from Madhya Pradesh, as does Lucky. They spend six months of each year plying their trade here, and for the other six they do the same in Khajuraho. Dhanur tells me he's a genuine music teacher, but selling drugs is a much more profitable, and poetic, business according to him.

'*Kya Ustaad*, so you've stopped teaching?'

'No, no, I still conduct class every day. Right now I have four foreign students.'

'What about Indians?'

'Chah!' he spits, 'what Indian wants to learn classical instruments anymore? Their only interest is Western culture. They want piano and they want drums and that damned guitar.'

'Don't you find it difficult to teach if everybody is stoned all the time?' I rib him.

'No, no,' he smiles back. 'They are very hard-working. Plus, I have my own secret methods. If I am pleased with anybody, I reward them with a free hit.'

'*Wah Ustaad!* If I'd had teachers like you, I'd have achieved academic greatness.'

'How much do you want?' he asks, having finished with the foreplay.

'How much per *tola*?'

'Normally I sell for not less than five hundred, but because you are Indian and on such a long pilgrimage I will give it to you for four hundred rupees only.'

'Two *tolas* should be good.'

'I made a big mistake today,' he says, weighing the hash on a delicate hand-held balance. 'One Italian man came and bought some hash from me in the morning, instead I gave him opium.'

'What happened?'

'What will happen? Big loss for me. Big headache for him. Ha, ha.'

I take the sixteen-gram black ball from the cup of his hand, thank him and then turn to my fortunate friend. 'Lucky, I have to ask you for one last favor. Can you show me the way back, please?'

From the terrace of the hotel Dwain and I cast our gaze over the river. The sun is sinking behind us. The dusty veil that hangs over the city begins to shimmer in the orange light. Bright color boats sway gently in the grey waters. From a distance the call for prayers floats in with the wind, and below us the ghats slowly come to life. A few minutes later, having barely descended the first step down to the river, I run into another Lucky who isn't Lucky.

'Hi friend, you want some good hash?' he asks without preamble.

'*Nahi yaar, nahi chahiye.*'

'You are Indian? Brother, you want to buy hash, I give you good price.'

'No, thank you, I just bought some.'

'No problem. I can see that you are a man who appreciates quality. You have to try my hash. I assure you it's the best you'll find here.' He takes my hand and places in it a small amorphous black substance the size of a pea. 'Go on, just have a taste.'

'I really don't want to buy any.'

'No, you don't pay for this. It is free sample. You like, you buy more.'

'How will I find you?'

'Don't worry about that,' he assures me dramatically. 'If you are on the ghats, I'll find you.'

This is a completely novel and wonderful experience. Drug peddling with customer service. The best part being that you don't even have to look for it. It comes looking for you. With free samples.

A couple more steps and a flood of offers follow. Not just drugs. As Lucky pointed out, everything is for sale in Varanasi. I ignore them, as far as such a thing is possible. The scenario is most neatly summed up by the T-shirt every other backpacker in Varanasi seems to be wearing. Running down the front, the T-shirt reads:

No Boat

No Room

No Postcard

No Drugs

No Sex

NO PROBLEM.

The T-shirts don't seem to be helping anybody.

Another step. The air is saturated with the ripe scent of ganja. Instinctively, my eyes look to the dark corners. I forget where I am. In Varanasi you don't smoke in the shadows. This is Shiva's city. Sitting on the ghats running down to the Ganga, sadhus spark their *chillums*, heads held high looking to the heavens, faces glowing red in the fiery light of the cheroot before disappearing in a plume of smoke. Locals approach them casually, foreigners curiously, and pilgrims hesitantly. Everyone shares the one blessing, bound by one sacred duty. Selecting a suitably eccentric baba, Dwain and I hunker down as well.

'Om Namah Shivaya!'

'Boom Bholenath!'

'Boom!' The ritual chant echoes, with every lighting of the *chillum*.

This city so full of life is also a city of the dead. Deceased Hindus come from all over the country to be cremated on the ghats of Varanasi; some of them come while they are still alive, with the express purpose of dying here. Death in Varanasi is apparently good for the soul. We approach Manikarnika, one of Varanasi's famous 'burning ghats', just as they are preparing a body for cremation. People sit at a discreet distance, taking in the drama.

'Dwain, I'm not so sure about this . . . it seems a bit insensitive,' I say, thinking of the grieving family.

'I don't know about that,' he shrugs. 'It seems alright.'

'Well, is it alright?'

'Why the hell are you asking me? I'm the foreigner.'

'Well, you guys seem to know more about these sorts of things than we do.'

'Hmm—'

'Excuse,' a voice interrupts from behind, 'do you want a good place to watch the cremation from?' We turn around to see a middle-aged man, dark and skinny, yet muscular like a laborer. Tangled hair pushes out from his unbuttoned maroon shirt, which he's knotted at the ends and tucked into a blue and white checked dhoti. 'Come with me, I take you to best spot,' he offers. Sensing my doubt, he adds, 'People come from all corners to watch these cremations. It is good for your karma and for that of the departed soul.'

The funeral platform stands on the edge of the river bank, the sacred waters lapping at its base. Flames from the pyre reach for the skies, licking the air and consuming it with a burning passion. Only in India can a funeral become a tourist attraction, I muse, perched on a balcony overlooking the platform. All I need now is a bucket of popcorn.

Kilometer 7338

At dawn, the 'City of Light' comes into its own. Just before the appointed hour, thousands of devout Hindus gather on the ghats in anticipation of *suryodaya*, when the first rays of the new sun will purify them, and the waters of the Ganga will wash away their sins, leading to salvation. Personally, I'm not big on salvation, interrupting the continuous cycle of life-after-death. You'd think the natural tendency would be to keep on living, but no, the ultimate aim of every Hindu is to stay dead forever. According to us, nothing is as bad as life in the present age.

And so I stand, witness to a timeless vision. The orange fire of belief rises up to the sky, and the fervently waiting silhouettes bathe in its sanctifying light. Bells chime and ritual fires burn. Metal urns glint in the light as the Brahmans pour water over their heads. Sadhus, arms folded above their heads and standing on one foot, slowly lowering themselves into the river. Women struggle in their cumbersome saris, protecting their modesty, holding hands as they take the three plunges. Offerings of flower and fruit float away from the banks.

Aah, the blessed irony. The holiest icon, of the 'purest' religion, of a pollution-phobic people, is also the filthiest place in the world. According to Dwain's *Lonely Planet*, this stretch of the River Ganga is the most revoltingly dirty river in the world, with pollutant levels 1.5 million times above environmentally acceptable standards. I repeat: *1.5 million times above acceptable standards*. Near where we stand, a corpse wrapped in white cloth and weighted with a stone is dropped into the river from a boat. A few feet away, the ashes and un-charred remains of a cremated person are scattered into the river. To the left, buffaloes bathe and empty their bowels in the water. Dhobis do their washing on the ghats. Garbage floats by in miniature armadas. Further ahead, the black sewage of the city empties into the Holy Ganges.

And amidst all this I watch the devout. Stepping into the river. Taking a few sips of the water with unaffected veneration. For them, the Ganga is pure.

What do I believe?

I close my eyes and step forward, plunging into the . . .

If you think we are an apathetic people, let me confirm that indeed we are, but in this particular case certain attempts were made to clean up the Ganga. One of the imaginative solutions was to introduce turtles into the river to eat the undestroyed flesh. Unfortunately, somebody ate the turtles.

. . . dripping diseases, I emerge from the waters.

Feeling more putrefied than purified, I race for the shower.

We spend our last evening in Varanasi invoking Shiva on the ghat, and run into three Brits on the steps, playing the tabla and the mandolin, and smoking *chillums*.

'We've been here for months,' the tabla player says.

'Yeah man, it doesn't matter how long you are here, there is still something new to see each day,' the mandolin player adds.

'I've overstayed my visa and I'm out of money,' the unoccupied third rues. 'The only way I can get back to England is to somehow find a way to Nepal.'

'The real problem is bringing yourself to leave this place,' Tabla says.

'It's magical,' Mandolin concurs.

'Damn right,' Unoccupied agrees.

Before returning to the guest house, I buy a floating lamp from a young girl, light it and gently set it down on the water. I follow its flickering path, until it disappears into the darkness beyond.

Life always needs a bit of magic.

Kilometer 7541

Kaya was back on the road after three days of rest and recuperation. She had a few minor repairs carried out in Varanasi, but the front shakes hadn't left her. Still, there was nothing wrong with her heart, and the engine purred contently as she cruised towards Ayodhya. I, on the other hand, rode with disaffection eating my heart. For me, Ayodhya symbolized the end of innocence.

On December 6th, 1992, a large gathering of Hindu mentals – let's drop the *funda* part, they have none – converged on the city of Ayodhya, at the supposed birth place of Lord Rama; born lord-only-knows when, never died. By noon, a string of the finest political and religious thinkers completed their rabble-rousing speeches. At 12:30 the first *Kar Sevaks* eased their way past the police cordon protecting the inappropriately positioned mosque. By 12:35 the saffron banner fluttered atop the mosque's magnificent domes, with a sense of accomplishment akin to the Soviet flag over the ruins of the Reichstag. At 12:36 the first pickaxe blow fell, shattering the ancient brick and plaster. When the dust settled that evening, the 436-year-old Babri Masjid ceased to exist.

On December 6th, 1992, India was torn apart, like it hadn't been since the Partition. Riots broke out in cities across India – Bombay, Surat, Kanpur, Ahmedabad, and Delhi – leaving 2,000 dead. The country began its relationship with bomb blasts the following year, when they claimed 250 lives in Bombay. In Babri Masjid, terrorism in India had found its martyr. A decade later, a train returning from Ayodhya was set alight. More death, more killing. All this violence over an ancient pile of brick and mortar standing on an imaginary birthplace of a mythical character. To the mentals, destroying the mosque was 'an act of balancing history'. Unfortunately, you can't balance history by repeating its mistakes.

Kaya stops before the uninviting metal cordon around the disputed site. Standing here, all I can see is ugliness. Coils of barbed wire and a network of iron bars; gun-toting security forces standing in readiness. God the protector or god the protected? Leaving Dwain with Kaya, I step through the channel of barricades. Before I can enter the compound, the guards perform a body search. It can't be for bombs, since nothing remains to be destroyed. They are looking for cameras, which are barred from entering the premises. So great is the shame, and fear, no one has been permitted to photograph the site since the outrage.

It is too late, though. What are they trying to protect now? Not hope, not trust, not goodness, not god. All that is rubble. What lies before me is the pitiful wreckage of the national, or should I say Hindu, conscience. No temple has come up in place of the mosque. On a small plastic-wrapped platform rests the garlanded idol of Lord Ram. A priest watches over it, pocketing the money the trickle of misled pilgrims offer. Where is the glory in any of this? All we have raised in Ayodhya is hatred. My stomach churns, and I fight the urge to retch on this 'sacred ground'. I have no interest in being lynched. Restraining my treacherous tummy, I turn my back and walk away.

Back astride Kaya, I stayed quiet as she headed for Lucknow. I can't recollect much of the ride, or the spaces we passed through. Dwain sensed my disquiet, but I didn't bother explaining it. I didn't expect him to understand what I lost at Ayodhya.

On December 6th, 1992, I became different from a Muslim. One day of dying taught me what 13 years of living hadn't; that we weren't all the same. I'd known I was Hindu, but as far as I cared it was simply another thing handed down from my parents, like their palate for spicy food and penchant for pointless arguments. Religion was something performed for a few minutes but never carried out of the temple; it held all the appeal and devotion of a visit to the barber. I'd never tagged a person to their religion. And it never occurred to me that a friend might belong to one or the other.

Like the caste system, religious distinctions didn't exist in my developmentally-challenged mind. But then Ayodhya happened, introducing me to communal violence. In the madness and mayhem that was to follow, I unfortunately learned a lot: to look beyond the architectural differences between domed and spired building, to tell people apart people by their names, to realize my neighbor was actually my Muslim neighbor.

Sometime not long after Ayodhya, I was talking to my dad about our school's new cricketing talent while we drove to a restaurant. 'We have a new bowler in our team, Feroz,' I informed him. 'He's a Muslim,' I then added with no particular intent.

My father pulled the car over to the side and turned to me. The look of disappointment in his eyes will last with me forever.

As will his words. 'Do you think it makes a difference if he's a Muslim? Do you think religion makes a difference to how well he can play?'

I lowered my head to hide the tears welling up.

'Then why do you want to label him as anything? He is your teammate. A friend. And that's all that counts.'

I am grateful for those words, but it didn't make the knowing go away. The knowing that sharp differences exist, which can tear neighbors and classmates apart. The realizing that swathes of this country prescribe to these differences. The feeling that in some way I was tied to the tag Hindu, regardless of the penury of my faith. Perhaps the emotion is misplaced, but my resentment towards Ayodhya has never dimmed.

Two months after our visit to thc site, the makeshift temple was attacked by Islamic militants firing guns and hurling bombs. All six terrorists were gunned down. Two police personnel were critically wounded. One pilgrim died.

Kilometer 7745

Mid-April summer sun escorted Kaya along the Lucknow–Agra highway. The air burned 42 degrees and the road probably a hundred. It was the kind of heat that made the tar melt and tire tubes explode. Kaya's tank sizzled. Her engine fumed. Dwain lowered his head in fatigue. Near fainting, my heat-muddled brain distracted itself by musings on our magnanimous nature.

A fine example is the Residency in Lucknow, the battle-scarred walls of which stand testimony to the heroic British resistance against mutinous sepoys during the revolt of 1857. Revolt? Mutinous Indians? Gallant British? We might as well be singing 'God Save the Damn Queen'. 'The Revolt of 1857' is how my history books in school referred to the incident, and that's the way my high school teacher taught it. And yes, she called the Indians mutinous. In most countries, an incident involving fourteen drunken colonials, three dead natives, and one dead chicken is generously called a War of Independence; in all likelihood, even the chicken is turned into a martyr. But not us, we call a bloody struggle for freedom that extended across half the country a mutiny.

One particularly fine tourist article I read about the Residency begins, 'It is a visual commentary on one of the most poignant incidents during the British Raj.' It then goes into evocative detail about 'courage shown by British soldiers', 'Union Jack flew proudly', 'ruthless Indian assaults'. It was an exceptionally well-written article, making me want to leap to my feet and cheer the redcoats. An Indian wrote it.

Only in recent times has the term 'War of Independence' begun to replace revolt in popular usage. Still, the event receives little recognition. As a nation we have more celebrations and holidays than some countries have people, yet none commemorates 1857. It remains an event that invokes little passion, and no monuments have been raised in recognition of the fallen. In fact, the biggest memorial to India's War of Independence *is* the Residency. And this is dedicated to the British.

As memorials to the dead go, our next destination was home to the grandest of them all; one dedicated to love rather than war. Fighting her way through the bewildering confines of Taj Ganj, Kaya rolled to a halt by the banks of the river Yamuna, the world's most photographed dome mirrored in her murky waters.

Dwain and I watch the sun slowly sink along the river's length, disappearing behind the red bastions of Agra Fort, orange skies gently dissolving into purple mist. Behind rolls of barbed wire and fortified walls, the marble surface of the Taj Mahal glows blue. Between wire and wall stands a tented outpost, surrounded by sandbags and settled by gun-toting guards. We fall into conversation with 34-year-old Kishan, of the Special Tasks Force. Coming from Orissa, where his wife and two school-going sons still reside, he has spent the last fourteen months at this post. When I recollect passing through his home town of Brahmapur, he is so pleased he might have grabbed me to his chest, except for the barbwire separating us.

'Why is there so much security here?' I ask him.

'Few people are aware, but this is amongst the most sensitive places in the country,' he tells me. 'We receive frequent reports of terrorist threats against the Taj Mahal from Pakistan-based outfits. There is even danger of Hindu fanatics trying to damage it because of its Islamic heritage.'

'Has anything untoward happened while you've been around?'

'Not even the slightest. You know what? I think she is too beautiful for anyone to bring themselves to harm her.'

As we prepare to leave he tells us not to visit the Taj the next day. 'Wait till Monday. I'm not sure exactly why, but the entry may be free.'

'Hey thanks, man,' Dwain smiles at him. 'If that's true, you've saved me 15 dollars.'

'What's there to thank me for? Besides, if you boys have the time to drop in again, your company is always welcome. There's not much for me to do around here.'

Kilometer 8141

Returning to the banks of the Yamuna at dawn, we take a boat out in the darkness. The silence is replaced by a rhythmic splash of water. When the sun comes up, the river turns to gold, and the Taj Mahal blushes pink.

A small temple stands by the river's edge, a flight of stairs running into the water; an ideal perch from which to gaze at the Taj in undisturbed leisure. I sit down on the dirty steps. Dwain, a little more concerned about the seat of his pants, begins to sweep the surface with his feet.

'*Oye, kya kar rahe ho*?' a frantic shriek rises from behind us. I turn around to see an agitated man emerge from the temple and stride menacingly towards us. '*Roko*,' he growls, his attention focused on Dwain.

'Dwain, stop kicking that stuff around,' I say, instinctively recognizing the cause for the man's distress. What Dwain is brushing aside with his feet is not just dirt, but also seeds scattered by devotees for birds.

'Forgive us, brother,' I say turning to the man, who is now standing inches from us, his face red. 'My friend here isn't aware that the seeds are offerings.'

'What forgiveness?' he screams, his face turning redder. 'What do you people think of yourselves? No respect for anything, you bloody scoundrels.'

'Listen to me, it was a mistake and I'm terribly sorry. Please let it go, he's a foreigner and isn't aware of our traditions.'

'Yes, but you are an Indian, at least you should know how to behave.'

'Bullshit!' Dwain, snaps suddenly. 'What are you going on about man? Do you want to fight? Come on, let's have it out.' A foot taller, he screams down into the man's face.

'Don't talk too much. It won't go well for you,' the man threatens Dwain. Their threats are meaningless seeing how both are shouting in different tongues. Realizing this, the aggravated man turns his anger on me. 'You are the worst kind of Indian, running behind these white people like a dog. You are so fascinated by them, you have no respect for your own culture.'

'What culture are you talking about? The kind where we fight over bird seed?'

'Oye—'

'What? I said I'm sorry, and I genuinely mean it. I guess your pride will not be satisfied until someone is lynched.'

'Just shut up and get out of here okay.'

'Come on, Dwain, let's go somewhere else.'

'No way, man, I'm not leaving because of this bastard. Who does he think he is?'

'Fine, you both can fight it out. I'm leaving.' I walk away, without looking to see if Dwain is following. A minute later, he catches up with me.

On the rooftops of Taj Ganj we escape the commercial bustle of the streets below, to sit back and enjoy the grandeur of the Taj Mahal while sipping a cup of tea. Here the morning air resonates with the flutter of wings and sharp whistles, as it has for centuries. The Mughal passion for birds found its expression in the sport of *kabootar bazi*, or pigeon fighting, and the tradition is alive and flourishing on these rooftops.

'While feeding the birds is repose for the soul, training them does the same for the mind,' explains Khalid, the manager of the rooftop restaurant.

I watch intently as expert *kabootars* wave sticks with a colored cloth flapping from it. They whistle and coo to their flock, while the birds fly in swooping circles above the roofs before returning to their homes to feed.

'So, which part of this is the sport?' I ask.

'The trick is to get your flock to combine with the opponent's flying pigeons and lead them into your coops,' Khalid tells us. 'The hijacked birds are then held for ransom, the winner's spoils.'

'Sounds like something that belongs in the terrorist Olympics.'

'It is very relaxing,' Khalid protests.

Later, Dwain and I visit Fatehpur Sikri, the victory city that was abandoned within 13 years because it ran out of water. We are mulling over the astuteness of Akbar when two security guards approach us. 'Show me the ticket for your video camera,' one of them addresses Dwain, pointing to the video camera in his hand.

'I don't have a ticket. This is a dual camera and I am only using it to take still photographs,' Dwain explains to them.

'Why are you trying to cheat us?' the guard says, shaking his head. 'Do you think we are fools?'

'Look, you can view the tape and check for yourself if there is any footage,' I offer.

'Why are you supporting him?' he barks at me, his unprovoked anger taking me by surprise.

'I . . . I'm not taking any sides—'

'You're all the same. Showing off in front of foreigners.'

'Listen, I—'

'Which state are you from?'

'Andhra.'

'Who is its chief minister?'

'What are you talking about . . . ?' I say, failing to understand where this conversation is headed.

'You don't know who the chief minister is, do you?' he smiles triumphantly. 'Do you know anything about your own country?'

For a second I'm too stunned to react. 'RAJSHEKAR REDDY, YOU ARROGANT SHIT.' My scream shatters the momentary silence. 'Who do you think you are?'

'*Chillana mat, bas niklo yaha se*,' he pushes me roughly towards the exit.

'What the . . . ?' Dwain jumps in and grabs his arm.

'Dwain, let him go.' My eyes are riveted on the guard. 'You touch me again and you're not going to have a job.' I glare at him, unwavering. My voice is calm, but the threat is implicit. 'I don't want to fight, but I'm not taking any nonsense from you either.'

'Just leave—'

'I am going to linger here till I feel like. If you think you can do something about it, you're welcome to go ahead and try.' As we walk away from them, I hear murmurings behind my back, and then nothing more.

Twice today I've been confronted by the same allegation. On both occasions it hit a raw spot. That Indians are fascinated-bordering-on-obsessed with white people is a national cliché, and logically I was immensely pleased to be accused of being a foreigner-lover. After all, I did want to be a real Indian, didn't I? It's the second part of the accusation which invariably hurt, that I didn't know my culture. Wasn't I the one on a journey to be the ultimate Indian? How dare these fools question my national integrity?

At 5:45 on Monday morning, Dwain and I are standing at the entrance gate to the Taj, where a large banner greets us, announcing sleepily: 'World Heritage Day'. And, as we discover, on this day heritage monuments across the globe are open to the public for free. In the fifteen minutes to opening time, an entire division of tourists has mobilized behind us, all of them as determined to get an unobstructed view of the monument.

As soon as the gates open I'm on a blind charge, running for the archway that opens onto the central courtyard. I step through it and pull up short. The sight of the Taj Mahal before me does not register in my mind. There isn't time for such irrelevancies. I lift the camera to my eye and reel off a couple of shots. I take a quick look at the output, make a minor adjustment to the exposure, and bring the camera to my eye again.

Hey, who stole my Taj Mahal?

I can no longer see her, my viewfinder filled with people.

The Taj draws more than 3 million visitors every year, which, assisted by some terrible mathematics, approximates to 10,000 a day. Undoubtedly the most popular destination for Indians, the monument draws visitors from every corner of the country. If at any point you get bored of staring at the cold marble walls, the Taj Mahal provides an impromptu cultural convention, with Rajasthanis in colorful turbans, Malayalis draped in cream saris, flowers in their hair, Tamilians with powdered faces and lungi-wrapped waists, Marathis donning Gandhi caps. All of them armed with picnic baskets.

Leaving the Taj, we head over to thank the security guard who'd tipped us off on the free entry. Kishan is delighted that we've dropped in on him again. Asking us to wait, he disappears into the tent and returns with a large tiffin box in his hand. He opens it and proffers the contents to us.

'*Rasagollas* from Orissa,' he beams. 'They are the best.'

LEG NINE

Salvation Comes Only Through Struggle

KAYA WAS GLAD to be back on the road, having spent a week in Delhi receiving some much needed rest and repairs. We left the dry heat and the dust-blown plains for the cool and lush environs of Uttaranchal, the start of a two-month sojourn in the mountains. But first, we were headed to Corbett National Park, India's oldest forest reserve and the launch pad for Project Tiger, in search of our national animal. My excitement grew as Kaya rolled deeper into the wilderness, accompanied by a tinge of foreboding, for, along with the wildlife, I was also about to have an encounter with Supermom.

And not just mum, but her sister and cousin were also going to join me for a couple of days, or, should I say, watch over me from the confines of their car. And no, they weren't holding me hostage; rather, I'd asked them to join me. Since one of my motives was to promote travel, home seemed a convenient place to start. I also hoped by sharing the experience with me, they'd understand my own motives better. Kaya comes to a well-behaved halt in front of my mum, at the entrance of Camp Forktail Creek, where I'd made reservations.

'Ooh! Look how thin he's become,' mum wails.

'Sheesh, see how shabby his hair is,' cousin grimaces.

'Tsk, tsk, why have you become so dark?' aunt scolds.

And that's not all they have to complain about.

'What do you mean we're staying in a tent???' my mum splutters in disbelief, on seeing the accommodation at Forktail.

'They don't even have attached bathrooms,' cousin adds in support.

'And I see that there a lot of flies around,' aunt grimaces in disgust.

Well, so much for introducing them to the pleasures of camping. Since the jungle camp has been vetoed, I make a halfhearted beeline for the Corbett Reception Office, aware of the improbability of finding last minute accommodation within the park.

'Sorry. All rooms are currently occupied,' the receptionist at the information desk says, confirming my worst fears.

'I see . . . well . . . is there nothing you can do . . . ?' I mumble dejectedly.

'I wish I could help but every ro— Wait, actually, we do have this one place. Tell me, do you have your own transport?'

'Yes.'

'There's a forest rest house within the sanctuary, at Sarapduli. Usually occupied by long-timers and forest officials, it's not part of the main tourist complex. I must warn you that there are no services there, so you have to cook your own dinner in the kitchen. Also, the bungalow is extremely isolated and there's no electricity either. Are you sure you want to stay there?'

'Does it have walls?'

'What??? . . . yes.'

'Excellent! I'll take it.'

I am forced to park Kaya at the forest check-post and get into the car with the ladies since two wheelers are not permitted into the core area of tiger sanctuaries. It's an illogical rule really. Why would a tiger want to harm a motorcycle? Or vice versa. Inside the park a dirt track winds its way over small undulating hills, through tangled forests of green and brown, past dry river beds, large white boulders gleaming under the sun. The traffic is heavy. We have to stop for a rampaging wild boar, skulking lizards, umpteen deer, and a peacock who wishes to cross the road, tail trailing.

Deep within the jungle, the old bungalow peeps through the thicket, standing on a small clearing by the banks of the river. No other sign of civilization exists around the whitewashed building. Inside, it has cold shadowy floors, a high vaulted roof, and two bedrooms the size of tennis courts, with large kingly beds.

'Ooh! What lovely bathrooms,' my aunt coos.

Everybody is satisfied.

The peal of a peacock rents through the pre-dawn stillness. I step out of the bungalow to find a herd of deer walking through grey mists, no more than a body length from me. The moist veil parts to reveal an elephant herd bathing in the icy waters, followed by a roll-in-the-mud on the opposite bank. From the depths of the forest rises a monkey's howl. Birds take to the sky. I thump my chest, feeling like Tarzan.

'Where do you think you're going without sunscreen?' my aunt calls after me.

Our search for the elusive tiger begins at Dhikuli, the main tourist center within the forest, where we first need to pick up a guide, and his gun. Driving around the core area is strictly prohibited unless accompanied by both, and while I'm totally on board with the presence of thc former, I can't say the same for the gun. This country is home to more than one billion people – classified as overpopulated. On the other hand, it shelters less than two thousand tigers – classified as endangered. So, tell me, where's the fucking logic in shooting a tiger to protect an Indian?

While the gun is troubling, the tourist complex is positively traumatizing. Sprawling over a fenced-in acreage, Dhikuli consists of a row of suburban concrete blocks set amidst walkways and lawns. It has a general store, a gift shop, and a restaurant. Five teenagers stand around a car, music blaring through its open doors. Bored drivers sit around smoking cigarettes and playing a game of cards. Three kids raucously chase an inflatable ball around the lawn. A couple strolls by holding hands lovingly; their free hands clutch coke bottles with equal ardor. The scene is straight out of my gated community in Hyderabad. Instead of escaping the city to a better place, we've transported the city to a better place. We've given the term 'urban jungle' an all new significance. And the people are loving it.

'Our bungalow has much more charm,' my mum observes, reflecting my very thoughts.

I reward her with a loving smile.

Over the next two days we patiently scout the web of tracks running through the forest and over the savannah grassland of the *chaurs*. Finally, around teatime on the second day, a tigress steps out of the bush, crossing a narrow stream no more than fifteen meters in front of us, her sinuous gold body flowing more than walking, the dark stripes forming ripples. The news of our spotting improbably broke the light barrier, for within moments a division of jeeps are recklessly charging towards us. A minute later, the wilderness has turned into a circus. As the tigress cowers in the bush, disturbed by the commotion, I am left wishing we hadn't spotted her.

'Okay, now that we've seen a tiger, can we leave, please?' cousin sighs.

'Ooh yes, we can spend the night at Nainital,' aunt agrees.

On our way out of the park I notice a pale and timid sign, half concealed in the foliage. 'Do not enter forest area,' it says. I ask the driver to stop. Getting out of the car, I clear the weeds around the sign. Then, using my cousin's red lipstick, I overwrite: 'Non Animals Not Allowed'.

Kilometer 8805

Stalked the entire time by the Qualis carrying my family, Kaya took a lot more than the prescribed two hours to reach Nainital. And within a minute of getting there I was desperate to get back down. Nainital is a paean to Popcorn Tourism – like a visit to the cinemas of late, where after a few cheap thrills you find that the only thing the movie has going for it is the popcorn.

Once an evocative lake hemmed in by green hills, today Nainital is a festering clog of thoughtless development. A volcano spewing molten concrete would have created a better town than the crush of rundown buildings and rain-eaten plaster that had taken over the hillside. Neon advertising lit up the slopes like a cheap Christmas tree, and every lookout came with a side order of dangling electricity cables. A hundred tacky restaurants rim the lake, but not one had a view of it. Hawkers sold bags of chips, *bhel puri*, and *'garma-garam' bhutta*; the leftovers of which tourists generously shared with the lake. Multi-hued plastic swan-boats bobbed amidst the debris.

'This place is wonderful,' my mum exclaimed, undoing all the good karma she had accumulated in Corbett.

Bidding farewell to my folks, Kaya and I headed out by ourselves. Escaping from Nainital, for the first time in all these kilometers it was just the two of us. I felt lighter, freer. The road immediately became more personal. We passed Almora, following a serpentine route over crests and troughs, the rolling hills carpeted by golden terraces, deodar woods, groves of oak and fir, and thick swathes of pine. A cushion of brown leaves covered the forest floor and paved the roadsides. Blue monals and black babblers swooped down in front of Kaya. Heavy clouds hung low over the vistas, concealing the glacial peaks beyond. And then we passed Pithoragarh.

Looking down from our lofty heights, I saw my path extending for miles along the hillsides. We followed the meandering course of the river, deeper into the mountains. Where the pines disappeared, entire slopes had been turned into terraced fields, like large golden steps descending the face of a hill. Stacks of hay stood in tepee-shaped piles. Blue and gray skies. Green rivers. Autumnal leaves. Golden fields. Red earth. The colors of life.

Having threatened all along, the rain gods finally struck, catching us out in the open. Within seconds I was soaked to my chuddies. The visibility dropped to wherever Kaya's front tire landed. Then the cold set in.

Spotting a solitary house by the side of the road, Kaya pulled over.

I squish over to the house's awning and take shelter under it, trembling. I blow into my numb fingers, trying to get some feeling back into them. Suddenly, an elderly woman sticks her head out of the open door and waves me over.

'Why are you standing there in the cold?' she berates me. 'Come inside, come inside. And bring your motorcycle under the awning. Look how it's getting wet.'

From where I sit, on a wooden stool, I can see only one other room in the small house. There might be more, but I don't think so. It is gloomy inside, grey light diffusing in through two windows. The power is out. The floor is clean and the walls aged. One corner of the room belongs to god. On a small stand sit the idols and lithographs of the usual suspects. A dulled calendar of Lakshmi graces the wall, a shower of gold coins falling from her palms. Its dates belong to 2001. The only other adornment on the wall is a photograph of a young man in military attire, the elder son serving with the army.

A large trunk rests in another corner, on which two elder men sit. The second son stands by the door leading to the inner room, which I think is the kitchen. A young woman sits on a floor mat. The elder lady who'd invited me in puts a cup of hot tea in my trembling hands. Five sets of eyes are trained on me.

'Look at him,' my benefactor says. 'He's shivering so much he can't even hold the glass.'

'Where are you going?' the young man asks.

'Munsyari.'

'I doubt you'll make it there tonight. The road ahead gets really bad.'

'There's still a fair bit of light,' I reply optimistically.

'Yes, but it's an unnecessary risk and there isn't much around if you have a problem . . . god forbid.'

'Yes, yes, it is not safe,' my benefactor affirms. 'You should stay here and go in the morning.'

'You . . . well, yes . . . if you need to, you can spend the night in our house,' the old man offers, more hesitantly than his wife.

'Oh no, that won't be necessary,' I jump in, trying to bail him out. 'It looks like the rain will let up soon. I'm sure I can make it to the next town, if not Munsyari.'

'Yes, Didihat,' he confirms, seeming much happier with this option. 'You will get to Didihat without difficulty. It's about forty kilometers ahead and they have a traveler's house there.'

I tell them about my travels around the country and they talk to me about their son's travels with the army, and then we run out of things to talk about, but the five sets of eyes continue to devour me. It's only the easing of the rain that rescues us from the silence, and I take my leave. I am about to get onto Kaya when my benefactor comes scurrying out of the house and hands me a rag. 'To wipe the wet seat,' she tells me. I am gripped by a desire to hug her; rather, I remove a bar of well-watered Dairy Milk chocolate from what I'd thought all along was a waterproof jacket pocket and, placing it in the cup of her palms, I fold my hands over hers. She lets out a childlike giggle.

Getting back on Kaya, I feel surprisingly warm.

Kilometer 9302

Kaya and I made a lazy exit from Didihat in the morning. The ride to Munsyari kicked off just swell, got progressively better, and before long bordered on stupendous. It began with a 'shortcut' through the fringes of Askot Wildlife Sanctuary. And like most ill-considered detours, the only thing it was short on was sense. Kaya chose a furrowed dirt track climbing the wet hills, cutting through shadowy jungles and pools of stagnant sludge. Slippery, it was a torturously cautious ride.

Real travelers must always take shortcuts – even when they can't find one. Why? Because shortcuts invariably make the journey longer. The more shortcuts you take, the longer you travel. The longer you travel, the further you go. The further you go, the more you see. So despite visiting the same destinations as everybody else, a shortcut traveler sees more and travels more. Besides, shortcuts provide great opportunities to get lost, and have numerous time-consuming mishaps, while you try to find yourself again.

Past the sanctuary, Kaya encountered the first strip of paved road, but it didn't last long, bifurcating into a dirt track, which led into a tranquil valley. Mountain goats and pack mules were our only companions, their master lost somewhere in the herd. As we ascended to ever greater heights, the air got crisper. Gentle slopes gave way to sheer crags, the forests replaced by scrubby grass. Streams plunged down the cliff to join the river – tall, short, nearby, in the distance, wide, narrow, trickling, and thundering. One cascade arched over the road, forming a watery gateway for Kaya to pass under. Pebbled streams flowed across our path. The world grew more isolated.

Kaya squeezed past an army mule-train and entered Munsyari, coming to a halt in front of a guest house.

Munsyari, a tiny settlement scattered along a slope facing the snowy peaks of Panchchuli, is on the very edge of habitation; the base camp for a seven-day trek to Milam Glacier. After checking into a dorm, I promptly lug my backpack onto my shoulders and head out to find a guide. Having decided to exercise my legs all the way to the glacier, this is my last ditch effort at 'getting fit' for the forthcoming ordeal. Barely a kilometer later, I stagger into an establishment called Adventure Treks, gasping for air and sounding like Darth Vader on a respirator. I half expect the guide to shoo me out in disgust. Instead, he welcomes me in, offers me some water, then a cup of tea, and launches into a pitch on the wonders of the trek.

'So, when can we leave then?' I ask.

'We can't, at least not yet,' he smiles calmly.

'What do you mean?'

'See, the path, which is snowed in during winter, is usually cleared by this time of the year, but what to say, we've had a particularly harsh winter. And now this rain, it has delayed everything.'

'When do you think the trail will be cleared for us to go?'

'Oh, I'm sure it will be okay in a week or so.'

'A week! What will I do here for that long?'

'You can relax till then. Munsyari is very peaceful,' he suggests sympathetically. 'And I can get you good hash.'

Carrying my backpack, my disappointment, and the hash, I trudge to the edge of the hill and sit on a rock. The five pointed peaks of Panchchuli ascend 6,500 meters to the skies, not that I can confirm the fact with the summits lost behind dark grey clouds. Icy tendrils flow down the jagged face, creating a narrow white valley, leading deep into the frozen heart of the mountains. Gazing wistfully at the trail I'm hoping to follow, I roll a joint.

Having just created a few of my own clouds, my paranoid ears pick up the shuffle of feet behind me. I casually drop the joint at my feet and turn around. Shit! Two uniformed men are standing over me. The beginnings of a false smile is cut short by the moustached one.

'You're smoking ganja?'

'Who me . . . no, sir, not at all.'

'*Chodo yaar*, why are you lying? I can smell it. We just want a couple of drags.'

'Oh!' I'm not sure I believe him, but with little real choice, I bend down and uneasily pick up the joint. I look up to see the uniforms smiling at me. I smile back, relight the joint and hand it to Mr. Moustache.

'Why did you get so scared on seeing us?' Moustache asks.

'He must have thought we're cops,' Clean Shaven laughs.

'Ha, ha, yeah? So you thought we were the cops?'

'Er, no . . . not at all,' I mutter, still clueless about who they are.

'We belong to ITBP. Our military base is just around this hill. What about you, where have you come from?

'Hyderabad.'

'Andhra Pradesh! Hey, we have a guy from your state in our unit. I'm sure he'd like to meet you. Just stay here okay. We're heading back to the base, we'll send him out.'

'Yeah sure, I can wait.'

They disappear around the hill, the men from Indo-Tibetan Border Police, who have the distinction of guarding some of the most extreme regions in the world. Ten minutes later a solitary figure emerges from the same direction. Hailing from Vijayawada, Narsimha Chary is tall for a South Indian, but his features are unmistakable. He sports a thick moustache. Mournful eyes stare from under bushy brows. A sharp nose and a prominent jaw complete the face. We talk in Telugu.

'You must be mad to come here by motorcycle,' he laughs at me.

'You must be mad to come here with the army,' I dish back.

'I have to agree,' he says wistfully. 'I grew up in forty degree heat, and now I have to freeze in the negative forties. I hate this job.'

'Then why did you volunteer for the Special Forces?'

'Better pay. Earlier retirement. You'd be surprised how many South Indians are posted in these places. Besides, not all the postings are as bad. My next transfer will hopefully take me somewhere nice in Ladakh or Kashmir. That's like a summer on the plains in comparison.'

'Does it get very dangerous out there?'

'Sometimes. The snow glare is so fierce we can never step out without protective goggles, otherwise you'll get blinded. And the featureless expanse plays tricks on your mind. It's quite easy to get lost, and it does happen that sometimes soldiers disappear. Mostly, though, it's a dreary job. We spend our time watching movies and playing cards.'

'But what about the enemy?'

'Who, the chinkies? They are a tough lot, and the bastards seem to handle the cold much better than us. Anyway, they don't trouble us too much. Sometimes we meet up just to maintain friendly relations, share a cigarette and stuff like that. Then again, you get too close without the proper signals and you'll have unwanted Made-in-China objects flying at you.'

'Ha, is there anybody else from Andhra with your unit?'

'Right now, no. There are a couple of Kannadigas. It's the same for a lot of us. We all come from different places. The only time I get to talk in Telugu now is when I call home. That's why it's always nice to run into somebody from home. Besides, I'm not going to see a new face for the next six months.'

'Why is that?'

'We are moving out to Milam Glacier tomorrow.'

'Milam! But the path is closed. I planned to go there myself, but I was told it's still unsafe. And look at this weather.'

'Maybe it's closed for civilians. But we will have to leave tomorrow. The previous unit has spent an entire winter in that frozen hell and we were meant to relieve them two days ago. It can't be delayed anymore.'

'What if the weather gets worse?'

'We leave tomorrow morning,' he says evenly. 'I'll give you my home address. When you pass through Vijayawada you should stop over and say hi to my family.'

I sit alone for a few minutes after he's gone. Then, picking up my pack, I start the breathless walk back to the dorm. Two minutes into my struggle, it begins to pour.

I'm back at the same perch at 5:30 in the morning, praying for an interesting sunrise. The light diffuses in slowly. The world before me is . . . white fluffiness. At 6:30, the sun is M.I.A. Meanwhile, the fluffiness has come together at the top to form an ominous grey. At 7:45, I shrug off the summits as a lost cause. Half hour later, I see a human train slowly making its way down the slope, to the bottom of the valley and towards the white beyond. It's the army unit on the move. I yell to them and start waving. A number of hands wave back . . . maybe one of them was Narsimha's.

I make up my mind to leave as well, only I'm going to stay on the road.

Kilometer 9453

Over the next three days Kaya followed a constantly changing river across the mountains, from the eastern rim of Uttaranchal to her western borders. Economically a 'backward state', the geographical conditions are not conducive to commercial agriculture, and the hill towns exist on subsistence farming, and on sons donated to the armed forces. Meanwhile, industrialization is as conspicuous as acne on a movie star. The towns are small and scattered, few buildings grow more than a story tall. With barely any private vehicles to speak of, we have the road to ourselves. Sporadically, collective jeeps pass by, the passengers precariously dangling out of them. Even rarer are the public buses, groaning up the slopes, nudging everybody else to the edge of the narrow roads. Time moved at a more leisurely pace here, and while the state might be poor, I saw little poverty . . . little ugliness.

When I finally returned to the plains, it was also a return to the usual signs of urbanization: chaos, filth, and poverty. Originally known as Mayapur 'the magic city', Haridwar, located at the foothills of the Shiwalik Range, is the gateway to the 'abode of gods'. Here, the holy Ganga, descending from its glacial source, touches the plains for the first time; carrying with it life, laying down silt, watering the lands that formed the cradle of Indian civilization.

All in all Haridwar is pretty sacred, and seeking salvation, at daybreak I step onto the ghats to bathe in the gentle gaze of the sun and the icy flow of the river. Emerging from the waters, I console my freezing body that any sin attached to me has to have shriveled up and died. Around me, the pious go through the numbing ordeal in unmindful ecstasy. On the ghats are as many sadhus and temple beggars as pilgrims, squatting on the paved banks, praying for charity while also praying to their *chillums*. I donate breakfast from the Bharat Scouts and Guides *langar* to a group of ten sadhus, sharing the insipid *khichdi* and *halwa* with them. In gratitude, they later share a *chillum* with me.

Behind the ghats runs a crowded market, rows of lean-to stalls facing each other, the narrow path between them canopied by blue and yellow plastic sheets. Pyramids of vermilion powder spill out of shimmering steel bowls. Bags of dried fruits stand by the tables. Shelves display cheap plastic trinkets, kitschy images of gods, and audio cassettes of devotional music. Shopkeepers call out to me, offering prayer materials and amulets. Though I keep walking, there are hundreds of other devout victims to keep the merchants happy.

A white cow is also on her morning stroll through the market, her ample size taking up most of the path. But she doesn't seem to mind. Neither does anyone else, except for a cycle-rickshaw driver, who, in a rush to get past the cow, bumps into her. He then makes the grave error of stopping to hurl abuses at the bovine pedestrian. Like Superman of the speeding bullet fame, a shopkeeper leaps from his stall and, grabbing the rickshaw driver by the scruff of his collar, gives him a resounding smack. I wince just from the echo of the blow.

While global awareness on what a Hindu is and where these bizarre people might come from is minimal, almost everyone seems to know that in India the cow is sacred. And for once it's no exaggerated stereotype, for no animal in the world is held in such high regard, aptly illustrated by the first poem I learnt in Hindi class: '*Gai Hamari Mata Hain*'. Indians have probably fought more wars over cows than the rest of the world over oil. During Islamic reigns, militant cow-protectors became the greatest rallying point for Hindu communities. Our First War of Independence had more to do with cows – and pigs, of course – than any sense of nationalism. More recently, Gandhi is supposed to have said, 'Hinduism will live as long as there are Hindus to protect the cows', which honestly makes no sense; you'd think 'Hinduism will live as long as there are Hindus', period. In any case, if Hindus fail to perform their duty, the cow is also protected by the Indian Constitution. It's probably easier for a cow to get justice in this country than a human.

So the beating the cyclist is receiving should surprise no one, and though my heart goes out to him, my cowardice keeps me from interfering.

'That's right, teach the scumbag a lesson,' a voice encourages.

'He must be the same bastard who hurt the cow previously,' another voice calls out. The mob is now gripped by bloodlust.

Smack! 'You people only understand force,' the shopkeeper screams at the cowering cyclist, striking him again. 'Learn to behave according to your status. If I see you around here again . . .' he warns, shoving him against the rickshaw.

His cheek buried in one arm, the cyclist pushes his rickshaw a few feet before getting back on and riding away. People carry on grumbling behind his back. The cow, meanwhile, has continued on her stroll, quite unperturbed by all the fuss.

At sunset, the ghats echo to the ritual Ganga prayer. Pilgrims, hundreds of them, sit on both banks of the river. Others wade into the gushing water. Before the temple, priests perform operatic ceremonies with grand props. My search for a convenient perch is waylaid by a well-groomed man in a silk *kurta-pyjama*.

'Looking for a good place, eh? Come with me,' he says without preamble, and grabbing my hand, pulls me through the crowd. 'Have you performed the *pooja*?' he continues before I can recover from the kidnapping.

'Uh . . . not really.'

'Oye *chotu*, bring the *pooja* material,' he shouts to a kid buzzing around purposefully. 'Well, here we are.'

As promised, he has brought me to an excellent spot by the edge of the river, just beside the main ghat where the ceremony is taking place. An instant later, I'm holding a basket of votive offerings in my hand and he's prattling in Sanskrit. It's all so slick I haven't had the chance to react, let alone make a decision. I feel foolish, annoyed, and trapped, all at the same time. And I also feel unsure. I can't snub him in the middle of a prayer, can I? That would be rude . . . and blasphemous.

His cell phone rings. He halts the prayer to answer it. He is sharing a joke with the person on the other end. My eyes wander. They are everywhere, his ilk, wearing expensive silks and gleaming jewelry. Their watches look flashy, as do the constantly interrupting cell phones. They remind me of hotel receptionists . . . and of hyenas.

'How much will you donate for Ganga Mata's sari?' my priest asks me.

'Er . . . nothing,' I barely manage, stumped at the idea that a river needs to be clothed.

'How many kilograms of ghee will you donate to the holy mother?'

'I . . . uh, zero. Listen, I don't want to do this.'

'*Chalo theek hain*,' he brushes aside my objections. 'But you must at least feed some Brahmans?'

'Fine,' I relent.

'How many would you like to feed?'

'Five.'

'What is five?' he smiles, making me want to throw up. 'You should feed more.'

'Alright then, ten. What is this going to cost me?'

'One thousand five hundred rupees.'

'*How much!*'

'One thousand five hundred rupees,' he repeats casually.

'What are you talking about? I fed ten sadhus for two hundred and fifty rupees just this afternoon.'

'Those are beggars,' he corrects me haughtily. 'You feed them out of pity. We are Brahman, the caretakers of religion. To feed the Brahman is your duty. You will be blessed.'

The sense of relief is rapturous. The shackles of guilt, ingrained fear, and inculcated reverence have finally fallen off, and for the first time I understand the priesthood for what it is: a career. There is nothing pure or sacred about a priest, as I'd foolishly believed. 'Brahman' is nothing more than a job description, and as in any job they are only entitled to the respect and reward as the service provided.

'How much for this prayer material?' I ask, indicating the basket in my hand.

'Thirty rupees,' he replies.

I put a fifty rupee note in the basket, hand it over to him and walk away, quite pleased with myself. I should have also thanked him for opening my eyes.

At the end of the ceremonial Ganga prayer, crackling public speakers announce to the gathered pilgrims that representatives will come around to collect money and all true believers should donate freely. The anonymous voice reiterates what a wonderful thing it is to donate money here. 'It is a great blessing, and those who give generously will most certainly find happiness.' They even give you a receipt. Maybe it can be traded in for karma points.

Kilometer 10030

From Haridwar, over the next thousand kilometers Kaya joined a steady stream of taxis and tour buses dragging themselves up the northern mountains of Uttaranchal along one of the principle Hindu pilgrim circuits, to the sources of four sacred rivers: Yamuna at Yamunotri, Ganga at Gangotri, Mandakini at Kedarnath, and Alaknanda at Badrinath. The roads are passable only for a few months a year, and during that period Hindus in the tens of thousands make the annual journey to these glacial peaks.

Kaya climbed higher than ever before. The mountains grew taller, hemming us within narrow corridors. Glaciers hung from snow-covered crests, their thawing bodies morphing into sanctified rivers. Conical conifers rolled down the lower slopes, spilling onto the river bed. The ground was a carpet of grass and pine needle. Shimmering streams cut a white course through the green, feeding the river below. We flowed to the river's source. The river flowed away from us. Through plunging ravines, across gentle sandbars, and over rocky beds.

Hanuman Chatti, where most pilgrims halt for the night, signaled the end of the road for buses and cars to Yamunotri, beyond which extended a steep dirt track accessible only to four-wheel drives and horses. And to one intrepid and slightly overweight motorcycle. Bouncing along the furrowed path, Kaya suddenly started to emit a rasping noise from around her rear tire. The culprit was a menacingly long nail, which had pierced clean through the rubber of the tire, miraculously leaving the tube untouched. Having extracted the nail from the tire, Kaya moved gingerly over the last few kilometers, coming to a relieved halt at Janaki Chatti.

Janaki Chatti, all of one ashram and two hotels, is where a vertical seven-kilometer hike to Yamunotri begins. I pitch my tent beside a gurgling stream, a soft carpet of grass my floor, the snowy crown of Bandar Poonch Parvat (Mount Monkey Tail) shimmering behind. Falling asleep while dusk's soft glow still permeates the valley, I am woken to the squeal of tires rushing past the tent. I poke my head out to find dawn fast approaching. It's time to start walking. Leaving Kaya and my bags at the ashram, I join the human chain that is already winding its way to the glacier.

Logically, the way to go about a trek is to put one foot in front of the other, and repeat until satisfactory results are achieved. Oddly, a substantial percentage of the population seem to find the idea preposterous. Scores of horses and mules crowd a clearing at the base of the climb, while the elderly, overweight, unfit, or just-plain-lazy haggle with the owners over a good price to have the animals carry them to the top. For those who find the horses expensive, or uncomfortable, a cheaper option is to sit back on a palanquin while four others do the walking for you. Even cheaper is the *pittu*, a human mule who single-handedly carries you up the mountain in a basket slung over his back. His asking price is a hundred and fifty rupees but, judging from the negotiations, it appears he can be had for a discount. People being carried – a sight from hospitals and funeral processions. I hurl looks of disgust at the pilgrims using palanquins and *pittus*, disparaging them under my breath. Have they no principles? My agonizing is interrupted by one of the porters.

'Sir, would you like to sit on the palanquin?' he asks me politely. 'It is very comfortable, sir. We will get you up in no time.'

'No, thank you, my brother,' I reply righteously.

A minute later someone else approaches me. 'Sir, take *pittu* sir, I'll carry you on my back,' he insists. 'The walk is very difficult. Why put yourself through the trouble?'

'No, brother, I'm quite capable of walking,' I wave him away, still smiling. I begin to walk, feeling good about myself.

'Sir, it is very cheap,' another person offers. He is the tenth person to approach me in as many steps. 'If you like, I give you discount . . . yes?'

My arrogance has crumbled by now. I hear the pleading in his voice. I see the expectation in his eyes. Just then, a pilgrim comes up and asks the porter to carry his child. The porter smiles at the pilgrim with genuine relief. He smiles because he has found work. Because he can now take home some money. For all my moralizing, I'm the one contributing nothing to their lives.

'Sir, you want to sit on palanquin,' the next porter has arrived, full of hope.

'I . . . I'm sorry . . . I want to . . . I can't.' I'm no longer smiling, only confused.

Lowering my head, I join the other walkers. The human chain coils up the steep slopes, each link distinct, with its own appearance, its own style. Forged in diverse regions, they reflect the forger's hands – Gujaratis, Bengalis, Kannadigas, Punjabis. As I move forward it feels like I'm slipping from one pocket of the country into another. Even on this common quest I find myself the odd one out, the only person traveling alone. At first, people assume I'm extremely pious. When I tell them about Kaya's pilgrimage, they decide I'm simply extreme.

'Why are you alone? Where are your family and friends?'

'What? You've left them all to travel for a year?'

'What about your studies and your responsibilities?'

'Nobody is paying you to do this? Then shouldn't you go get a job?'

'And why aren't you married?'

'Oh, by the way, you must visit our town on your travels. It is very beautiful.'

'For five years my wife and I saved money to make this pilgrimage,' an old pandit from Madhya Pradesh tells me, 'but she passed away last summer. Heart attack . . . it was very sudden. My son doesn't have the time, so I had to come with some other people from my town. It is a sad fate to be alone.'

Most of us on foot are simply out of shape – with a scattering of the very young, old, and infirm – but together we make an epic out of the journey. The ground beneath our feet is uneven, rising sharply, hard rock with no grip, slippery sand, loose pebbles. The air gets thinner and weak knees turn weaker. But through it all flows this wonderful sense of camaraderie and goodwill. We stop, we enquire about each other's wellbeing, we compare experiences, we share our beliefs, and we share our desire to get to the top.

As I wrestle over every step, calves tight, legs turning to jelly, my breath escaping in short gasps, my mind weeps for the unsung heroes carrying human burdens to their liberation. They push their bodies to the limit, faces grimacing and taut, their muscles straining till the veins throb purple. Their struggle is superhuman, and some of the pilgrims appreciate this. A grandmother admonishes her palanquin bearers for not taking sufficient breaks, assuring them she's in no hurry. People share with them food and water. I spot one old man sharing his cigarettes.

Our exultation is one when we reach the sacred source of Yamuna, her green waters gushing out from the mouth of the glacier that trails up the mountain. A temple stands beside it, saffron flag fluttering from the white spire. Yamuna is the sister of Yama, the god of death, and anyone who bathes here is spared a painful death. Though, if you ask me, freezing in her frigid waters is about as painful as death can get.

Just watching others take a dip gives me hypothermia.

'Be brave, son,' a woman laughs, amused by my hesitation. 'Isn't this what you've come for? Mother Yamuna's touch is purifying.'

It's not what I've come for, but I hold my breath and step in. My feet feel like they've been set on fire. I quickly splash three jugs of water on myself and run for succor. Magically, as if created specifically for wimps like me, a hot spring emerges from the ground a few feet in front of the temple, and the water is drained into tanks for the people to bathe in after the frigid blessings. The water is so hot, the temple priests use it to boil rice and potato, which is then served to pilgrims as sacrament.

Warmed up and back on my feet, a few minutes into the return trek I meet an old lady sitting by the side of the slope, her husband, son, and daughter-in-law beside her. 'Son, is it much further?' she asks me through tears. 'I don't think I can walk much more.'

'*Chinta mat karo dadi*,' I assure her. 'You are almost there, and it's very rewarding.'

Kilometer 10258

From Yamunotri, Kaya flowed on towards Gangotri. Just past the town of Gangauri, timeless waters of the Ganga rushed down to greet us. Unlike the Ganga I'd seen so far, muddy or downright filthy, the water was pristine and sparkling green. Here she was youthful and beautiful, glowing in her innocence. The Ganga of the later stage is much older and wiser, more solemn, having witnessed life and death, carrying man's sins and his refuse.

Still twenty-five kilometers from Gangotri, the rain forced me take cover at a tea shop in Harsil, an idyllic little village with a silvery waterfall for a backdrop. On my third cup of tea the rain relented and I returned to the road, but barely five kilometers out, Kaya's rear-end started to sway like a drunken sophomore. Her back tire had gone flat, and darkness was upon us by the time I pulled out the offending nail and changed the tube. Then, it began to rain again, forcing Kaya back to Harsil.

'You can put your tent up on our porch,' the tea-stall owner offers, showing me to his house. Two babyish and bemused faces peer shyly through the window as I set up my tent. To break the ice between us I hand them a bar of chocolate each, and before long they've taken over my tent, screaming ecstatically in the claustrophobic space, leaving me with the impression they've never seen a tent before. Only when their mother shoos them away do I have a moment's peace.

'I hope you liked our dinner,' she says. 'Rice and vegetable is simple food, but it's very healthy.'

'It was lovely, thank you. I'm going to sleep a satisfied man.'

'Wait, I'll get a blanket for you.'

'Thank you, but I don't need one. This is quite comfortable,' I reply, pointing to my sleeping bag which is rated as 15 degrees below zero.

'This, what will happen with this,' she smirks, lifting it up. 'It is too thin for our climate.'

'No really, this will do fine.'

'It's up to you,' she shrugs, but returns a couple of minutes later with a blanket that weighs like it is lined with lead. She also hands me a large tarpaulin sheet. 'For the motorcycle,' she points out, 'it's getting wet.'

I wake the next morning to the sound of a couple of scamps unzipping my tent. I stick my head out to find the mother is waiting with a cup of tea.

'My husband has gone to the shop,' she informs me.

'Is it very busy around here?'

'Harsil is the only real town near Gangotri. During the pilgrim season there's quite a bit of traffic on this road.'

'What about winter time?'

'We manage. Our son lives in Uttarkashi and he sends some money, especially since the grandchildren stay with us.'

'Grandchildren! I thought they were your kids.'

'You're joking,' she giggles in embarrassment. 'I'm forty-five years old.'

Back on the road, it led all the way to Gangotri. No walking required. The temple stood in the shadow of giants, a simple white structure that seemed to reflect the purity of summit and water. Another freezing holy dip was in the offing, and despite a genuine effort, I failed to convince myself that I had nothing to fear from harmless old H_2O. Embracing cowardice, with cupped hands I carefully splashed water on my head, making sure not a drop rolled down my neck.

Other than washing away sins, the Ganga also possesses healing capabilities, though no one's really sure what it heals you of. Amongst its special properties, the water at Gangotri contains zero impurities – yes, this is the same Ganga of Varanasi – and inexplicably remains uncontaminated even after several years of storage. Recognized internationally for these features, the science chaps have conducted numerous inconclusive tests on the water.

It is because of certain herbal secretions, biologists have pronounced.

It is due to the mineral contents of the water, geologists argue.

Devout Hindus just laugh. Don't those fools realize the Ganga is divine?

Kilometer 10535

Leaving the Ganga behind Kaya set out in chase of the Mandakini. Riding along the hills of Chirbhatya, a shadow flew over us, and then, with the flutter of wings, a large vulture dropped down from the skies into the valley below. Looking up, I saw a lot more of them, circling the sky, their wings outstretched. Occasionally one of them peeled off and descended to the river banks, where more of its brothers stood on the water's edge. A bus carrying thirty members of a wedding party had gone off the cliff the previous day. The vultures were discovering the bodies.

Kaya continued riding, until we reached Gaurikund.

Gaurikund is the base for the long ascent to Kedarnath, and hundreds of cars and buses clog the approaches. People drop out of them like bombs from a B-52. The settlement is in the firm grip of chaos; the lone street, narrow and dirty, crammed with people trying to find a place to stay. A dozen Made-in-China speakers crackle, hiss and spew devotional songs. Noise and disorder are of mythical proportions that will amaze even the gods. All rooms are 'fully occupied'.

People huddle next to small cooking fires, sleep in buses, lie on the roads, or wander about helplessly. Thinking of going back a few kilometers to find a more comfortable camping ground, I return to where Kaya stands. What the hell! Her rear tire is flat. Damn, she'd been perfectly fine when I'd parked her here. Annoyed by this development, I get down to removing the tire. Before very long, a group of amused drivers is gathered around me.

'Look at his tool kit. I don't have so many things in my car,' one jibes.

'Forget car, my bus doesn't have so many tools,' someone else laughs.

An hour's struggle and I have another nail in my palm, by which time it's too late for me to go anywhere. 'My bus is empty. You can spread your bag in the aisle and sleep there,' a bus driver offers.

I awake before dawn, to the loud crack of my skull striking against a foot rest. I stumble out of the bus with a splitting headache and set off on the thirty-kilometer return hike. Far more grueling than Yamunotri's fourteen kilometers, otherwise it's a reenactment of the same drama – the panting pilgrims, the struggling palanquins and *pittus*, the unhappy horses.

At each break there's a conversation with someone new, as soon as we catch our breath. The Kannadigas and Telugus are thrilled when I speak in their tongues.

'Our son is in America . . . Chicago,' an elderly couple from Andhra informs me. 'We got our daughter married in January.

Now that we've completed our worldly duties, it is opportune for us to devote time to spiritual matters.'

'Excellent!' a man from Hosur claps his hands. 'You know Kannada and you smoke ganja, come on, let's share a *chillum*.'

'Why are you spoiling children?' his wife chides him.

'Spoil? Woman, this is the blessing of Lord Shiva. Ha, ha.'

I'm kept busy on the trek, as the unofficial photographer for all and sundry, an unintended job thrust on me ever since Yamunotri. The smiles out-dazzle the peaks, three generations framed in a portrait: children, parents, and grandparents. The faces before are beginning to look familiar. I recognize this camera in my hand, and the family posing before me. I have seen all these people before, along this sacred route.

Finally at the summit, with up to 40 feet of snow falling each winter, huge slabs of ice still cover the ground. Most impressive of the Char Dhams, the ancient stone temple to Shiva stands etched against a background of lofty snow-covered peaks. Of the hundreds of temples I've seen, in hundreds of spectacular places, none compare to this for location. From behind the temple, the Mandakini begins its sacred descent, but sacred or not, it's too goddamn cold, so without hesitation I skip the holy dip.

Most people opt to spend the night in the ashrams that have sprouted near the temple, but by early evening I'm halfway down the mountain, where I bump into an old man who I'd met earlier at Yamunotri. He is struggling to breathe and coughing as we rest under a 'restaurtent'.

'Why don't you take the *doli*?' his concerned son urges him.

'Yes, grandpa, it is difficult for you,' a porter suggests. 'We won't charge too much.'

'It's not about the money,' he says calmly. 'This is the way it's meant to be done. Salvation comes only through struggle. If god wants me to make it, he'll make sure that I do.'

Kilometer 10882

Onwards Kaya went, to the origins of Alaknanda, through luxuriant green meadows and thick rain forests. On the way I met two enormous, super friendly dogs with crude metal collars around their necks, thick with vicious spikes pointing outwards. Sheep dogs, the owner told me. The collar protects them against leopards and other predators that go straight for the jugular. The elder of the two had a run-in with a leopard once, coming out of it with both life and pride intact.

Open vistas and great white summits run along the horizon. Past the town of Joshimath, the road was perilously steep, multiple switchbacks running along the bleak, grey mountainside. In the first ten thousand kilometers Kaya's tire hadn't gone flat once, but in the last few days she'd run into three nails. Two blow outs and one near miss. And always just as we neared one of the three river sources. With Badrinath fast approaching, I wondered if lightening could strike a fourth time. It played on my mind.

Halfway along the slope, lightening did strike.

The flat cost me three hours, but when I got astride Kaya, it was with the honor of knowing that the gods wanted to communicate with me. Four trails. Four nails. How surreal is that? This couldn't be a coincidence, no, it had to be a sign from above. The gods were undoubtedly trying to tell me something – the problem was figuring out what they were trying to say. From the available clues all I could come up with was: *Stay away, we don't want you anywhere near us*, and the more profound: *Life is full of holes*.

Near Badrinath the grey gave way to white. The river ran under ice. According to legend, Badrinath was originally home to Shiva and his wife, Parvati. Lord Vishnu visited them in the guise of a small child, who Parvati took into their home against Lord Shiva's advice. One fine day, on returning from an outing, they found the child transformed to Vishnu, who refused to leave, forcing Shiva and Parvati to move to Kedarnath. Well, it just goes to show that land-grabbing is a legendary profession in India and sanctioned by none other than the gods.

In front of the colorful temple flows another sacred river, demanding another icy dip. I'm glad this is the last of this nonsense. There has to be an easier way to salvation, like saying three Hail Marys.

Having completed the pilgrimage, we had a long ride back to Haridwar, and while I made my way out along the one road, a stream of vehicles surged their way up, the numbers growing even as I watched.

Yamuna, Ganga, Alaknanda, and Mandakini – four divine rivers that purified the faithful Hindu. But while the rivers performed the favor of cleansing us, who was going to clean the rivers? All four destinations were fast turning into garbage dumps, the rivers clogged with plastic. Polythene bags stuck to the rocks like moss. Food wrappers, soap covers, and cigarette packets washed up on the banks. Discarded bottles littered the river beds, outnumbering the pebbles at stretches. It was an agonizingly Indian sight.

Each winter, when we leave these hallowed grounds to the gods, we also leave them all our rubbish. Unfortunately for the gods, they have no idea what to do with the damned plastic. How could they, when they aren't the ones who created the stuff in the first place. And so it remains, till the next summer, when a new group of the faithful comes along and adds to the mess. And adds, and adds. At some point we will be no more. The plastic, though, will outlive us all. Maybe in some ways this was an apt resting place for it, amongst the immortals.

Strange ways we have of showing our reverence for the sacred. We call the river 'mother', swear by her, adore her and worship her. We aren't meant to think a bad thought in her presence. Or say a harsh word. Even going to the extent of removing our shoes to keep her temple unpolluted. And then, with gay abandon, we dump all our trash into her, destroying what we came here to worship, the river's purity. If these rivers really are the route to salvation, then rest assured, for treating them the way we are, in our next life we are going to be reincarnated as anal-dwelling tape worms.

The problem is also much greater than just the litter. In none of the four destinations did I witness any signs of order, or organization. If any institution existed to manage the Char Dham, it was doing a marvelous job of keeping a subterranean profile. Lean-tos and buildings sprouted like fungus on a dead rainforest tree; the unruly crush a blight on the landscape. If permitted to continue in a similar fashion, soon there would be little of beauty remaining. What chaotic infrastructure did exist was incapable of supporting the growing number of pilgrims – not the crumbling hotels, not the waste management, not the narrow roads. More importantly, does anyone know how many pilgrims make this journey each year, and what is the environmental impact of supporting this annual influx of humanity? What if this fragile ecosystem cannot endure our unrestrained veneration?

Kilometer 11685

Kaya crossed the Uttaranchal border, and an hour later she halted for the night at Lake Renukaji, surrounded by wooded hills, a temple reflecting in its still waters.

A sign stands by the water, half-embarrassed half-ashamed. 'Centre for Aquatic Sports', it reads. Next to it lie a few overturned pedal boats, pretending to be dead. I walk over to the one little shop.

'*Bhaiyya*, can I have a packet of Gold Flake Kings?' I ask the young chap manning it.

'I'm about to take a ciggie break myself,' he smiles. '*Chalo*, let's smoke one together.'

'Sorry, I don't smoke cigare . . .' I blurt without thinking.

'Oh . . . Oho!' He gives me a knowing smile. 'Then would you like to smoke a special one with me, brother?'

'Of course I would,' I say and reach into my pouch for the weed.

'What *maal* do you have?' he asks with palpable excitement.

'Ganja that I picked up from sadhus at Kedarnath.'

'No, no. That just won't do,' he shakes his head in disapproval. 'I have something better.' Opening a cash box, he produces a small black ball and holds it out to me. 'Malana Cream, the world's best hashish,' he grins.

Welcome to Himachal Pradesh.

LEG TEN

Don't Touch! Don't Touch!

AFTER A NIGHT in the lowlands, Kaya ascended the mountains again. I could tell Shimla was a popular place even before we got there. It became obvious when, still miles from the hill station, touts started leaping through the unrolled windows of the cars in front of us. Kaya skillfully evaded the plucky bastards, only to realize they'd been standing there for a good reason. In the time of the Raj, to escape the heat, the Viceroy and his entire government migrated from Delhi to Shimla during summer; now, all of North India seemed to be doing the same. So finding a reasonable, aka affordable, hotel in Shimla was like searching for an honest politician: frustrating and futile.

We spent three hours wandering around the small town, stopping at every hotel that wasn't disguised as a chandelier showroom. I've noticed that hotels with too many lights are always expensive, probably has to do with their electricity bills. Over the course of my search I rode through five tunnels, only to discover later that Shimla has just the one. Eventually, I wound up in what was probably the town's filthiest hovel. A medieval dungeon really, with a shared toilet that had my bowels in mutiny, citing unnecessary humiliation. One look at the squatting-bowl made me wonder if all our countrymen are directionally challenged. Or perhaps we are preconditioned to believe that any water emerging from the ground is sacred. Why else would no one aim for the hole? Incidentally, Shimla boasts more than a thousand hotels.

One thing harder to find in Shimla than hotels was parking space. Most buildings simply clung to the slopes in desperation, making very little provision for such luxuries. And the town's designated parking lots stood a long way down the hill. In all of India, this was the only place where a room didn't necessarily come with a place for Kaya to rest. In fact, what convinced me stay at the Should Be Condemned Hotel was that the owner had kindly provided space for me to leave Kaya. So what if that space was in the gutter in front of the hotel.

While the town still retains a smattering of its Victorian charm, including Christ Church and the Viceregal Lodge, present-day Shimla's pulsating center is the Mall Road. From what I've observed, town planning in Indian hill stations is quite simple, and all of them seem to be following the same ingenious manual. First, select a particularly nice looking hill and destroy it – generally achieved by removing all signs of nature from the vicinity. Then, chalk out one 'wide' road which becomes the tourist hub of the town. Next, name the above-mentioned 'Mall Road' and promptly ban all vehicles from using this one reasonable stretch of tar. At this point, throw away the plans and let the rest of the town go to hell.

So, here I am, lost in the by-lanes of Shimla, when something quite remarkable happens. No, I didn't find my way. That would actually be astoundingly remarkable. Rather, I bump into Jemma and Scott, an English couple I'd met many miles and weeks ago in Lucknow.

'Hey, surprise, surprise!' I grin. 'So, how's India been treating you both?'

'Why don't you come up to our room and we can talk some more,' Scott suggests. 'I picked up some tea leaves in Darjeeling, if you fancy a drink?'

'I picked up some THC leaves in Kedarnath, if you fancy a smoke?' I reply.

Scott, a tea connoisseur, is carrying an assortment of leaves he's picked up on his travels, from Sikkim, Darjeeling, and Assam. We swap travelogues, sip tea and smoke weed in their cozy room at the YMCA, a charming colonial mansion overlooking Mall Road and the lower slopes of Shimla, with carpeted wood flooring, an unused fireplace, and a gleaming toilet. And it costs half what I'm paying.

'Why don't you get a guide book, it makes things so much easier,' Jemma suggests.

'Ah, you see, but they make things *too* easy, upsetting my credo that if it's comfortable, it's not travel. Besides, I feel like most people with guide books tend to follow the information blindly, almost like an instruction manual. I've met travelers who won't eat or stay at any place that's not in the *Lonely Planet* and, carrying a copy that's five years old, they spend most of their time grumbling over how people are trying to charge them more than what the book ordains. On the other hand, when you don't have a clue what to do, that's when you're forced to go looking, and unless you really look, at the end of all your travels you've seen nothing.'

'Good speech. Nonetheless, wouldn't you be happier with a clean commode?'

'Yeah sure,' I shrug, 'but your hotel doesn't have a gutter to park in.'

When I step out of the hostel, the moon is hovering high in the night sky. The streets wait, dark and soulless. I look to the left and see a maze of unrecognizable lanes. Balls! It's the same on the right side as well. While I now know the way to the YMCA, I still have no clue how to return to my hovel. Maybe I can find someone to ask for directions. Just then it strikes me that I don't know where to ask directions to. I've forgotten the name of my hotel . . . in the one town that has a thousand of them.

I select left and start to walk. Two hours later, at 3:30 a.m., I stumble upon it. I don't recognize one thing about the hotel. What catches my eye is the unusual sight of a motorcycle parked in a gutter.

Kilometer 11976

From Shimla, Kaya traced NH22, running across the valleys of Kinnaur and Spiti, following the centuries-old trade route between India and Tibet. Once a journey of courage and endurance, through some of the most inhospitable and extreme terrains of the world, for Kaya it was a journey of sheer exhilaration. Though still few and far between, here, for the first time, we started encountering other motorcycle-tourers. Mountains extended endlessly. Serrated ridges and bare gorges, the soil stripped off the surface to expose sharp rock. The muddy waters of the Sutlej raged through the funneling valley, eroding deep gullies as it swept past. Kaya flowed upstream along the river, towards its source at Mount Kailash, the permanent residence of Lord Shiva.

Its primitive beauty marked by an extravagant backdrop of snowy peaks and undulating valleys, the village of Sarahan is dominated by the twin pagodas of an ancient Bhima Kali Temple, their overhanging wooden rooms crowned by sweeping slate roofs. As late as the 19th century, the temple courtyard witnessed human sacrifice, until the meddlesome British put an end to the ritual. It's a pity, really, because all the sacrificial burden nowadays rests on the shoulders – or should I say, necks – of goats and buffalos. Imagine if we still lopped off the occasional human head to make it rain. Think of the amazing impact it would have on tourism. Considering how many travelers are drawn to the exotic and shocking, I'm sure this would be a most sought-after destination. We could make it an annual event and have box seats, international television rights, corporate sponsorship, and special edition Coca Cola bottles with tops that resemble the sacrificed head.

Beyond Sarahan, the ride through Kinnaur was a hair-raising cliffhanger. The road was untamed, not cut along the slope, but carved into the cliff wall, forming a ragged, three-sided tunnel, a dizzying drop where the fourth side should be. Roiling and roaring, the river dashed against the rocks below. Wooden bridges traversed it, corroded by extreme weather, land spills, and floods. Much of this raw beauty disappeared even as we rode past. The valley reverberated to dynamite blasts. The cliffs shuddered, and then shattered, leaving behind gaping holes. Bulldozers hacked into the rock, burrowed into it, with reckless abandon. Dust clouds billowed as trucks and diggers tore into the ground. Cranes stood ready to raise the dams. Where Uttaranchal had opted for small-scale hydro-projects, Himachal Pradesh was out to squeeze every bit of energy from its water sources. Soon all of Kinnaur was going to be one big generator.

Approaching Sangla, the road climbed at a gravity-defying angle. Kaya had to run at full throttle just to keep us stationary, and all forward motion was provided by my frantically pedaling legs. Just as we reached the crest, from where I'd hoped momentum would be on our side, our path was blocked by a ghost. It turned out to be a sadhu, unintentionally disguised as a ghost, but the result couldn't have been much different. Kaya came to an abrupt halt and I was driven crotch first into her tank.

'Take *Mata's* blessing and go,' Ghost Baba smiles through his pearly white beard. 'She will keep you safe on the road.'

'Mmmmm . . .' I manage through the pain. When I can finally think again, I shuffle about a bit to confirm that all is in order. Reassured that I'm still a man, I push Kaya to the cliff's edge and park her there, leaving sufficient room for oncoming traffic to pass by.

Slightly wider than a phone booth, and a lot shorter, a shrine balances precariously on the thin strip of lay-by. Behind it, the world plummets a thousand feet to the river that cuts through the narrow valley. Across the road, a niche in the cliff face is walled around, creating a tiny cave-room. The latter is Ghost Baba's home, and the former, his work station, beside which he now stands, waving me over.

Long silvery tresses cascade down his back. The beard dangles to his chest. From under all this hair emerges a long nose followed by a pale face, time lines firmly etched and brows furrowed. His eyes spark with manic energy. A streak of vermillion powder runs along his forehead. He wears white, rather than the traditional saffron of sadhus, but I can tell he isn't a priest. The hippy hairdo is a dead giveaway. Besides, his smile doesn't remind me of car salesmen. *What the heck*, I think, walking over to join him before the idol, *he looks like a mad enough chap.*

Bundled under multiple layers of cloth, the idol of Goddess Kali stands on a small pedestal, her fearsome eyes trained on me as I approach her. Picking up the oil lamp burning before the deity, Baba circles it in front of my face thrice. He then applies a *teekha* to my forehead, before finally placing a handful of the *prasad* – a potpourri of sugar crystals, dried fruits and nuts – into my cupped palm.

At this point, instead of making a demand for money, he grins and says, 'Will you smoke *chillum* with me?', confirming that he's indeed not a priest.

Boom Bholenath! Boom Shankar!

Boom!

Into the shrine. Then out he shuffles. Restless. Adjusting the goddess's attire. Picking through the sacrament. Energetic. More like a hopped-up crackhead than a brain-dead pothead.

'Ha, ha, we smoke more *chillum*, ha, ha,' he laughs, 'we have good time.'

He crushes some weed. Stops. He remembers something.

'Baba make first-class coffee,' he announces.

The half crushed weed is now in my hands. He's gone. He's back. I hold a cup of coffee in my hand. The weed is in his.

Boom Bholenath! Boo—

'Wait, someone's coming,' he interrupts.

He's gone again. Work beckons.

Scurrying into the shrine, he returns with the tray of *prasad* and *kumkum* and stands on the road. A bus inches over the crest, engine screaming, eking every ounce of power, clawing for the peak before gravity can drag it down.

'Don't worry,' Baba screams to me over the din, 'you keep smoking *chillum*. I just need to distribute the non-intoxicating *prasad*, ha, ha.'

I tense up, concerned for the welfare of Ghost Baba, sure that the bus driver was going to abuse him, or even squish him. Nobody, especially not a bus or lorry driver, struggling up a slope like this appreciates being pulled over without a bloody good reason. I watch the bus flatten out as it reaches the top, and with a loud sigh squeeze its way past Baba. And then, to my utter surprise, the bus comes to a halt, its center directly opposite the shrine. The driver folds his palms together and raises them to his bowed head. Most of the passengers do the same.

While the bus idles, regaining its breath for the next push a few meters ahead, Baba steps under the driver's window and holds up the tray to him. The driver applies the *teekha*, takes a fistful of *prasad*, and exchanges quick pleasantries with Baba, who then unhurriedly goes around the front of the bus and steps inside. Walking along the aisle, he holds out the tray to the passengers. He seems to know most of them. Everybody accepts the *Mata's* blessings. A few people drop some spare change onto the tray, the rest don't. As the bus wheezes on, Baba rejoins me where I sit beside the temple. He places the tray down and picks up the interrupted *chillum*.

'We smoke now, ha ha.'

Boom Bholenath! Om Shankar!

Boom!

We do smoke, albeit with multiple time-outs. This is the only road heading in or out of Sangla valley, and though traffic is sparse, the odd vehicle passes by every fifteen minutes or so. And despite the inconvenience of stopping here, everybody invariably does; taxis, the rare private car, buses, and even trucks. Most people are regulars on the road and stop of their own accord. Newcomers don't have much of a choice really; it's either stop, run over the Ghost, or run off the cliff.

One man is in a hurry. He offers a quick bow to the idol, and waving to Baba drives away. A private car pulls up angrily. The driver refuses to acknowledge the goddess. His wife, on the other hand, insists on saying a long prayer, and before leaving she drops a ten rupee note onto the tray, probably a bribe to make up for her husband's arrogance. Three foreigners pull up in a cab. They laugh, take photographs, and then drive away with red foreheads and sweet tongues.

Om Namah Shivaya!

Boom!

I've lost track of time.

'Baba is very happy here,' Ghost Baba informs me, always referring to himself in the third person. 'Can you feel the goddess's energy? Whatever Baba needs is at hand, regular supply of food, regular supply of ganja, ha, ha. Once in a while loneliness sets in, but then travelers like you come along.'

'Did you build this shrine, Baba?'

'No, no. It was already here.'

Baba tells me he's originally from M.P., which he left when still a young man. In the process he also left his wife. For thirty plus years he wandered around the country by foot, meditating, learning from wiser sadhus, and then one day the path led him to the *Mata*.

'She was abandoned, and her shrine left neglected,' he says. 'Baba felt the urge to tend to it. That was five years ago. Only last year, with the money people donated, Baba repainted the shrine and bought new clothes for *Mata*. People give more rupees than Baba needs, ha, ha.'

'How come everybody stops, Baba?' I ask

'Before, many accidents happened on this road. Now that the *Mata* is being cared for, the number of accidents has drastically reduced. The travelers feel much safer. See, Baba do good, ha, ha.'

Rarely respected, mostly ignored, today the sadhu is little more than a curiosity or a tolerated anachronism. But on these slopes, Ghost Baba has become more. People wish him well and seek his blessings. A lady from Sangla hands him a few candles on her way out of the valley. Three youngsters come down from the village to give the Baba cigarettes. In return he offers them a *chillum* and a great cup of coffee. A trucker parks his lorry half a ways up slope and walks to where we sit. He brings with him some sugar and sits down for a chat. The *chillum* passes through his hands as well.

Boom Bholenath!

Boom!

The day has passed me by, and the mountains cast long shadows across the valley when I finally get up to leave. 'Why do you want to go?' Baba asks. 'You can stay here. The room is small, but Baba has fire inside and it gets warm. We tell stories, and we smoke lot of *chillums*, ha, ha.'

'Maybe I will take you up on the offer on my way back Baba. Thank you for everything,' I say, removing fifty rupees from my pocket and proffering it to him.

'What is this?' he says. 'No, no, this is too much. You are trying to spoil Baba, ha, ha. What will Baba do with so much?' He refuses to take the note. 'For the *Mata* you leave some change in the tray. If you want to give something to Baba, on your way back you bring little gift okay, and you stay in Baba's house.'

Back on Kaya, I eased on towards Sangla Valley.

I found something comforting in Ghost Baba's presence on that slope. Our highways have become a tribute to exacting time-is-money schedules, to hurried existences, to the present on steroids, where we fuel our selfishness, our aggressiveness, and our anger. But here, Ghost Baba put the brakes on any hurried journey. And it was this simple slowing down that reduced the number of accidents on that bend. Situated on a blind turn of a particularly steep slope, Baba's temple did what the 'Blow Horn' and 'Reduce Speed' signs failed to. The traffic, which hadn't slowed down for the signs, now automatically did so in anticipation of the temple and *Mata's* blessings. While the locals, and Ghost Baba, credit the divine for the fewer accidents, it is Ghost Baba himself who is the cause.

Ten minutes past the shrine, a tremendous rumble reverberated through the narrow corridors, followed by a petrifyingly loud crash. Instinctively, Kaya slowed down, and I looked up. No, the skies weren't falling on our heads. The stillness returned. Thinking nothing of it, I raised Kaya's throttle, and off we went. As far as the next bend, beyond which the highway ran head on into a pile of restless-looking rocks. While I scratched my head in wonder, the dust from the landslide settled on us softly.

A Maruti car pulled up beside Kaya, and the driver casually informed me that the mess would be cleared in good time. He was the principal of Sangla's primary school. The person beside him was a military officer. They both wore vermillion *teekhas* on their foreheads. A bus, two trucks, and a shared jeep added to the stuck traffic, but no one showed any annoyance. People milled about, waiting patiently. Somewhere up the slope, a road gang had been at work, and within the hour a bulldozer turned up on the opposite side of the now-settled rocks, followed by a lean-bodied Bihari workforce. While the machine crushed the larger boulders and pushed them down the gorge, some of us joined the Biharis in moving the smaller debris. Before long, there was sufficient space for Kaya to squeeze through.

Kilometer 12329

At 3,500 meters, this valley is higher than most mountain peaks, covered in lush fields and blossom meadows, scattered with orchards and deodar. The aquamarine Baspa River meanders through, glaciers running down the slopes to meet it. Ancient villages lay strung along the valley floor, traditional wooden houses on stilts, with grey slate roofs. In the Tibetan language, sang is 'light' and la is 'pass'. Sangla, the 'pass of light', a beacon for people who crossed these mountains.

Snuggled in the far reaches of the valley is Chitkul, the last village on the Indian side of the old Hindustan – Tibet trade route; a settlement of twenty wooden homes and a few small plots under the timeless gaze of Mount Kinner Kailash. The closest I've come to the word idyllic, Chitkul provided glimpses, ephemeral ones, of an older world, and for two days I sat on a rock overlooking the village and watched nothing happen. Streets and lanes were conspicuous by their absence, and in all the time I spent there I saw not one other vehicle. The houses were of mud, wood, and slate; the cozy, low-ceilinged rooms warmed by wood stoves. A stream, diverted into a network of tiny channels that flowed all over the town, provided each home's running water supply. The town's 24-hour flour mill was a box that stood over the stream, the two wooden rollers turned by the flowing water. It belonged to no one. It belonged to everyone.

The town elders wore a look of serenity, always smiling, just like in the images that grace tourism brochures and travel books. The women were beautiful, achingly so. I fell in love with three or four of them, but none asked me to stay. The unruffled pace of the day was punctuated in the evening by an excited game of volleyball played by the young men of the village. Volleyball appears to be the game of choice in the mountains, and for good reason, without enough flat ground for cricket and soccer, or enough men. Undoubtedly my image of Chitkul was superficial, and heavily biased by the eyes through which I was perceiving it, still I wistfully hoped this older world would withstand the winds of change blowing through.

But I knew this piece of paradise was already looking outward, or forward as some would have it, to the regular world. My presence here was as sure a sign as any of the coming change. The impact of tourism on Chitkul was palpable, and irrevocable. As yet, few travelers came here, but the transformation of the dirt track into a paved highway signaled the expected surge in numbers. Where the town offered me three accommodation options, no more than spare rooms in traditional homes, as I watched, frantic construction was underway on four purpose-built hotels.

True, travel the world and the experience will change us, but as surely, we also change the world we travel through; 'leave nothing behind but footprints' is little more than a clever catchphrase. At the volleyball game a few kids had gathered around me, fascinated by my camera. I'd delighted in showing them how it worked, even letting them use it. But then, I found myself battling guilt. Was I corrupting their simple lives by bringing this alien object into their world, creating a new desire? My guilt turned out to be needless and foolish, laughable really. Wandering around the town a short while later, I noticed a smooth little saucer clinging onto the roof of a house. It was a satellite dish. Chitkul had cable TV.

On my way out of the valley, I stopped at a store in Sangla and bought two packets of Good Day cookies, a few bars of chikki, an assortment of Cadburys, a box of tea, and some sugar. I'd decided to take Baba up on his offer and stay the night in his Babacave.

Soon, I find myself sitting in the shadows of the narrow space – the lantern only bright enough to create dark shadows – sipping coffee, pulling on a *chillum* and listening to the ghost's tales as a sudden storm lashed out at the valley.

Boom Shankar!

Boom!

'Baba has walked over these mountains to Gangotri,' he boasts, and detecting the hint of skepticism in my smile, makes me spread out my map. 'Show me Sangla on this map,' he says. When I point it out, he traces the path just over the mountain and asks 'What place is this then?'

'Gangotri.'

'Yes, Gangotri, ha, ha. I can walk from here in four days.'

'That's how long it will take by road.' I'm duly impressed.

'Babas are good walkers.'

'Tell me, why did you decide to become a sadhu? What'd you do before that?'

'Baba does not think about his past. The material part of life is forgotten . . . dead.'

'Come on Babaji, what are you hiding?' I tease. 'Eh, what are you running from?'

'Running from . . . what about you, off on such a long journey, what are you running from? Ha, ha. Me, I wish I could run, but I can't anymore.' His voice turns longing, and the manic eyes soften. 'After all these years I feel the urge to move again. Alas, I can't leave the temple unattended. If I go away, who will watch over the travelers on this road? Who will keep them safe? Baba has become a prisoner. Ha, ha.'

Kilometer 12358

Kaya continued to follow the NH22 deeper into the mountains, past Kinnaur into desolate Spiti, where the road is more often than not missing. Snowed in, blocked off by spilling rocks, submerged by a flooding river, it has a very short annual life span. Every few kilometers, signs warned us to watch out for landslides. We stopped, looked up at the crumbling cliffs, waited for the separatist rocks to cross the road and then went about our way.

A few kilometers past the town of Puh, Kaya's progress was brought to a more resolute halt. The road had collapsed in tandem with the falling rocks. From the unperturbed manner that locals went about their business, I guessed this was a common enough occurrence, for which they had come up with an ingenious solution. They simply climbed over the rubble and into the bus or collective-taxi waiting on the other side, while those on the opposite side climbed into the ones emptied on this side. Landside or no, life carried on, as did the road.

Kaya, meanwhile, pulled a U-turn and headed back the way we'd come. She left the Sutlej behind her, swept down from the heights of Jalori, twisted along the thick forests of the Great Himalayan National Park, through woodlands and meadows of wildflowers in yellow, lilac, pink. Bridging the river Beas, we entered the *charas*-induced dream world of Parvati Valley. The world's premier *charas* producing region, here the grass is always green, until it is lovingly turned to black.

Kaya rolled to a confused halt at Kasol town.

Where the hell have I ended up now? Every person I pass is white or whitish, and they most definitely don't dress like Indians. The signs at the restaurants and hotels are in Hebrew. Fortunately, they also display English translations, advertising humus and falafel, and Israeli breakfast. Even the keyboards in the internet cafe are in Hebrew script. Did I take a wrong turn somewhere and get teleported to the holy land? Well, it's either that, or we've been colonized by the Israelis and no one bothered to tell me.

Kasol is little more than a cluster of restaurants, guest houses, and trinket stores flanking the principle road. All the shopkeepers are Indian, but they speak fluent Hebrew, as do the waiters, hotel owners, and taxi drivers. Apart from Hebrew, the air reverberates to the sound of Enfields thundering down the narrow streets. The sidewalks teem with happy hippy Israelis, laughing, running about, playing instruments, leisurely pulling on a *chillum*. They are at home here. No wonder other foreigners disparagingly refer to this area as 'Gaza Strip'.

I find a cozy guest house by the river, surrounded by tall pine trees and dwarfed by snowy peaks. A polite young boy guides me to my room, insisting on helping me with the luggage. He sings praises about the view from my room and then shows me to the terrace. After, he returns with me to my room and lingers about, making forced polite conversation. What does he want? I've already handed him a reasonable tip.

'Do you need anything else?' he asks.

'No, that will be all, thank you.'

'Are you sure there isn't something else I can get for you?' he asserts, eyeing me incredulously.

'Oh!' I gasp with sudden recognition. 'Malana Cream?'

'Yes,' he sighs, 'the best.'

Talk about room service. While luxury hotels generally come with a minibar and a basket of fruit, in Kasol even the most basic of them come with a supply of *charas*. And that's where the profits are. This room-with-a-magical-view only costs a hundred and fifty rupees. Meanwhile, an accomplished stoner, i.e. Israeli, will consume about five hundred bucks worth of *charas* each day. The economics of Parvati Valley are dictated by the narcotic.

Armed with my purchase, I step back onto the street with renewed confidence. Now I feel like I belong. It doesn't matter anymore that I can't speak Hebrew. After all, marijuana speaks a universal language, the ultimate icebreaker. All I have to do is find a suitably cool restaurant, and Kasol is overrun with them, carrying promising names like Third-Eye, Buddha Dreams, and Rasta Cafe. Settling on Dancing Shiva, I climb a narrow set of stairs to the rooftop restaurant.

A quick glance reveals about a dozen people, stretched out on mattresses spread across the floor, indulging in *charas*-inspired introspection. The long, low tables in front of them are cluttered with the tools of the trade: small crushing bowls, hash balls, *chillum*, hash sticks, stoker, hash chunks, *safi*, hash strips, cigarettes, and lighters. Wispy tendrils of smoke diffused into night sky, trailed by the repetitive thumping of techno.

With a casual head nod I join a trio at their table, or should I say their assembly line, for what I have the privilege of witnessing is the kind of precision and efficiency German factories strive towards. Each person a designated cog, they move like clockwork – powder, mix, fill, stoke, clean – not a wasted movement. The *chillum* burns endlessly, it burns beautifully. Until I join in that is, a spanner in the works, completely destroying their rhythm with my Indian precision. Having given me sufficient time to prove myself, one of them speaks out. Introducing himself as Itai, he politely asks me to stop helping. 'We make *chillum*, okay,' he tells me. 'No problem, you only smoke.' Smoke I do, late into the night, at some point learning that the other two are Ben and Ari. I also learn they are trekking out to mysterious Malana the day after. Following some initial hesitation, they invite me to join the group.

Kilometer 12917

The sun has barely woken when the four of us meet up with Kosi, our guide, at the town of Jari, from where the continuously uphill trek begins. Following the course of the Malana River deep into the woods, we reach the Malana powerhouse, where we are required to register our names before entering the valley, a provision to keep track of the occasional visitors who enter the valley and are never seen or heard from again. From the powerhouse it's a comfortable ten kilometer hike to the dam before the path begins a treacherously steep ascent. The only other settlement on our route is Chowki, and from what Kosi has to say, they avoid Malana like a lion would a bowl of Caesar salad.

It is late in the day when we finally approach Malana.

'Do not touch anybody or anything,' Kosi warns, for the tenth time.

'What do you mean by anything?' Itai teases.

'Nothing, okay? Please touch nothing,' he repeats emphatically. 'Keep your hands to yourself.' And then, asking us to wait, he goes into the town on his own.

'I don't like this waiting,' Ben grumbles impatiently. 'I'm tired and hungry.'

'Well, you know the rule,' I shrug. 'We can't enter the town till we have permission from the town elders.'

'What is Kosi up to? It takes less time to get past an Israeli checkpoint.'

As a people, Indians are at the forefront of eccentric behavior, but even by this country's standard the citizens of Malana are unquestionably absurd. To begin with, they don't even consider themselves Indian, instead claiming descent from Greek soldiers who deserted the armies of Alexander the Great in 327 BC. They've spent the millennia since mutinying against mankind as such. They live in suspicion of all outsiders and have written us off as inferiors. This disdain, and fear of defilement, extends to the point where no outsider is permitted to come in contact with them, or any of their belongings, in any way.

And they're not kidding.

Malana doesn't recognize the Indian constitution, nor its laws. They don't care to vote or pay taxes, and – as far as they are concerned – the less they have to do with the country, the better. The town follows its own system of justice and administration, guided by the spirit of the god Jamlu, who speaks to the elders through his oracles. Anyone defying the decision of the village council is thrown out of the valley. In extreme circumstances, such as theft or abuse of god's treasures, the wrongdoer is pushed down the mountain slopes, with a stone tied to his feet.

When Kosi returns and gives us the green signal, I walk forward with mounting excitement. Nothing could have prepared me for how the world's self-acclaimed 'superiors' live. The town's fifteen hundred citizens live in a haphazard cluster of stone and wood houses, the yard of each house a waterlogged mound of rags, empty wrappers, plastic bags, and rotting vegetables. Litter sluices through the tight, muddy lanes. My feet squelch as I warily step through the muck. The air smells rank with rot and filth. A woman dumps unidentifiable rubbish from the balcony. Who'd want to touch anything here?

Grimy and barefoot, children run around us screaming, 'Don't touch! Don't touch!' – probably the only bit of English they know. Ever so often someone sticks his head out of a window and enquires, 'Cream? Cream?', probably the only other bit of English they know. I am confronted by authoritative looking signs, haughtily hanging from the walls: 'Do Not Touch – Heavy Fines', they warn. Malana has only one option to accommodate visitors, a bare, musty guest house with the floor for beds. But it is ours and we can touch the walls if we want to. This I promptly go on to do, deriving great comfort from it.

It is only next morning that we get to walk through the field of dreams, the *forbidden marijuana plantations*. This is what we are here for. Renowned the world over, Malana's *charas* is collected by massaging the buds of ripe cannabis crops between one's palms and fingers. The dark resin that sticks to the hands is pure magic. Thankfully, the farmers of Malana don't mind people touching their plants, and I spend the next hour caressing the buds with a tenderness I didn't know I was capable of. While making your own *charas* is legit, photography is strictly prohibited. A rather inane precaution. This place is in the guide books for fuck's sake, and every cop worth his bribe is aware of it.

No trip to Malana is complete without buying a suitably weighty souvenir. Kosi comes to our assistance by taking us to his 'friend' to purchase the 'finest quality Malana Cream'. We argue over the price for a few seconds. He feigns poverty. We feign friendship. In the end, we conclude the transaction at the price he started with. It's all good. Dreams come cheap in Malana. The dealer indicates for us to wait and disappears into the house. He comes out a couple of minutes later, balls of cellophane-wrapped hash in his hand. Stepping up to us, he throws the hash at our feet.

I'm too stunned to react.

'Just throw the money on the ground,' Kosi instructs.

I'm still not sure what's going on.

'Here you go then,' Ben smirks, flinging the money down rudely.

The peddler smiles, bends over and picks up the money happily. It's just how they do business here. With no direct contact.

While leaving the town we are once again surrounded by children screaming, 'Don't touch! Don't touch!' Ari removes a fistful of Eclairs from his bag and offers it to them. They are ecstatic, but don't reach for it. Instead they point to the ground. Ari shakes his head in surrender. Itai laughs derisively. I wonder at the irony of being a superior race, so proud of their status, yet here they are, floundering in the dirt near our feet, for candy and outsider's money. If anything, their obsession makes them seem weak.

One thing's for sure. I'm never going to take a handshake lightly again.

Kilometer 12964

Heading back along the river Parvati, Kaya returned to Bhuntar, from there following the river Beas to Manali. I'd woken up with a headache that made my brain feel like the epicenter of a giant earthquake, and Manali only made it worse. The city looked like the aftermath of the earthquake in my head. It's incorrigible that people call it the valley of the gods. I doubt a deity with the least shred of dignity would want to live here. This was Nainital revisited, only on a grander scale. Unlike with Nainital though, a multitude of circumstances keep us from making a quick getaway. Kaya came to a timid halt in the parking lot of Hotel Broadways.

Stepping inside, I meet my personal hero, the man I've looked up to all my life. The man I call dad. Visiting Delhi on work, he's decided to catch up with me in Manali for a couple of days. It's all part of good parenting. Show support for your son's crazy schemes, and give him a pat on the back, even when you think he richly deserves a kick up the backside. His effort is all the more appreciable, considering how much he dislikes motorcycles. As a neurosurgeon, he sees plenty of motorcycle-induced head injuries. On the one occasion that he'd ridden with me on a motorcycle (and then, only because he had no other option), he came home and announced to my mum, 'Be prepared to receive a call one day saying your son is dead.' Apparently, he wasn't impressed by my riding skills.

So while he freshens up in the hotel room, I make arrangements for a taxi.

'Alright, where are we going then?' dad asks, stepping out of the shower.

'It's up to you,' I shrug. 'The taxi should be here soo—'

'Taxi! What for?'

'I thought . . . you . . . I mean, are you thinking of sitting on Kaya or what?'

'Well, isn't this supposed to be a motorcycle expedition?'

Kaya is under a lot of pressure over the next three days. Desperate to make a good impression on the patriarch, she rides cautiously, slowly, tentatively. Me? I'm overwhelmed by his trust.

Besides, it's a power trip knowing his life is in my hands, and not the usual other way round. We take short rides to nowhere, we visit a couple of temples and parks, but mostly we hang out at the cafes and play chess, with me trying to ignore the blazing *chillums*.

'Do you see a lot of these junkie types while you're traveling?' dad enquires, the question loaded with not-so-subtle connotations.

'No, dad, it's only around here,' I lie, a talent that doesn't come naturally. Then, thinking something more is expected from me I add, 'Don't worry, I avoid such people.'

'I hope you are not into drugs,' he glares at me.

The question doesn't come as a shock, just that it's dad posing it rather than mum. It pops up once a year, as surely as my birthday does. Usually, mum is holding the latest issue of *Cosmopolitan* or *Vogue*, the pages open to an article that says: 'Ten symptoms to tell if your child is on drugs'. Apparently I fit the description perfectly. I have never relented though and I have no intention to start now.

'Nooo, dad, drugs are foreign habits,' I protest my innocence. 'Indians don't do this stuff.'

On his last day in Manali, we rode high above the snowline, to Rohtang La at 3,978 meters; the first of four lofty mountain passes on the road to Leh. The road formed a thin black bridge across an ocean of white, hemmed in by sheer banks of snow, towering over us like waves. The favored destination for day trippers from Manali, a steady stream of taxis streaked past us on the sharp slopes. And at the summit, they all came together in an inextricable tangle, forming the world's most spectacularly located traffic jam.

A chain of mighty peaks loom before us, capped by hanging glaciers. The summits blaze a brilliant white, dissolving in their own radiance. Wisps of mist rise from them, the breath of titans, floating in the wind like fluttering veils. A stream of icy melt flow at their feet. And cutting a narrow channel between two 5,000-meter peaks is Rohtang, 'the pass of death' – or if you prefer the literal translation – 'pile of dead bodies'. For all its fearsome reputation, Rohtang has the atmosphere of a typical Indian picnic spot. And when Indians have a good time, we like to show it by leaving a trail of litter behind us. We've done such a fine job, it's time to rename the pass, from 'pile of dead bodies' to 'pile of undead garbage'. Or is it just me who thinks plastic has so much in common with a zombie – not alive, not dead, and extremely unkillable. The usual suspects lie scattered all around – Lay's packets, Kit Kat wrappers, Good Day covers, Gold Flake boxes, thousands of them.

The litter is normal enough, the bit that I find puzzling is the checkpoint at the foot of the ascent, where vehicles are stopped and searched for plastic bags. In accordance with government regulations, no plastic is permitted up the mountain, and visitors are obliged to purchase a cloth bag at the checkpoint to collect, and presumably bring back, their trash. But while plastic bags are banned, anything sealed in plastic is kosher. How can a restriction applying only to polythene change anything? What do our ingenious policymakers think, that the chips packet will self-destruct ten seconds after the chips disappear?

Amidst all the litter, I even spot a few discarded cloth bags.

If the apathetic Indian isn't bad enough, Mother Nature also has to deal with the international giants of insensitivity, Coca-Cola and Pepsi. If anything is more plentiful in this country than gods, people, and coconut trees, it is cola commercials, and seeing how Rohtang is high on Tourist Receiving Point (TRP) ratings, the narcissistic colas had to make their presence felt. Until 2002, the Coke and Pepsi logos greeted visitors along the fifty-kilometer stretch to Rohtang, not from billboards or posters, but boldly emblazoned in chemical paint across 45-million-year-old rocks. The emperors of consumerism had become common vandals. Taken to court, and faced with media outrage, the Cola Criminals decided to erase the advertisements. With gallons of paint thinner. They've created such irreparable damage, even moss is terrified to grow on those rocks now.

I look out longingly beyond Rohtang, an escape to purer spaces. A solitary road meanders deep into the mountains, through the eternal snowfields of the upper Himalayas. Open for five months a year, this high-altitude road squeezes through the highest passes in the world and over the loftiest peaks. Higher than any mountain in Europe or Australia or Africa, the oxygen too thin for petrol to burn, too thin for us to breathe. A three-day journey over 450 kilometers, with no civilization, no petrol bunks, no mechanics, no hospitals, no help.* This is the ultimate road trip.

It is a road I hope to follow. As soon as I find someone to travel with. For good reason, not many people make the journey alone, especially if, like me, they can't tell the difference between a spark plug and a carburetor. The vast majority of motorcyclists head out with friends, or in tour groups that bring along a mechanic, and even a support van. The operated tours are a little too sanitized for my liking, so back in Manali I wander around the town looking for any group heading for Leh, hoping to tag along with them. But with the road having opened only a couple of days ago, there are still few bikers to be found. As for me, I've fantasized about this journey for too long to sit about waiting.

'Dad, I'm going to leave for Leh in the morning,' I announce at the dinner table, 'alone.' Silence. I wait, steeling myself for the protest, the command to reconsider.

'Fine, let's go shopping,' he says eventually, his voice even. 'We should get you some extra pairs of socks, medicines, chocolate bars . . .'

Looks like he's been making his own enquiries.

On returning to our hotel we complete the check out formalities. 'Can you call a taxi for me at nine in the morning, please?' dad requests the manager. 'I have to catch a flight from Kullu at noon.'

---

*Well, there's one petrol bunk at Tandi, but anyone who's done the ride knows what I'm talking about.

'And what is your plan, sir?' the manager asks, turning towards me.

'He's leaving for Leh tomorrow,' dad replies on my behalf.

'So, he's found someone to travel with then.'

'No. He's going to do it by himself.'

'Oh! You are a brave man, sir,' he says to dad, shaking his head gravely. 'I would never let my son go alone.'

I fight the urge to reach over the counter and smack him in the face.

LEG ELEVEN

We Are the Military, We Can Do as We Wish

IT TOOK KAYA four days to reach Leh. Mountains went by in a blur, like the sails of giant ships. The landscape alternated between sublime and surreal. A Daliesque wasteland of misshapen rocks and jagged boulders. A high-altitude desert with dusty, wine red slopes. A shimmering expanse of unbroken white. The road plummeted, it disappeared, it reappeared, it crumbled, it submerged, it turned to ice, it climbed and it climbed.

It turned out to be a pretty uneventful journey. I got trapped by a miniature avalanche. I had to cut frozen socks off my feet. I set fire to my clothes for warmth. I fell, many times. I bled, from many places. I became delirious. I could have met an icy death. I'm not getting into the details since this isn't a tale about how wonderfully brave and adventurous I am. Besides, it'll take too long to describe how wonderfully brave and adventurous I am.

Oh, and I learned a lesson in humility. Having reached Taglang La – at 5,328 meters, the highest pass on this route – I got off Kaya, puffed my chest out proudly and took in a deep, satisfying breath of air. I'd set out by myself and conquered the most extreme road in the world. I felt like a hero. Until I caught sight of a solo rider, coming from the opposite direction, and slowly making her way to the summit marker. She was riding a cycle, the kind that needs pedaling. I'm not being sexist, but really, with people like her around it's hard to feel like a hero these days.

From Leh, Kaya headed west on the 434-kilometer 'Treaty Road', along the historical trade route between Srinagar and Ladakh. For me this was also a personal journey. When this impossible road was first conceived, my late grandfather, a civil engineer with the Border Roads Organization, had served with the team that made it possible. Across yet another surreal, desert landscape, I carried my *tata's* memory with me.

The wind swept along the bleak hills. Kaya swept along cliffhanging roads. From these Martian summits, I saw like the Hubble telescope, far. The road carried on, without end. Slowly, trees reappeared, running along the river bank, a scattering of green. The cliffs were softened by a veil of moss. Slopes turned into terraced fields, the ground into pastures. Approaching Kargil, we left a barren red world and entered a vibrant green one. We also left behind a land of peace to enter a war zone. Graceful mosque minarets and graceful artillery barrels appeared at regular intervals, both looking skywards. When one speaks, it signals a call of prayer. When the other speaks, it signals the end of prayer.

Located on the Line of Control, Kargil burst into the Indian consciousness during the 1999 incursion by Pakistani and Mujahedeen forces. Discovered by shepherds, rather than our intelligence agencies (who are remarkable only for their complete lack of any), no one appreciated the gravity of the invasion until the shelling of the town. Suddenly, the entire country woke up to a place called Kargil, and though few knew where it was, or what was there, every armchair patriot wanted it defended against those evil Pakis, 'at any cost'.

The cost was 527 unquestioningly brave soldiers. My generation's introduction to war, 'Operation Vijay' was hot news. Friends who considered reading a disease could no longer live without the daily paper. We cheered as our army defended the towns, and retook the hills. The media screamed themselves hoarse with jingoism. We won the battle. A day later, Kargil was relegated from the front page to the corner of page eight. We put aside the paper. Kargil lay buried in my memory, forgotten, until I reached the war memorial at Dras. I'm reminded of superficial patriotism. I'm reminded of the price tag of war.

A few kilometers past Dras, Kaya's path was blocked by a wall of sheep. While the sheep moved towards the greener grass on the other side, three shepherds moved towards me, dressed in long kurta, loose pantaloons, and sleeveless vest. The tallest of them shouted in an incomprehensible tongue, while waving his staff.

Not sure if he was addressing me or the sheep, I stayed quiet. He screamed again, and I picked up one word: '*dawai*'.

Medicines. That's what they were after. Well, they'd come to the right man. A traveling pharmacy – with a bag full of painkillers, bandages, antiseptics, sleeping pills, and laxatives – I was more than happy to play drug dealer. The difficulty lay in explaining the purpose of each medicine, especially when they showed little inclination to learn, instead staring at the *dawai* like a child who's stumbled on Santa's workshop. Words failing, I tore out a piece of paper and drew a few disturbing images depicting bowel movements and the like. First, they eyed me like I belonged in a straitjacket. Then, they shared a good laugh at my expense. Resigned, I left my entire supply of unprescribed prescription drugs with them, well aware how difficult it is for people in these remote recesses of our country to access medicines.

A few kilometers past the sheep, we came within sight of the military check-post at Zoji La. In that same instant, I also spotted a mounted machine gun, needlessly pointed at me.

Pulling over near the barricade, I start to get off Kaya when the soldiers gesture for me to take her further back. One of the soldiers walks over and informs me that I would have to return to Dras and come back the next morning. Traffic is restricted to only one way at a time for two short periods each day, and I was too late. As always under these circumstances, I promptly launch into a speech about Kaya Dreams. Eventually, I am taken to meet the officer in charge, who asks me take a seat, offers me a cup of tea and makes me repeat my story.

'Why are you traveling alone? Where's the fun in that,' he thunders, his voice echoing around the narrow valley.

'I tried to get friends on board, sir. But it never worked out.'

'It's nice to see what you're doing though,' he nods approvingly. 'Nobody cares about the country anymore, and the young chaps nowadays have no courage.'

'Thank you, sir.' An embarrassed smile appears on my face.

'But tell me, why aren't you riding an Enfield? Now *that's* a real bike. A man's bike.'

With the officer's approval, the barricade was lifted, and back on the road I had to spend the first few minutes of the ride handling Kaya with kid's gloves, just in case she'd heard the last part of that conversation. It wasn't the first time I've been accused of not being a 'real motorcyclist' because I'm not on an Enfield. Well, if being a real motorcyclist involves less riding and more pushing, then I'm quite happy not to fall into the category. Clinging on to old world charm and old world parts, the Enfield is a wonderful bike really, except that it feels obliged to have a break down more often than a high-strung actress. And every time the manufacturers attempt to improve the Enfield's reliability, the fans scream bloody murder. 'It's no longer a classic,' they bemoan. Ostensibly, a motorcycle is a classic only if it doesn't run properly. As much as I'm charmed by the Enfield, I'd rather ride a bike I can trust. I'd rather ride Kaya, who has twice the heart of any motorcycle I know.

Beyond Zoji La, the soldiers were everywhere, armed to the teeth and watching the road intently. They stood in pairs at every bend, near every lookout, more regular than the milestones. I waved to them as Kaya rolled by. Every one of them returned my greeting, accompanied by bemused smiles.

Kilometer 14352

Kaya raced down from the pass, anticipating the exuberant green floor of the Kashmir valley. Instead the meadow was torn, marked by hundreds of tents, pitched row after row. People milled around in the thousands. A cloud of dust rose up to meet us. Grey trails of smoke climbed skywards from numerous cooking fires. Barbed wire and mesh fences cordoned off the area. Armored trucks passed between the barricades. Armed soldiers stood on the ready, searching every individual who passed through.

Despite the appearance of a refugee camp, Baltal is in reality a pilgrim camp, the starting point for the Amarnath Yatra. The Guantanamo Bay style military deployment is explained by the fact that this is Kashmir, a favored destination for any ambitious Pakistani insurgent – and what juicier target to make a political statement than Hindu pilgrims. Consequently, on August 1st, 2000, two bearded men in green fatigues emerged from the jungles and entered the camp at Pahalgam, indiscriminately opening fire on pilgrims headed for Amarnath. Five grenades hurled, 570 AK-47 rounds fired, 30 people dead, and 60 grievously injured.

Kaya rent through the cloud of dust and pulled over at the vehicle dump – it would be too polite to call it a parking lot. The guards pay special attention to me at the barricades. Once inside the camp, having barely taken a few steps, another guard comes over and goes through my bags again. He asks a lot of questions, giving me the impression he finds me unsavory, suspicious even. It has to be the long hair and bushy beard. The terrorist's style statement aside, there's something about long-haired men that instinctively aggravates certain Indians, compelling them to put us in our place. Satisfied that I'm only a social deviant, and not a terrorist, the soldier lets me go find a tent for the night.

At dawn, pilgrims gather in the hundreds near the barbwire checkpoint at the start of the trail, watched by machine guns. When the barricade lifts, the ecstatic crowd surges forward with a collective cry. Praise the lord. An hour into the walk, I fall in with a group of uniformed soldiers, three Sikhs and a Rajput, making the trek solely to visit the shrine. Discovering that I'll be in their home states soon, they begin to list out places that I just have to visit. The list is long, and helps keep my mind off the agonizingly long climb. As we come out of a particularly steep slope, they step off the trail and find a discreet place for a breather.

'Do you smoke?' one of the Sikh soldiers asks me, proceeding to extract a ball of hash the size of a grenade. When we commence the walk again, I feel distinctly light headed. Unfortunately, I also feel heavy footed. The walk gets progressively tougher.

Deep within the heart of the mountains, surrounded by pristine white snow fields, icy peaks, and cascades of glacial melt, the yawning cave of Amarnath is an impressive sight. As for the 'miraculous' 14-foot-tall snow-lingam formed naturally each year . . . well, it's not all that incredible when you consider that a phallus is not a very complex shape. Besides, I didn't share the nation's 'shock' when it was revealed that the shrine board had a helping hand in the 'natural creation' of the lingam, much like making a snowman. The authorities' excuse for this 'first time' gaffe was 'lack of snow due to global warming'. Who knew even our gods are subject to environmental disasters?

Following a rushed and crowded *darshan* of the sacred lingam, I begin the seventeen-kilometer walk back to Baltal. Less than halfway there, my body is a mass of aching muscle. I've pushed myself to the limit. Now I push beyond it. Still a fair distance from the base, my left knee finally gives out with an excruciating tweak. I rest for a while before trying to walk again, only to collapse in pain at the very first step. The problem isn't simply fatigue, and every time I bend my knee I feel a sharp stab of pain. Witnessing my agony, a passing pilgrim lends me his walking stick, and for the remaining distance I'm left dragging the leg rather than walking on it.

A wave of relief washes over me as I approach the checkpoint, physically drained and mentally frayed. The only thing that's keeping me going is the thought of the tent and my sleeping bag waiting for me inside.

'STOP!' I hear a scream behind me, but I don't bother, too dazed to see if it has anything to do with me. 'STOP!' The voice rings out again. This time I turn around, to see a soldier striding determinedly towards me. 'What's your name?' he asks tersely.

'You don't have to stop me just because of my long hair,' I snap, awed by my stupidity even as the words are spilling out my mouth. No one appreciates a long-haired smart-ass, especially not someone wearing a uniform and holding an automatic weapon that demands automatic respect.

From the look on his face, I might as well have shouted Long Live Pakistan. His face turns a distinct red, and the rage is expressed in his response. '*Bakwas bandh kar*. What do you think of yourself? Come on, show me some identification.'

Resigned, I pull out my driver's license and hand it to him.

'*Yeh kaun hain?*' he sneers, and before I can begin to defend my youthful gawkiness, he's called a fellow soldier over and they're having a good laugh at my expense. For good reason. I've carried this license on me since 1994, and in this time it's received several washings, gone for a swim in the ocean and – on one exceptional night of drinking – was bent in half and dunked into a pint of beer. The well-abused photograph reveals an acne-riddled teenager with a crop-dusted moustache pretending to be twenty-one. Regardless, traffic cops all over the country have never objected to it.

'At what angle does this picture resemble you?' the soldier asks, all serious again. 'Do I look like a fool? I want to see some other form of identification.'

'What other identification?' I argue, continuing down the path of idiocy. 'I'm an Indian, so you tell me, what other form of identification do we possess? At least I have a license. Why don't you stop somebody else, and see if they can show you even that.'*

'*Bahut ho chukka tumhara hoshiyari.* I've stopped you, not somebody else. Do you have any other identification or not?' The spittle is flying off his lips.

'I have ten different letters of introduction, but they are in my tent. I can go bring them if you want.'

'I'm not letting you go anywhere.'

'Listen, I've got nothing to hide and no reason to escape. You can accompany me . . . or send someone to make sure?'

'We have better things to do than entertain the likes of you. Do we look like an escort service? If you really have these papers, why aren't they with you?'

I don't have a reply, instead getting angrier at his pig-headedness.

'I don't believe anything this chap is telling,' he says to the other soldier. 'There's something suspicious about him.' Then turning his attention back on me, 'What's in that bag?'

'Only my camera.'

'Give it here. I want to take a look.' Without complaint, I hand him the camera bag and watch as he pulls everything out, examining the USB cable, memory chips, extra lenses, and spare battery with suspicion. The most distrustful look is reserved for

* With aadhars, pan cards, and voter IDs, today an Indian has more forms of ID than Jason Bourne, but even as recently as 2005 it was a simpler world where a majority of the people had no real way of showing they existed.

the lens cleaner fluid. 'What's all this for? Why do you need all this to take a photograph?'

'This is ridiculous! They're just camera accessories. I can't make a bomb out of them.'

'Bomb!' he gasps. 'I've had enough of you,' he sputters. 'You're coming with me to the holding area right now.'

'No, I'm not,' I wave him off and turn to walk away. My brains must have flown the coop at some point.

'What are you doing?' he screams, sounding more surprised than angry, and grabs me by the arm roughly. He looks like he might explode. 'Do you think this is a joke?'

'Why should I fear you when I've done nothing wrong? I'm telling you I have the required papers in the tent and you're not willing to be smart about it.'

With this last bit of lip, all diplomacy comes to a resolute end. The grip on my hand tightens, and I'm drag-pushed towards the 'interrogation room'. Images flash through my head – a gloomy cell, a single chair, a lone dangling bulb, walls stained dark by dry blood. Instead I find myself in a tidy green tent with a new table and a reasonably comfortable chair.

'Let me go. I've done nothing wrong. You've no right to—'

'We are the military. We can do as we wish,' he threatens.

'Look at his eyes,' his partner says. 'I'm sure he is on something.'

Yeah, on the *charas* that your friends shared with me, I want to say, but decide my mouth has gotten me into enough trouble already.

He asks me to remove my jacket. I hand it to him, wondering if I'm going to get busted for the possession of illegal narcotics, given to me by his fellow soldiers as a gesture of friendship. Despite the circumstances, the irony isn't lost on me.

'Aha! What do we have here?' he says, slamming a rather heavy object down on the table. Oh damn it, not the Leatherman. 'What are you doing with this?'

'It's my tool kit.'

'With a Rambo knife in it?' the other one sneers. 'We should search him properly.'

'No way!' I rise up from the chair, more panicky at this point than angry. 'I want you to call a superior officer because I'm not listening to you anymore.'

'What do you think you can do about it?'

'I'm not nobody, okay,' I say, ashamed of myself for playing the I've-got-influence card. 'Not only do I have letters from the central government, one of my introductions is from an army colonel.'

He hesitates, unsure if I'm bluffing, and then turns to his companion. The sidekick shrugs and heads outside the tent without a word, leaving the two of us glaring at each other, until he returns with an officer in tow. My interrogator salutes the man. I greet him as sir.

'What's happening here?' he asks in a smart, educated voice, clearly used to asking questions and getting answers.

I jump in and explain the situation.

'So, what's the problem then?' he says, turning to the soldier. 'The boy is saying he's in possession of identity papers. Go with him to the tent and have a look at them. If you still find something wrong, then bring him back.' With that, he strides out of the tent.

My tormentor seems indignant, but resigned to his fate, he gruffly nods for me to follow him and sets out towards the checkpost. I'm too tired to gloat. We walk a few meters in silence when he suddenly stops and turns to face me.

'Are you sure you don't have any other form of identification on you?'

'Sir, if there was anything else, I would have gladly shown it to you,' I reply, speaking with the cordial respect I should have accorded him to begin with. 'Other than my license, all I have on me is my bank card,' I say, holding out my wallet.

'Show it to me.'

I hand over my Andhra Bank card to him.

'Is that you?' he asks, pointing to the 3mm/3mm smudge that looks vaguely like a human face.

'Yes,' I sigh, well aware how pointless the photograph is.

'Why didn't you just show me this before? You can go now.' With a quick turn, he walks away.

Too stunned to move, I stand there staring at his disappearing back.

Kilometer 14469

Kaya was pulled over twice as she approached Srinagar. On the first occasion, they searched my bags. On the other, the officer smiled and let her through. Inside the city, we were stopped twice more while looking for a hotel. Soon after checking into a room, I headed over to the barber shop. With my beard taken off, I stepped out of the shop feeling respectable. Five minutes later, I was pulled over again. I resigned myself to being a terrorist suspect until I left the city, or blew myself up, in which case they'd probably pat themselves on the back for being so perceptive.

Srinagar was a city under siege. Pillboxes and sandbags marked sensitive regions, armored convoys paced the roads, razor wire graced the sidewalks, and armed soldiers patrolled every street. This military presence only got heavier and more frantic as I neared Nishat Gardens, until, a short distance from the park, the road was completely cordoned off, with the traffic being turned around. A car bomb had exploded outside the gardens just as an army convoy drove by, killing nine soldiers and seriously wounding fifteen others, including a few tourists.

Remarkable in the eyes of someone who's not from here, despite the bomb blast right next door, the promenade of Dal Lake was overrun by Kashmiris determined to have a good time. Young boys sat on the embankment eyeing the beautiful women. Brightly lit shops lined the far side of the road, displaying Kashmiri shawls and handicrafts. Vendors filled the gaps with small carts, selling kebabs, popcorn, and *chaat*. The crowds and the action spilled onto the lake, a flotilla of *shikaras* vying for space and for customers. They have learned to go on, despite the violence, the repression, and the death, otherwise they would have no life. Besides, few Kashmiris had reason to shed a tear over our dead soldiers. As the sun descended, an orange orb in a blazing sky, the waters of the Dal Lake turned to fire. All else became faceless silhouettes.

I'd wanted to visit Kashmir since I can remember, but as Kaya made her way out I felt relief – to be leaving behind the guns, the suspicions, the fear. Baramulla, Sopore, Shopian, Pahalgam. Ninety-six hours in the valley had left me with an unsettling sense of claustrophobia. Big brother was watching, judging, in the crowded market place at noon, on the empty street at night. All that we take for granted as normal, for the Kashmiri was suspended: freedom of movement, freedom of expression, freedom of congregation. Freedom from disappearance. I couldn't comprehend living in this Orwellian world of uncertainty, not knowing which action of yours was deemed wrong, or if it even mattered. And perhaps that's what troubled me most, my own lack of understanding.

Why is it, when I think of occupying forces, my mind invariably turns to Palestine, when the world's most militarized zone – exact numbers be damned – is right here in Kashmir. Why does the *unbiased* lens of our liberal media see stone-pelting youth in Kashmir as villainous aggressors, and the gun-toting state as defender? Why are there so few who know that 70,000 Kashmiris have been killed since 1989, and even fewer who believe it? Why don't we see that 8,000 disappearances, 20,000 uncharged detentions, rapes, encounters, unmarked graves, and torture are too high a price to demand? Why do we fail to see what the Kashmiri wants?

During the summer of 2010, Kashmir erupted in widespread, intense, and sustained protest, unlike any witnessed over the last decade. Tens, perhaps hundreds, of thousands took to the streets to tell us what they want: *azadi*. Freedom. In response, the state crackdown left 122 Kashmiris dead. Meanwhile, the much-publicized Arab Spring witnessed 14 deaths in Sudan, 22 in Saudi Arabia, 8 in Algeria, and 120 in Bahrain.* While the sacrifices in those nations were rewarded with political reform, all the Kashmiri earned was false promises. Our democracy has shown itself to be more authoritarian than others' dictatorships.

Blame the separatists, blame external machinations, blame the militants – it doesn't matter. In the end, the protests were a cry against our tyranny. Whether Kashmir rightfully belongs to India – or not – as long as the military and the AFSPA remain, we will be nothing more than an occupying force. In protecting our interests, we have sacrificed those of the Kashmiri, but lest we forget, any strength derived at the expense of others is a sign of our weakness. Patriotism is derived from self-sacrifice, not demanding sacrifice from others. So, for every extrajudicial killing, for every human rights violation, for every political abuse suffered by the Kashmiri, it is not the army that is to be blamed but us, for our lack of moral courage and political integrity. And it is we who are responsible for the 7,000 martyred security personnel, including the nine who died that day.

---

* Without devolving into civil war, Egypt and Tunisia are the only countries to have spilled more blood than Kashmir.

The Jawahar Tunnel, as I approached it, reminded me of a prison break, an escape route that delivered you from the clutches of an oppressive warden. Except, of course, this tunnel was heavily guarded, and as expected my bags were searched before they let me pass. What made the experience particularly surreal was being pulled over and having my bags checked at the other end of the tunnel as well. Was there an arms dealer in the tunnel that I'd somehow missed? I mean really, what are the chances of somebody entering the tunnel with a bag of pears and dirty clothes, only to come out the other end armed with a bazooka and military secrets? It seemed like a fitting end to my Kashmiri sojourn.

'If there is a paradise on earth, it is this, it is this, it is this,' reads an inscription at Srinagar's Shalimar Bhag. Kashmir isn't paradise. It isn't paradise lost. Kashmir is paradise stolen.

LEG TWELVE

If I Become an Indian, I Become a Traitor

KAYA SWOOPED DOWN from the lofty heights and, after a short and unpleasant visit to Katra, we were in Punjab. It felt strange to be back on the plains. No more switchbacks and blind turns. No more precipitous edges and steep climbs. No more rarefied air. The road extended for miles in front of us, uninterrupted, flat. It was uninspiring. It was easy. I leaned back carelessly, and let my thoughts drift to Disha, my girlfriend of three years, and our anticipated reunion at McLeod Ganj the next day. The four-month separation having taken its toll on an already troubled relationship, we were hoping some time together would help fix it.

Screeeech! By the time I realized the lorry before me had come to a sudden standstill, it was already too late. I swung Kaya to the right, attempting to steer her past the stationary vehicle, but the handlebar struck the edge of the lorry, spilling me out of the seat in a magnificently un-acrobatic tumble. Experienced crasher that I am, I was back on my bloodied legs within seconds, dusting off my embarrassment. My real concern was for Kaya, who lay stricken beside the passenger door of the lorry, through the window of which the bewildered driver was looking down at her. Even as I tottered over, I could tell her front rim was a mangled mess. While the concerned lorry driver enquired after me, two motorcyclists pulled up beside us and picked up Kaya. To everyone's surprise, Kaya could still ride, but just barely, shuddering and bucking violently. It was like riding a drunken bronco.

The guilt-faced truck driver – after all, he'd stopped suddenly in the middle of the road to chat with a friend in the opposite lane – offered to load Kaya in the back and carry her the thirty kilometers to Pathankot. But I decided, wrongly as it turned out, it would be easier to ride there. With one of the motorcyclists escorting me all the way, the thirty kilometers took nearly two hours, and by the time I caught sight of the Bajaj Service Centre, my arms no longer felt like they were attached to the rest of me. It was nearly closing time when I stepped in and spoke to the service manager, but within minutes of explaining my circumstances, a team of mechanics was working on Kaya. At closing time they were still at it, and they continued well past. Even the manager, cashier, and accountant hung around, asking me about my travels. They served me lemonade and chips. At one point, the owner of the dealership dropped in to say hello and check on the progress.

I didn't hear anyone grumble. When the bill came, it didn't include any labor charges. The owner had left instructions to the effect, and they were billing me only for the spare parts. Then the manager showed me to a hotel run by his friend, a boisterous Sikh who insisted that after such a harrowing experience I deserved an AC room to unwind in. He also insisted that I only pay him the non-AC room tariff.

I concluded that Punjabis are the finest people on earth.

Kilometer 15398

Kaya showed no ill effects from the previous day's mishap when we rode out of Pathankot, and by mid-morning we had ascended the hills to McLeod Ganj.

Before I set out in search of a suitably atmospheric hotel though, I find myself doing something unexpected. I stop at a bookstore and buy a guide book. Guided by *Lonely Planet*, I find a charming guesthouse tucked away along McLeod Ganj's narrow lanes, where Disha joins me later that afternoon. The next few days go by in a blissful blur. We make no mention of the past. We don't discuss the future. We live in the now, riding around the Chamba Valley and Dalhousie, before returning to McLeod Ganj in time for the Dalai Lama's birthday.

Since the sixties, when the Dalai Lama fled Tibet and crossed the mountains into India, this has been his home and the seat of the Tibetan government-in-exile (officially the Central Tibetan Administration), an asylum for Tibetan refugees. Dubbed 'Little Lhasa', it is also home to Tibetan monasteries, Tibetan organizations, Tibetan shops, Tibetan restaurants, Tibetan monks, and a lot of Tibetans. The culture and arts of Tibet are preserved on these streets, kept alive as memories of a stolen home, and if the Chinese cultural revolution is anything to go by, you will, in all likelihood, discover more of Tibet's culture here than in Tibet. At the Tibetan Institute of Performing Arts, a new generation of exiles practice Lhamo, the arresting folk opera of Tibet. The Library of Tibetan Works and Archives stands as a repository for books and manuscripts. The Tibetan Cultural Museum provides a glimpse of rare and precious cultural objects. At the Tibetan Medical and Astrological Institute a monk offers to read our horoscope.

Tibetans aside, the rest of McLeod's population is also made up of foreigners. Pilgrims, tourists, travelers, and volunteers, all from the Western world, here in search of spirituality and an answer to life, the universe, and everything else. Some of them seem to have lived here as long as the Dalai Lama. A few odd ones think being a refugee is cool, and are upset that their own country isn't oppressed. And then there are the female volunteers, a fair number of whom believe the best way to ease the suffering of young Tibetan men is to sleep with them. Finally, we have the celebrity Buddhists, the Pierce Brosnans and the Richard Geres, whose photographs from their visit here grace the restaurant menus, along with a recommendation of their favorite dishes. Considering some the artistic abuse these actor types have subjected moviegoers to, it's perhaps not such a terrible idea for them to earn a few karma points.

While having lunch at a rooftop restaurant, Disha and I meet 22-year-old Karma, a student of *thangka* painting. With a small rounded face and straight black hair falling down the sides, he's dressed in a black Iron Maiden T-shirt that says Fear of the Dark. We are well met, and over the next two days spend a lot of time together.

'Sometimes I feel like I hate *thangka* painting, there are too many rigid patterns and principles,' he tells us. 'I'd like to paint with freedom. But what will I do with the paintings . . . it's a *thangka* every tourist wants as a souvenir.'

He spits the word tourist with such strong distaste it takes me by surprise. I've heard the tone before with reference to tourism.

'Uh, please don't get me wrong, I wasn't talking about you . . . it's just, I don't know,' he shrugs. 'The Dalai Lama claims it's important to keep up public interest in our plight, but I'm sick of being looked at like a victim.'

'I'm sure there are people who genuinely sympathize with your—'

'But I don't want people's sympathy. I had a girlfriend from Australia, and she was really nice, but . . . I don't know how to explain it, it was like, really important to her that I was her 'Tibetan' boyfriend. I see these girls, how they feel good about themselves for dating us. I just want to be Karma . . . not Karma the refugee.'

'So, you feel like a refugee in India?'

'All the time . . . though this is the only home I've known. Strange thing is, under Indian law I'm not even recognized as a refugee. I'm listed as a foreigner.'

'How long have you lived here?'

'I was born here,' he smiles sadly. 'I'm even eligible for Indian citizenship. But it's not as simple as that. If I become an Indian, in some ways, I also become a traitor.'

The sad irony of the Tibetan situation is that in becoming an Indian citizen they will be left without an identity. At least that's the fear. Approximately 1,20,000 Tibetans live in India, and less than one percent of them have ever applied for Indian citizenship. They represent a group that has voluntarily, or under pressure from the Central Tibetan Administration, maintained their refugee status for more than three decades. Karma was raised as a Tibetan, to be a Tibetan, and becoming an Indian will render him unrecognizable, belonging to neither. By gaining a nationality, he would lose a society. The Tibetans hold on to the idea that India is only a temporary exile, and one day they will cross the mountains to return home. So they remain, a people with a strong national identity but no nation.

'I love this country,' Karma says. 'You have willingly provided us a safe haven. But all that is changing, and it's only a matter of time before all support for our cause ends.'

'Why do you say that?'

'We'd suspected for some time that the Indian people have mentally accepted Tibet as part of China, but when the Indian government officially recognized it last year . . . that was the confirmation. Already it has become more difficult for refugees to enter the country. Our only real strength is the Dalai Lama, but he is an old man. I fear that all hope of Free Tibet will die with him.'

Our last day in McLeod Ganj coincides with the Dalai Lama's birthday, one of the biggest celebrations on the Tibetan calendar. The rain falls unremittingly throughout the morning, but it doesn't dampen the festive spirit. People gather around the main temple in the thousands, some wear raincoats, others hold up umbrellas or plastic sheets, a few embrace the rain as part of the festivities. The celebrations are simple, as is the man they are celebrating. Young monks dedicate songs to him, the schoolchildren put on a dance. And when the time comes, I bow my head and whisper a wish for him, just like all those around me.

For more than forty years India supported this hope, of a Free Tibet, until 2003, when Prime Minister Vajpayee signed a memorandum of understanding with China, recognizing the Tibet Autonomous Region as part of the territory of the People's Republic of China. It was India's first explicit recognition of the annexation of Tibet by the Chinese. In return, the Chinese government ceded all claims to Sikkim. Exactly a year, to the day, from when we rode out of McLeod Ganj, the Nathu La border between India and China was opened after nearly half a century, signifying the public recognition of the memorandum signed by the two countries. It's not really a coincidence that the event fell on the Dalai Lama's birthday.

Karma's fears turned out to be real.

Kilometer 16061

Kaya raced across the incongruously smooth asphalt of Punjab. The road shot across the plain, straight as an arrow, clean and fast. The wind was hot and humid, a natural sauna. The land of five rivers, irrigated fields extending for miles. This was indeed the breadbasket of the country. We went west, along the historic Sher Shah Suri Road. Built in the 16th century, this road was once South Asia's most important artery, and back then you could follow it from Sonargaon, in present-day Bangladesh, across the Gangetic Plain, all the way to Peshawar in Pakistan. Today, known as the Grand Trunk Road, it won't get you half as far as it did four hundred years ago.

Forty kilometers past Amritsar, someone has inconsiderately erected a barbed wire fence across the road. The road didn't end, no, it unerringly continued beyond the fence, only that stretch was Made-in-Pakistan. Welcome to the Radcliffe Line, on the other side of which live 180 million of my countrymen who are no longer my countrymen. Welcome to Wagah, the only 'legal' border crossing between India and Pakistan. Like a Picasso sketch, Mr. Radcliffe's line drawing has become a tourist attraction, a ceremonial border where soldiers on both sides of the fence put on a show of bravado; rather ironic, considering it's emulating a British tradition and is called 'beating retreat'. It's also irrational really, that we make an attraction out of a border we can't cross. It's like me going to a mosque just to enjoy the sign that says 'Non Muslims Not Allowed.'

A thousand Indians filled the stands on this side, while a matching number of ex-Indians filled the opposition stands. Before the actual ceremony began, a few visitors felt compelled to display their love for the nation – through frenzied waving of the tricolor, screaming anti-Pakistan slogans, and running to the gates to beat their chests in front of the opposing crowds. Ostensibly, the intention behind this show is 'promoting mutual respect'. It had all the mutual respect of a bitter divorce settlement.

Where the official ritual followed a similarly chauvinistic exhibition, it was fortunately devoid of real passion. When the border gates drew open, soldiers from both sides goose-stepped to the line, chests puffed out, heads held high. Stopping inches from each other, they glared into their counterpart's wicked eyes, and bellowed a string of sharp commands into the other's face. Boots were raised high and brought down with an unhealthy thump. Two limp flags descended the poles from which we hang our national pride.

I stared across the artificial separation, at the monsters on the other side. They sat expectantly, separated by sex, males to one side of the stand and females to the other. The men seemed a little less boisterous than our own, and the women a tad prettier. Beyond that I couldn't tell the difference. Yet we've spent sixty years hating each other, beginning with that original border crossing, which was accompanied by genocide. Though we don't like to use the term, what else do you call an act of politics that kills a million people? That's more than the combined British and American deaths from World War II, and we weren't even at war. It was civilians butchering each other, all in the name of an unresponsive god.

Other than prejudiced political rhetoric, neither of our countries has attempted to record, or reconcile, the event. Neither side has acknowledged guilt. Neither side wants to apologize for it. Neither side wants to forgive. Only forget. We have built no memorials for the dead. We do not mark a day to remember them. Nor do we teach our children about it. History class went something like this: 'Boys, the price of freedom was the Partition of India, and many people died during the process.'* I had to read a book called *Freedom at Midnight* by some French dude to get a real idea of what happened.

Does our silence come from the fear of our own role in the tragedy; that in remembering our loss, we must also recognize our crimes? Perhaps the reason we have no commemorations is because we are not only the victims, but also the villains. Unlike the Holocaust, there is no side to label as evil, and when we point a finger, we do so to a mirror. But we cannot deal with history through denial. By confronting it we might hope to learn from our mistakes. Rather than this saber-rattling display at Wagah – the marching, flag waving, and screaming that perpetuates our mutual animosity – we would be better served to build, on this line drawn in blood, a memorial of reconciliation. A memorial that stands not to assign blame, but to be a place where our collective sorrow can overcome our collective anger. It could remind us

* It can't be to protect our children from the horror of the events, seeing how they are exposed to gruesome violence and rape on a daily basis, thanks to Bollywood.

that nothing good ever has, nor ever will, come from our hatred for each other.*

A bright blue kingfisher swooped down and perched on the barbwire a few feet from where Kaya was. The bird turned its head, cast an eye on one side of the fence and then the other. With a flutter of wings, it flew across the border.

We, on the other hand, had to turn around and head back.

Kilometer 16413

Kaya raced like she'd never raced before, across Punjab and into Haryana, across Haryana and towards Delhi. Past mythical battlefields and real ones, embracing Punjabi hospitality and failing to out-drink them. The plains were an ocean of green, parting to let a straight black path run through them – four lanes of immaculately paved road, as unblemished as Aishwarya Rai's air-brushed face. This had to be the result of divine intervention.

Besides the Patiala peg, the only grief I faced along this stretch of the journey was from the two ladies in my life. Disha wasn't too happy about checking into hotel rooms as my wife, and my mum wasn't pleased about her checking into hotel rooms *without* being my wife. While I knew what my mum wanted from me, other than grumble, Disha never gave me a clear answer to what I was supposed to enter in the hotel register under the column 'Relation'. In Sirhind I let her take over the responsibility, and

* For those who fear that such a memorial will incite communal violence, let it be pointed out that the Holocaust Memorial is a place of sorrow and acceptance, not anger. Besides, communal violence stems from ignorance, not from knowing.

she filled in 'fairy godmother'. Obviously, the receptionist wasn't performing his duties properly.

Unfortunately, I've never been a competent liar and when you're as predisposed to getting caught as I am, you quickly learn that it's better to stick with the truth.* While most of my friends were still pretending like they were virgins – not surprising seeing how our parents regard premarital sex as a degenerative disease, for which if they ever found a vaccine, they'd administer it even before the polio drops – I very early in the game explained to my folks that I was in a live-in relationship. I had no choice really, not when I moved out of their house while living in the same city. Besides, I didn't like the idea of sneaking around in my own backyard.

'You're moving in with a girl???' my mother had asked deliriously, the tears pouring down her stricken face. I hadn't expected better, since live-in relationships are as few and secretive as plots to assassinate dictators. And like most coups, when the shit blows up you can expect a lot of suffering. 'Why are you telling me this?' she'd sobbed. 'Don't you have any shame? People usually try to hide this sort of thing.'

While the irony didn't escape me, she did have a point there. Disha's parents lived in Bombay and weren't aware I existed. The landlord of my 'love nest' lived down the street, and he wasn't aware Disha existed.

---

* The only thing I've never had the courage to own up to is the weed, and they're never going to know about it. Unless they are foolish enough to read this book someday.

'What kind of a girl is this?' my uncle roared. 'The fact that she's doing this reveals her upbringing. You're dragging the family name through the mud. This is not America for you to behave in such cheap fashion.'

I'd stuck with my decision, causing the family a lot of heartbreak and embarrassment. And for nearly two years things between us remained strained. Then I moved back home for a while. Things got better, and over time they've finally come to accept Disha, which is not necessarily a good thing. Now they're waiting for us to announce the wedding date.

So here I was, on a road that was kind, with a ride anything but smooth, dealing with incriminating registers and long-distance accusations. And if you find the following dialogue too dramatic, I doubt you have an Indian mother.

'What? What do you mean Disha's joined you? What is she doing there?' mum wailed.

'Ma, she's come to meet me and—'

'When is she coming back?'

'She's going to travel with me till Delhi, and then—'

'What? Shiva, Shiva, she's traveling with you on the bike. Oh god! What have I done to deserve this?'

'Relax, ma, it's only for a week, and—'

'How can I relax with a son like you? Do her parents know?'

'Uh . . . I'd guess not.'

'Ayayoo! Why can't you be like other children? Where did I go wrong in your upbringing? I sacrificed everything for you . . . sob . . .'

'Maaa, please stop crying. It's not such a big deal.'

'Who are you to tell me what to do? First you suck all my blood and now you want to steal my tears as well.'

You're sucking my blood. Now there's an accusation I've lived with since I learned the English language. While most mothers described their kids as princes and angels, I grew up feeling like Dracula.

'And what do you mean it's not a big deal?' she continued. 'Do you think it's a joke traveling with a young unmarried woman? Remember, you are the one responsible for her . . . and what if something bad happens.'

'Nothing's going to happen, ma. I promise to be careful which—'

'And what will people think?'

'How many bloody times should I tell you I don't care what people think?'

'Go on, shout at your mother. *Sob.* I'm here only for that. You don't care, but remember, I'm the one who's blamed for all that you do. *Sob.* I have to face society, the unfortunate mother who has to see her unmarried son carry on like this. As if it wasn't shameful enough that you lived with her. Now you are staying in hotel rooms together. Cheee! Just thinking about it is horrible. Whole of Hyderabad knows what you both were up to. Now you want to show the entire country. What is this, a honeymoon without a wedding? If you must carry on like this, why don't you just get married?'

'Maaa, I really can't have this argument with you right now, but I've told you, we aren't sure if we want to get married, at least—'

'Shiva, Shiva! Then what are you doing with her? Everybody knows what kind of relationship you had with her. If your intentions aren't honorable, why have you carried on so openly? Why did you tell us?'

'I don't believe this . . . ha. So, you're saying I should lie and hide things from you?'

'At least that way it shows that you have some respect for our feelings.'

'What kind of fu— logic is that?'

'What is so logical about what you're doing? How can you be so heartless? Sometimes I wonder if you are really our child. Your father is such a principled man and look at you. After all you've done with that poor girl, now you just want to leave her.'

'Maaa, why do you want to make me the bad guy? It's not like I'm trying to cheat Disha. She doesn't want to get married either.'

'Hah! How can she not want to? Any proper Indian girl who has . . . been with a boy obviously hopes for a future with him. What will people think of her otherwise? Do you think anybody else will want to marry her?'

'I don't care about—'

'It doesn't matter if you care for the society or not. You can't escape the fact that you are part of it. You live in a country with strong social ties. I don't know where you get your ideas from, but they aren't Indian. Your thinking is like a foreigner and you—'

'Ma, don't go there . . .'

'There's no use getting angry with me. It's how everybody feels about you. Growing your hair. Getting tattoos. Living with a girl. And now this great bike ride. You talk about understanding our culture, but you don't want to behave anything like an Indian.'

'Ma, enough . . .'

'Fine, fine, but promise me you'll be extra careful while she's around.'

'I promise.'

'And promise she'll travel as your wife. I don't want her to be put in a shameful position.'

'She doesn't . . .' I began to explain, but gave up. 'Yes, yes, I promise.'

'And promise me she's returning home from Delhi.'

'I promise. Besides, she has to get back to her job.'

'Good! But seriously, you're twenty-six years old, why don't you just marry the girl . . .'

And how did Disha feel about the situation? Why, she was delighted that my mother was so concerned about her welfare. And she hated me because I introduced her everywhere as my wife.

It sucked to be me.

LEG THIRTEEN

God Willing, It Will Be a Boy

KAYA EKED HER WAY past the stately walls of Red Fort, fighting a stampede of metal and flesh, before finally pulling up in the parking lot of Delhi's Nizamuddin Station. I breathe a sigh of relief, consequently inhaling a lung full of the world's most polluted air. The relief is brief.

'Love . . .' Disha purrs, as we stand on the platform from which her train to Bangalore is going to leave in ten minutes.

'Yes, dear?' I reply dutifully, sensing imminent trouble.

'I don't think I want to go home yet. I've always wanted to visit Rajasthan, and it's a shame to miss out when I'm so close.'

'But . . .'

'What is it? Don't you want to travel with me any longer?'

'Of course I do, but . . . but what about mum?'

'Well, what about her?'

'You know . . . I promised her you'd go back from Delhi.'

'Come on, you can convince her. Besides, it's only a matter of a few days, just Jaipur and maybe Pushkar, and then I'm gone. Who knows when we'll meet again? It feels like we haven't even said bye properly.'

'But . . . oh well, fine then.'

Within the hour Kaya was headed out of the city towards Rajasthan, Disha easing back in the pillion seat. I didn't have to look back to know she wore a satisfied smile on her face. Well, at least one of us was happy. The road, one side of the Golden Triangle, was well-paved and fast. Cars screamed past us. The wind slapped against my exposed face, carrying with it monsoon's wetness. A featureless expanse broken by dark ridges, a fortress perched atop, abandoned, graying, crumbling. Just one, amongst the hundreds that litter the Rajasthani landscape.

After all, this is the home of warriors, land of the Rajput, who lived with pride, and very often died from it. If the fortresses don't succeed in convincing you of war's place of pride in their lives, a quick visit to the palace armory museum should: swords with gem-studded handles and engraved blades, gold gilded guns, carved ivory powder horns. For the bon vivant or hedonist, Rajasthan – with its outpouring of palaces, havelis, and castles – is a window to the extravagant pageantry and debauched lifestyle of the infamous Indian Maharajas. Even better, for a reasonably exorbitant sum of money, you can live like royalty for a short while. Proud and mighty Rajasthan has become one big historical theme park.

We enter Jaipur under the watchful gaze of the hilltop fortress of Nahargarh, the imposing ramparts standing sentinel, as they have for the last three centuries. The city is an eyeful of tapering columns, honeycombed *jharokhas*, graceful archways, and colonnaded bazaars, all of it doused in pink, the warm shade of hospitality. Jaipur took on its color back in 1876, when Maharaja Ram Singh ordered the entire city painted pink in honor of the visiting Prince of Wales. Today, the city maintains the tradition, as mandated by the government, in honor of the visiting tourist.

Wandering the street in front of the iconic Hawa Mahal, we are accosted by a young man of genial smile, disingenuous eyes, and swirling moustache, who, ignoring our ignoring of him, falls into step with us.

'You know something,' Stalker Guide whispers conspiringly, 'the real name of the Hawa Mahal is actually Hawas Mahal . . . the palace of lust.' His tone is mischievous, his expression a mock apology in case he caused embarrassment to Disha.

'And why would that be?' she asks.

'Because this was an extension of the king's harem. There is a water tank in the center. It is where the maharaja would celebrate Holi with his women, in the nude.'

'Sounds like fun,' I retort, wondering if it might not be a bad idea to hire the informative chap.

Disha is not amused.

Jaipur's other big draw is the City Palace, dutifully shocking in its excessiveness, where the star shockers are two giant silver urns standing at the entrance to the Diwan-e-Aam 'hall of public audience'.

'These vessels are the largest silver objects in the world,' Ex-Stalker Guide points out with pride. 'It is in the *Guinness Book of Records*. They were used by the Maharaja Sawai Madho Singh to transport drinking water on his trips to England.'

'The maharaja carried water from India, to England???' Disha splutters in astonishment.

'Yes, he would take water from the Ganga with him because he didn't want to risk being polluted by foreign waters.'

'Let me get this straight. You're telling me he transported Ganga water all the way to England, believing that it was cleaner than the water they were drinking in England.'

'Yes, of course.'

'*Our* Ganga?'

'What is this question?'

'Tell me, did the maharaja die from dysentery by any chance?'

Now it is Mr. Ex-Stalker who isn't amused, though I'm not sure what he finds more upsetting: Disha's disrespect for a paranoid king or her blasphemy against a pure river. The guards and guides at the City Palace are as much a part of Jaipur's history as the palaces themselves. Sprouting grand handlebar moustaches, and dressed in regal white robes topped off by traditional red turbans, these men are descended from families that have served the royal household for generations. To this day they take pride in their loyalty to the royal family – who live in a separate wing of the building while they battle over property rights.

'What duties did your family perform during the kingly days?' I ask a particularly impressive guard standing at his post, the door to the museum.

'My ancestors were the king's most trusted *dwarpals*,' he says smartly.

'What did they do?'

'They stood by the palace doors,' he beams.

His forefathers stood guard for kings.

He stands guard for King Tourist.

Kilometer 17578

From Jaipur, Kaya rode east to Bharatpur, and then in a southerly direction through Sawai Madhopur to historic Bundi. The rain followed us, reminding me that not all of Rajasthan is desert like we perceive. A meandering path alternated along open plains and small undulating hills, past tangled bush and dark woods, rain-soaked lushness and pools of water. Occasionally, ghostly ruins rose over the otherwise unmarked surroundings. A deer leaped onto our path; an Indian tree pie fluttered over our heads.

It is our last night in Bundi, and we are having dinner on the terrace of our haveli, under the gaze of the imposing fortress, its sheer walls crowned by delicate domed kiosks, reflected by the dark green lake at its foot. Our solitude is disturbed by the mutterings of a man, his smooth face dominated by a magnificent moustache. He staggers over to our table, holding a bottle of

Kingfisher lager in one hand, and a dying cigarette in his other. Placing the beer down next to my bowl of piping hot *dal makhani*, he pulls up a chair and makes himself comfortable. His eyes are blood shot, his breath is intoxicated.

'Hi fraínds, I's Mister Ranbhir,' he grins foolishly. 'Yous is liking Bundi?'

'*Haan, yeh bahut khoobsurat jagah hain*,' I reply in Hindi.

'Me ij very sorry, boot I knowings no Hindi, oonly Inglis.'

Not knowing where to go with this conversation I stay quiet.

'So, ij yous marrying to sister,' he says, indicating Disha.

'No, he is just a friend,' Disha replies emphatically, ruining the opportunity for me to practice my lying skills.

'What??? Haw many years yous have?' he asks me, pointedly ignoring Disha.

'Me, twenty-six.'

'What, you have toonty six and no marrying,' he shakes his head disapprovingly. 'I ij toonty seven and I justly having three babies. All are boyj,' he adds, the last piece of information accompanied with a twirl of the proud moustache.

'How old were you when you got married?'

'Twenty.'

'And your wife?' Disha asks softly.

'Sixteen. She ij moost bootiful girrul in village,' he says, finally looking at Disha and giving her the once over. Then turning back to me, 'Yous must marrying sister fastly . . .'

What I really must do is finish my *dal makhani* and leave.

Leaving Bundi, Kaya headed back towards Jaipur, along a shorter, more direct route. Where this road was similar to our earlier one was that it continued to course through Rajasthan's red belt of underage marriage. While Bihar is the nation's offender-in-chief, Rajasthan has a firm grip on second place, and as we made our way through the state, we met a number of Mister Ranbhirs, not necessarily drunk, but still very concerned about our marital status and lack of progeny. We were in our twenties, single and childless. Surely we suffered from serious physiological and psychological problems. Alternately, we must have terribly irresponsible parents.

Poverty, tradition, gender norms, family honor – the factors driving underage marriage are plentiful, but in the end the victim is one, the girl child. Married at ten and widowed at fourteen. A bride at twelve, mother by fourteen, and dead by sixteen. Wed at eight, abused by fifteen, and broken by eighteen. Stolen childhood, imprisoned present, and blighted future; these are glimpses of everyday India. The victims aren't nameless. Any name will make these tales real. According to UNICEF's latest report, around half – 2.3 crore in absolute numbers – of married women between the ages of twenty and twenty-four were married before their eighteenth birthday, placing us right up there with the who's who of dysfunctional nations.* In parts of Rajasthan, where we were just then, the number of child brides was closer to 80 percent,

---

* The key indicators to measure the incidence of child marriage is the percentage of currently married women in the age group 20-24 years who were married before the legal age of 18 years. The advantage of this method is that it gives a good measure of prevailing conditions by keeping out historic trends.

of which 56 percent were wed before their fifteenth year and 15 percent before they turned ten. Eventually, despite being twice as likely to die at childbirth when compared to adult women, half of all girls end up pregnant between the ages of fifteen and eighteen.

The first attempt to address the problem dates back to the Child Marriage Restraint Act of 1929, legislated by the British Indian Government, and – seemingly impressed by the effectiveness of the law – it was another eight decades before our independent government decided to strengthen it by passing the Prohibition of Child Marriage Act, 2006. And why would our lawmakers and law enforcers care; after all, most of them are male. Besides, child marriage is part of our proud tradition. We even have an auspicious special day for it, the festival of Akshaya Tritiya, when mass child weddings are celebrated openly, with ministers, police officers, and government officials in attendance to bless the new couples.

It was during the Akshaya Tritiya celebrations of 1992 that Bhanwari Devi, a Dalit grass-roots social worker employed by the Women's Development Project, spoke up against the planned wedding of the nine-month-old granddaughter of Badri Gujjar, the headman of Batteri village. His pride sullied, Badri Gujjar, his son, nephew, brother-in-law, and the priest from the village temple assaulted Bhanwari and raped her. In her quest for justice, she was humiliated by the police, ignored by the medical examiners and ostracized by her village. In 1995, the judge hearing her case declared the accused not guilty. According to this judge, it was unimaginable that respected higher caste men could ever bring themselves to rape a Dalit woman, or that a temple priest could participate in such an atrocity. A member of Rajasthan's Legislative Assembly organized a victory rally through Jaipur to celebrate the verdict.

When we made our untroubled way past Batteri village – where Bhanwari Devi continues to live and defiantly work towards women's empowerment – thirteen years after the incident she had yet to receive justice. Instead the government has given her a bravery award and one lakh as compensation. The child marriages continue. The rape of Dalit women continues; one every third day in Rajasthan.

Kilometer 18621

Kaya raced against time, striving to reach Jaipur station so that Disha could catch her train back to Bangalore. Two hours after leaving Tonk, we saw the first signs of the city, right on schedule. I was about to congratulate myself on a job well done when I felt Disha lean forward, and then I heard her purr in my ear.

'Love . . .'

No way, I couldn't believe this was happening.

'I've been thinking about it,' Disha says. 'I've never been to the desert before, and it would be a shame for me to miss out on this opportunity.'

'What are you talking about? I almost got us all killed trying to get here in time for your train.'

'It was truly wonderful riding, love, but what does that have to do with anything?'

'Nothing,' I sighed, 'nothing at all. But what about your job?'

'Since when did you care about my work?'

'I don't . . . uh, I mean, I . . . yeah, deserts are awesome.'

Kaya rode west. The breeze was pleasant, but only as long as we kept moving. Small hills rolled by, stunted trees, pools of stagnant water, scattered fields. As we entered Ajmer District, green and brown, the two worlds collide, the former giving way to barren plains, arid hills, and strong gusts of wind. Dust rose in billows, sweeping across our path with a sting. By mid-morning were in Ajmer, an overwhelmed oasis embraced by a ring of barren hills, with the Dargah Khwaja Sahib as the focal point of veneration for millions.

The most important Islamic shrine in the country, the *dargah* contains the remains of Moinuddin Chisti, a famous Sufi mystic who resided in Ajmer in the 12th century. Second in importance only to Mecca, this shrine is so sacred, it's even sacred to Hindus, and they flock to the tomb in equally large and excitable droves. And really, there's no reason to get excited over a Hindu bowing before a Muslim deity, it's a common enough sight all over the country. When we're used to praying to a multitude of deities, how does it matter if some of them aren't ours? Besides, our millions of gods can be explained by the fact that we've assimilated every belief we've come across into our own. This Hindu dichotomy is something I've grown up around. My mother, who unfailingly prays twice a day to Lords Krishna and Shiva, also makes it a point to visit church every Thursday and light a candle before the idol of Infant Jesus. I guess, the way we see it, there's no harm in getting all the assistance we can. Just in case my god is busy, maybe yours is free to help.

Still, it surprises me as we approach the shrine how much the scene outside resembles that of temples. Located at the conjunction of three bazaars, the narrow streets surrounding the *dargah* are lined with shops selling flowers, incense sticks, and votive offerings. Before we've so much as looked at the building, we are assailed by a throng of persistent hawkers.

'I'll look after your motorcycle, brother,' a squeaky voice offers. 'Otherwise police will take it away.'

'Brother, buy some flowers,' a young girl pleads.

'Mister, you want guide,' another voice offers.

'Handkerchief. Handkerchief.'

'Ah yes, two handkerchiefs please,' I say to the little kid selling them, seeing that we're required to cover our heads before entering the *dargah*.

'I good guide, make sure you get all blessings.'

'You must offer flowers to the saint.'

'Somebody will steal your slippers from the gate. Let me look after them. It won't cost you much.'

I feel a familiar sense of dread, and I haven't even entered the place yet.

Just past the entrance, on both sides of the gateway, rest two of the largest cooking vessels I have ever seen. Donated by Emperor Akbar and his son Jahangir, they are capable of cooking 4,480 kilograms of rice, or a full-grown elephant, if the need were to arise. Back in the day, these cauldrons performed the noble function of preparing food distributed to the poor and needy. Today they serve as donation bowls, performing the noble function of collecting money from pilgrims, to make them poor and needy.

The central courtyard bustles with activity and resonates to the high-pitched voices of the *qawwali* singers. But there is little opportunity to appreciate any of it. Every time we stop, someone automatically presumes we wish to dispense with some of our money.

'We are direct descendants of the saint,' one man tells us, long flowing beard bearing the tinges of age and henna, a velvety cap on his head. 'He was a great man who could perform many miracles. But he only used them for the benefit of others. His own life was completely austere,' he says with pride.

'You must be following in his revered footsteps.'

'Yes, of course.'

'Then you probably don't need money either.'

'The money I ask for is not for me, son. It is in the name of the saint, and goes to charity. If you don't want to make a donation just say so.' He walks away in a huff.

Meanwhile, Disha has gotten herself into trouble. Looks like miracles still take place at the *dargah*; for example, a registry book that turns into a donation book as soon as you sign it. Disha witnesses this extraordinary occurrence with her ordinary eyes. After all, it was her signature that brought on the transformation.

'How much money are you giving?' the registry man asks her.

'Money? What for?' Disha says in surprise.

'You've made an entry.'

'But you asked me to register my name.'

'Yes, to make a donation.'

'You . . . but . . . you never said anything about donations. I thought you wanted my remarks.'

'Now that you have made an entry, you must offer something. It is bad luck to scratch it out. Give whatever you feel like.'

'But . . .' she looks to me for help. I shrug. 'Fine . . . it's all your money anyway,' she shrugs back at me, '. . . here, take twenty rupees,' she offers the registry man, wrestling a scruffy-looking note out of the pocket of her tight jeans.

'No, no,' the man draws back in horror. 'What are you doing? Just take a look at the previous contributions.'

We scan the list to witness yet another miracle. Not a single entry on the page displays a sum of less than five hundred rupees. 'What is this? Only millionaires visit this place or what?' Disha asks, looking at me helplessly.

'I guess only they can afford to,' I smirk.

'Well, this is all I can give,' she says, placing the twenty rupees on the register and ignoring its unhappy protestations.

Once inside the tomb, every step I take costs money. First step. A man smacks my head with peacock feathers and holds his hand out for a donation. I put ten rupees. Second step. A man smacks me on the head with something that looks like a dust mop and holds his hand out. I lose another tenner. Third step. A man places a cloth on my head and holds his hand out. I have no more change, damn. I lose twenty rupees this time. Still, he's not happy. Fourth step. I pay for having successfully reached the tomb.

Fifth step. A guy points to the exit and holds his hand out.

Kaya roared out of Ajmer, leaving behind a trail of furious dust. Having never before experienced such flagrant venality at Muslim shrines, I was left wondering if perhaps the large number of Hindus visiting the *dargah* were bringing their bad habits with them.

Kilometer 18904

Sitting by the ghats that lead to the holy water, Disha and I bathe in the predawn serenity of Pushkar, watching the radiant resurrection of the sun. The stillness gives way to the stirring resonance of temple bells, and the footsteps of pilgrims.

'Love . . .' Disha says softly, 'I'd like to take a small detour on our way to Shekhawati.'

'Sure, where to?' I ask, pouring over the map unfolded in front of her.

'Deorala.'

'Deorala . . . Deorala . . . hmm . . . haven't heard of it. What's there?'

'Here, read this.' She hands me the book her nose has been embedded in these last few days, William Dalrymple's *The Age of Kali*, a collection of stories on India that she picked up at a book exchange in McLeod Ganj. 'Go through the chapter titled 'Sati Mata',' she tells me.

I do.

In the morning Kaya followed the road north, past Jaipur and towards Deorala. Dish was quiet, pensive. The air got warmer and the surroundings drier. Brown. Baked. Uninviting.

On 4th September, 1987, Roop Kanwar, a beautiful young woman, stepped out of her haveli dressed in her bridal finery, and set out on a final walk through the unpaved lanes of Deorala. The village folk gathered at their doors or watched through windows in reverence as she made her way past their homes. By the time she reached the village cremation ground, a crowd of more than five hundred followed in her footsteps. Once there, she sat down on her husband's funeral pyre and placed his head on her lap. Her sixteen-year-old brother-in-law then set fire to the logs. Half hour later, all that remained was ash. Roop Kanwar had been married for eight months. She was eighteen years old.

Sati, another truly Hindu concept that makes you wonder if perhaps it's not better to be born a cow in this country rather than a woman. Derived from the name of Shiva's first wife – who committed suicide to honor her husband's reputation by jumping into the sacrificial fire – for upper-caste Hindus *sati* is just a convenient method to get rid of inconvenient women, ingeniously packaged as an act of pride, supported by tradition. Within two weeks of Roop Kanwar's death, more than 7,50,000 people had poured in from the surrounding villages to pay homage to her. The site of the pyre was turned into hallowed ground, and Roop Kanwar had become a goddess, *Sati Mata*.

My skin burned under the fierce gaze of the desert sun. Heat rose off the ground in shimmering waves. Little else moved across the barren expanse, other than swirls of dust that tattooed against our skin. There was no life here, just rock and sand. And our thoughts, as harsh as the world we rode through.

During the early decades of the 19th century, the British documented as many as five hundred *sati* a year in the state of Bengal alone, before finally abolishing the practice in 1829. But proscribing the tradition didn't necessarily make it disappear – or, for that matter, make it disreputable – and in the years following independence nearly fifty cases of *sati* have been recorded, mostly in Rajasthan, where the cult of *Sati Mata* is still strong. The burning of Roop Kanwar, though, evoked shock on the front pages, following which, urban India dutifully expressed its outrage, and all of two thousand people, mostly women, marched on Delhi in protest. Forty years after independence, it finally occurred to our progressive government to introduce the Commission of Sati (Prevention) Act, wherein the act of *sati*, its glorification, and its worship became illegal. In response, over a hundred thousand villagers marched to Jaipur to protest the new law. Ostensibly, for every horrified liberal Indian, there were a hundred prideful traditional-Indians.

I felt Disha grow tense behind me as Kaya entered the town. She was reflecting my own sense of disquiet. What were we doing here? What had we hoped to find? Demons maybe, men with fangs and women with horns. Something to point a finger at and say, see they aren't one of us. But Deorala was no different from any other village I had passed through. A barefoot boy ran across the street. A turbaned man sat at the entrance to a house. A young woman watched us go by, an infant cradled in her arms. We didn't stop. We spoke to no one.

What was there to ask them? How had 500 of them stood by and watched as an eighteen-year-old girl had been burned to death? How had 500 of them chanted praises while she turned to ash? After the incident, it was accused that Roop Kanwar had been drugged and forced onto the pyre. Thirty-two men were tried for murder, but the allegations proved to be baseless and all of them were acquitted. Were we asking the wrong questions of the wrong people? Instead of looking to the village folk for answers, asking why they did it or why they let it happen, maybe it would serve us better to question Roop Kanwar's motives, and perhaps we should ask ourselves what kind of a society we live in if it can drive an eighteen-year-old girl to willingly immolate herself.

I don't believe Roop Kanwar committed *sati* because she had been given no option; rather, she did it because it was the best option. Depending on which society in India you have the misfortune of being born into, there are few things worse than being a widow. Regardless of the fact that she was only eighteen, her culture deemed that Roop Kanwar no longer had a future, and harshly enforced its oppressive norms of widowhood. What she faced was a life without color, confined to wearing only white, a life devoid of comfort and companionship, to be excluded from social gatherings, her mere presence inauspicious. To live out her days in isolation, forbidden any pleasures – of taste, of touch, of sound. Dehumanized, no longer 'she' but 'it', viewed as a burden and living at the mercy of others. Death must come as a relief.

The cremation ground stood at the far end of the town, open, isolated, and sun-burned. All that grew there was a scattering of trees and a huddle of *chattris*. And an unassuming pile of *sati* stones daubed in vermillion. At the height of the controversy, the site was protected by Rajput villagers brandishing swords. But no worship can take place openly anymore, only furtively, like something of shame. According to the people of Deorala, Roop Kanwar's death has brought pride to their village name, but in reality Roop Kanwar most probably died so that she could escape their pride.

Disha never said a word throughout. She didn't break her silence as we rode out either, but under that calm I sensed simmering disquiet. Leaving Deorala behind, Kaya entered the region of Shekhawati, a relatively recent discovery of the tourism industry. The landscape remained bleak. A semi-arid region flooded by sand and sprinkled with scrub. In sharp contrast to the monotonous, monochromatic surroundings, the havelis of Shekhawati grow out of the barrenness in a cacophony of vibrant hues and bizarre themes; every available surface covered in paintings – the ceilings, pillars, doorways, windows, and unlike elsewhere, even the exterior walls. Oases of color, they represented man's victory over the dreariness of the desert.

A single-lane highway carries us into the small towns, from where a maze of pathways guides us to a state of confusion. I receive confirmation that we are going around in circles when we come across a mural of an Indian sepoy bayoneting a British officer in his nether regions while Gandhi looks on in amusement.

Is seems unlikely that two buildings could showcase such a unique artistic expression. We are pondering how to tackle this labyrinth of treasures when Gaurav comes to our rescue. A clean-cut, broad-shouldered young man, wearing tight blue jeans and a yellow shirt, he stands a head taller than me and speaks careful English.

'Shekhawati is a fairly large region, and there are interesting buildings all over the place,' he tells us. 'If you want, I can guide you around and show you the important sites.'

'Sounds good, but how do we get around. Uh . . . I guess all three of us can squeeze onto the bike,' I say, turning to Disha for approval.

'Oh that won't be necessary,' Gaurav says. 'I have my own ride. Please wait here and I'll be back in a minute.' He disappears around the street, and returns a few moments later, mounted on a horse. 'Shall we go then?' he asks nonchalantly, like strolling down the streets on a horse is perfectly natural here. I follow the horse.

'In the 17th and 18th centuries, Shekhawati was a prosperous region that fell along the major trade routes passing through the desert. When the caravans died out, the Marwaris spread out across the country in search of business, but they still sent money back to their ancestral homes, where the rest of the family continued to live,' Gaurav explains when we aren't on our mounts. 'These havelis became a symbol of their family pride. But now everybody has moved to the cities, and all that's left behind are empty shells and old caretakers.'

The neglect is clear to see, with most of Shekhawati's buildings dilapidated and decaying. Doors are barred and *jharokhas* boarded shut, the elaborate woodwork stripped off and sold to antique dealers. The frescoes have faded. While the visitors are only just trickling in, with the prospective lure of tourism in mind, many of the havelis are being reopened and painstakingly renovated.

'These murals formed a visual narration of the changing times,' Gaurav informs us. 'The early motifs were based on the mythological themes, before family portraits and scenes from daily life became popular. Towards the later stages you will notice the appearance of white-faced, gun-toting soldiers, along with men in suits and women in gowns listening to gramophones and riding cycles.'

Along with paint, what the people of Shekhawati have in abundance is eccentricity. The themes vary from the curious – the Wright brothers in flight, to the erotic – sexual positions only to be performed by experts, to the bizarre – Lord Krishna sitting on an airplane, to the ridiculous – a bewildered Indian staring at a Western toilet. The most recurring image, though, is of the train, a reminder of the awe and fascination it must have evoked when it first rumbled across the countryside.

'What's up with the horses?' I ask Gaurav, watching a group of foreigners pass by on horseback.

'Other than murals, Shekhawati was always famous for its horses. Back in the day, we produced some of the finest cavalry in the country. The Indian Army still recruits a large number of soldiers from this region, but unfortunately they don't have much use for our horses anymore. So, nowadays they are best used for tourist purposes.'

'Does the horse belong to you?'

'Yes, she's part of my family,' he says with affection, 'like my own child. Do you and sister have any children?'

'No . . .'

'How old are you?'

'Twenty-six.'

'And you don't have any children yet? I am also twenty-six, and my wife is carrying our third child.'

'Congratulations. How old are your other kids?'

'Five and two, both girls. But this time, god willing, it will be a boy, the family's pride who will carry on our name.'

I feel Disha's nails dig into my shoulder.

Leaving horse and rider behind, Kaya rode deeper into the desert. A colorless world. Emptiness, vast spaces of it. Every creature and every race is naturally preoccupied with propagation of the species, but the anomaly in India is our unhealthy obsession with only one half of the species. After child marriage, the other major statistic of Indian chauvinism is female infanticide and feticide. In all fairness, Rajasthan doesn't find itself at the forefront, with a fair number of states in the northern belt deserving rich credit for this process of 'gender cleansing'.

Viewing a girl child as a burden, the popular option is to dump the problem before it can come to bear, though you also hear frequent stories of a girl child being drowned, suffocated, or starved to death. A UNICEF report states that, in Jaipur, prenatal sex determination results in the abortion of 3,500 female fetuses annually; while in Bombay, of the 8,000 abortions conducted in one year, only one was male. India is one of the rare nations where the ultrasound has been turned into a weapon of mass destruction, forcing the law to step in and make it illegal for doctors to reveal the sex of an unborn child. What changed is that female fetuses began turning up in toilets, drains, and garbage bins.

Aborted, starved, drowned, and choked, females are steadily disappearing from the country. Presently, India champions amongst the most distorted sex ratios in the world – fourth nation from the bottom to be precise, with a national average of 933 women to 1,000 men. This translates to an impressively macho shortfall of four crore women. In Rajasthan, the state ratio is 922 to 1,000, with some regions like Jaisalmer recording figures of 810 to 1,000. But nothing competes with neighboring Haryana's statewide ratio of 877 to 1,000 and dropping as low as 750 to 1,000 in certain districts. What all this implies is, soon India can take pride in being the first all-male nation of the world, with every citizen twirling his moustache. Beyond that, who knows?

Perhaps we also become the first all-gay nation of the world.

Kilometer 19451

Kaya brought us to the city of Bikaner. Near the gateway of Junagarh Fort, I noticed a stone slab covered with impressions of small, dainty hands. 'This is a *sati* stone in honor of the brave ladies who committed *sati* when the maharaja passed away,' a palace guard informed us, his voice thick with reverence. For a second there, I thought Disha was going to throw herself at him and rip the moustache off his lip, but she didn't. Walking away without saying a word, she sat down by a doorway with her face buried in her hands. Kaya took us away from Bikaner.

Sati, female feticide, child marriage, and dowry harassment – all reflections of a woman's stature in India, mirrors to their daily struggle for basic dignity. Since Deorala, five other widows have burned alive on their husband's funeral pyre, quietly, without much media fervor. A month before our visit to Rajasthan, the state tourism department released a guidebook extolling the virtues of the women who had committed *sati*, promoting these funeral sites as sacred destinations. The minister for tourism defended the worship claiming, '*Sati* is seen as the source of strength.' This minister, I must add, is a woman.

While literacy and economic opportunity will go a long way, by themselves they cannot assure the women of India their dignity. In his *capabilities approach*, Amartya Sen gets to the heart of the issue – we need to ask not what resources are available to the person, but rather, what is this person able to do or be? It is about the liberties available to a woman, and her ability to choose the life she wishes to lead, on her own terms. Remember Roop Kanwar – she was reasonably wealthy and well-educated, yet her societal circumstances provided little choice. The real challenge is that our prejudices are deeply rooted within our traditions and culture, and further packed-down by our pride in them. Laws, money, education – none of this matters unless accompanied by social change. The question remains: Do we have the moral courage to recognize the flaws in our culture, and the strength to break down the barriers erected by it? As a society, we need to see a woman as independent from her relationship to a man, or her family. We have to separate her chastity from her honor, or her family's. Most importantly, we need to separate her person from her body. And as men we need to learn that the emancipation of women doesn't necessarily mean our emasculation. The change is not going to be easy, for, consciously or subconsciously, our biases against women permeate every aspect of our life, at every level.

And, as I soon discovered, I was as good a misogynist as anyone else.

Thirty kilometers south of the city, the inconspicuous little town of Deshnoke is home to the conspicuously curious temple of Karni Mata, and its resident twenty thousand rats. The rodents, preferably identified as *kabals*, are everywhere, doing what any honorable member of the species does – feed, drink, sleep, play, gnaw, fight, poop, and a few things better left unmentioned. The rats, though, are not really rats, but more like, well, humans in transit. According to the Charans – a community of bards, writers, and storytellers – these rats are the souls of dead Charans until they are reborn. So, when you spot a furry little squeaker at Deshnoke, you might actually be staring at the next Tagore.

At the feet of the primitive idol of Karni Mata sits a plate of *prasad*, from which the *kabal*-rats take unhurried nibbles, while devotees expectantly queue up to get a piece of the offering, now sanctified by rat-dribble. Now, if you are the faint-hearted types, like me, who find the idea of eating out of the same plate as a rat unappetizing, an alternate way to receive the rat's blessing is to get one of them to run over your feet. In the process though, please take care not to squish one of them under your feet. It's not a polite way to treat your host, and it's considered really bad for your karma. Fortunately, if you are sufficiently careless to commit the aforementioned sin, atonement awaits in the form of a gold rat. Kept on hand for just such an occasion, you can buy the gold idol of a rat from the temple and donate it back to them. Who knew rats could be bought off with gold as well. Only in Incredible India!

As for the skeptics who question the divinity of a rat, how else do you explain the fact that, despite their numbers, none of them ever step outside the temple boundary? And in all these years there has never been a growth in their population (as discovered by the temple census, I assume). Furthermore, the temple never stinks as would be expected from a rat infestation; it is always sparkling clean, and there's never been an outbreak of any rodent-related diseases here. On the contrary, during the outbreak of the plague in Surat in the nineties, concerned citizens visited this temple, to seek help from the rats. Godly or not, perhaps our government can learn a lesson or two in family planning, communal hygiene, and disease prevention from the *kabal*-rat.

Beyond, on the road to Jaisalmer, the so far half-assed desert became real desert-like; desolate, dusty, and featureless. Not a blade of grass grew anywhere. There were no rocks, no stones, not even dunes. There was nothing, excepting the straight black line that split the flat expanse of endless sand into two. The road was as characterless as the surroundings. Not even a small pothole or unmarked detour. Occasionally, the desert spilled onto the road, reclaiming its lost territory. Everywhere I looked I saw sand, probably because a lot of it was in my eye. The only source of excitement was the vultures, which were the liveliest creatures along this stretch. Actually, they were also the only live creatures along this stretch. Everything else around was mostly dead, accounting for the vulture's liveliness.*

Pokhran, the first real town of any description along the road, was, in terms of personality, quite similar to the vultures: ugly, an omen of death, and full of energy, albeit the radioactive kind. This is ground zero of India's nuclear program, the test site for our weapons of mass destruction. And that's one of the strangest things about nukes. Unlike conventional bombs, which we liberally drop on real and perceived enemies alike, the only place nations ever detonate nuclear bombs is in their own backyard – or, in the case of England, in their friend's backyard. The Americans, for example, have blown themselves up nearly one thousand times in exchange for the two they've dropped on Japan. Russia, meanwhile, has inflicted more than a thousand

---

* I'd never considered the fate of deceased cows before, simply presuming from our veneration of the animal that most of them would receive grand funerals, and Taj Mahalesque tombs. So it came as a surprise to find along this road the carcasses of cows, rotting under the sun, and torn by scavengers. Since it is an act of impurity to handle the carcass, only the casteless can perform the duty. But if there are no Dalits around . . . well, the vultures enjoy a feast. What an unholy end for the holy cow.

explosions on itself – a couple of them accidentally – without once using them on an outsider.

Yet, for inexplicable reasons, we Indians felt left out of this self-destruct party, and on 11th May, 1998, our newly formed BJP government decided to send a message to all the big nations, and to one small neighboring country in particular. The message read something like: 'We have developed the power to kill a lot of people, bwah, ha, ha, haaa . . . uh, by the way, what now?' Over the next two days, four more underground nuclear detonations were carried out, under the code name 'The Buddha Laughs', with the test shaft being dubbed 'The White House'. Somebody in the program has a seriously devilish sense of humor.

For a short period of time following the detonations, Pokhran became India's most talked about place, and played host to a uniquely Indian farce. A few misguided chaps, namely those belonging to the VHP (which I like to think of as the saffron version of the KKK), got it into their fanatical heads that the explosions were divinely ordained. Using logic as toxic as radioactive waste, to them it apparently signified the rise of Hindu power, and therefore called for a rewriting of the constitution to declare India a Hindu state. In the immediate aftermath of the detonation, radioactive sand from the test site was distributed as *prasad*, and a plan was drawn up to take the 'sacred sand' on a pilgrimage around the country. The VHP even intended to build a temple at the site, to a deity called 'Atomic Shakti'. If the shrine ever did come up, Kaya simply rode past it.

The 800-year-old fort of Jaisalmer emerged from the desert plains without warning, a mirage growing out of the golden sands, and in that instant we were teleported into the pages of the *Arabian Nights*, except the skyline was marked by spires instead of domes. The Sonar Quila, or golden fort, is the last of the living forts in the country, occupied by the same families from centuries ago. Beyond the fort flowed the sands of the Thar, across the border into Pakistan. Founded on the lucrative trade routes passing through the desert, it acquired great amounts of wealth during medieval times, and the picture that greeted us was almost identical to the welcoming sight that would have awaited the merchants as their camel trains traversed the desert.

The city of Jaisalmer can be neatly divided into two zones. There's the fort, which forms the historic center, and there's everything new that sprawls around it for no apparent reason. Passing through the imposing gateway to enter the citadel, it felt like we were slipping between times, from a nuclear present into an unclear past. A traveler's fantasy, this was the Disneyland of fortresses, yet reminiscent of Varanasi, sans god and water. The same maze of streets, crush of ancient buildings, welcoming faces, tourist traps, sense of mystique. And the same holy cows loitering in the streets. In an otherwise traffic-free world, the narrow passageways resonated to the rumble of Kaya's engine.

Our search for accommodation was long and hard. We couldn't decide between carved stone and frescoed plaster, between balcony-overlooking-desert and balcony-overlooking-palace. We stayed at the fort for four days, and changed *havelis* four times. By day three, it appeared that everyone knew us. Our carefree wanderings, though, ended on the third day when my aunt (the same one as earlier), my cousin (a different one), and my cousin's husband arrived at the fort intending on traveling with me for the next week. This wasn't an altogether pleasing development, since I hadn't yet confessed to my mum that Disha was still around. Nor had I confessed to Disha that I hadn't confessed to my mum. And as far as my aunt was concerned, I had no business travelling with a woman unless she was my wife. At this point, the sensible move would have been to confess all and sundry, but then again, no one's ever accused me of being sensible. What I decided instead was to come clean to Disha, but to keep her hidden from the family.

'You're a dumbass,' was all she had to say about the plan.

Kilometer 20436

By noon on their second day in Jaisalmer, bored with sightseeing, my aunt and cousin headed out on a shopping frenzy, intent on buying out every artifact store. Fearing bankruptcy, my cousin-in-law announced that we would be leaving for Jodhpur after tea, a decision which left me in a tight spot. Presuming we were spending another night in Jaisalmer, my master plan involved getting an early start the next morning and reaching Jodhpur well ahead of them.

Kaya exited the fort in a mad rush, roaring at full throttle, blazing a trail to Pokhran, completing the 110 kilometers in an hour. Never much of a speed fiend, I was riding outside my comfort zone. Soon it would be dark. Realizing that regardless of the progress we'd made so far it was only a matter of time before the car caught up with us, Kaya pulled to a sheepish halt at the bus stop on the outskirts of Pokhran.

'I'm sorry, but I don't think I can keep up this pace for much longer,' I tell Disha. 'I think it's better if you take the bus.'

'I told you—'

'Listen, this isn't the time for that, okay,' I cut her off brusquely. 'Just bear with me, please, and get onto the bus.'

'Yeah great, but how will we catch up in Jodhpur?'

'Don't worry about that. I'll stay right behind the bus the entire time.'

'Well . . . fine, whatever.'

'I'll also talk to the conductor and ask him where you should get down . . . uh, in case we get separated.'

'What do you mean—'

'Relax, it's just a precaution,' I assure her, and then approach the bus conductor. 'Brother, what time does this bus leave?'

'Any minute now,' he replies.

'And what would be the ideal place to get down at Jodhpur without going too far into the city?'

'There's a large flyover just as you enter the city. You can't miss it.'

'If something should happen and I lose you, just wait for me there, okay,' I instruct Disha, and then, turning back to the conductor, 'Brother, can you please let my wife know when the stop arrives?'

'What happened? Why aren't you taking sister with you on the bike?'

'Uh . . . it's developed some mechanical problems and I'm trying to nurse it to Jodhpur.'

'Andhra Pradesh motorcycle? Have you both come riding from so far?'

'No, no,' I lie for no apparent reason, 'we're only visiting Rajasthan, just a short vacation.'

'How long have you and sister been married?'

'Uh . . . well, actually we were wed just last month.'

'Ha, ha, I thought as much,' he laughs. 'It's your honeymoon, eh. No wonder you're so concerned. But who goes on a motorcycle for a honeymoon, you young people also. *Chalo, chinta ki koyi baat nahin*, I'll make sure she gets down safe and sound.'

'Thank you, brother, that's a load off my mind.'

Making Disha take the bus was an inspired decision. Barely twenty minutes after the bus departed Pokhran, with me in tow, a white Toyota Qualis drove up beside Kaya and a pair of dark hands aggressively flagged her down. Needing to keep up with the bus in front of me, I tried to ignore them. The hands were determined, and succeeded in bringing Kaya to a halt.

'Rama! Rama! What is wrong with you?' my aunt screams at me.

'I do—'

'Why on earth are you riding so fast?'

'The thin—'

'Is this how you're always riding?'

'But—'

'Well, don't you have anything to say for yourself?'

I watch helplessly as Disha's bus disappears over the horizon. Damn, there's going to be trouble waiting for me on that end as well. 'You can carry on and I'll catch up with you at Jodhpur,' I say.

'We aren't letting you out of our sights,' she replies firmly.

'No, really, there's no need for you to slow down. I was only trying to get as far as possible while there's light. Now that it's dark I'm going to take it extremely easy.'

'I don't think so.'

'Honestly, there's nothing to worry about. It's going to be hard for the car to keep such a slow pace, you're unnecessarily making it difficult for the driver.'

'Hmm . . . okay, but you promise to ride carefully.'

'Yes, yes, I promise.'

I knew the car would shoot past the bus at some stage, but despite a crazed ride Kaya never did, and we entered Jodhpur without any sign of the bus. As for the flyover, I could see no signs of it either. The roads were deserted, and it didn't seem like the place for a girl to be alone at night. I was hit by a wave of panic, and with it suspicion about the conductor. Fuck, fuck, damn. How could I have trusted him so blindly? And he did look a bit dodgy. Bloody hell, what if he's harmed her. Could that be the flyover, but there's nobody there. Oh man, oh man, oh man. I'll kill that guy if anything's happened to her. Please, please, I hope she's safe. 'Fuck, fuck, fu—'

'OVER HERE . . .' a piercing scream penetrates my fragile sanity. I trace the source to a pair of hands waving to me from the shadows. It's Disha, and she isn't alone. The bus conductor has gotten off along with her to make sure she's alright, even though this isn't his actual stop. All I can offer in return are a few hollow words.

'Thank you very much, brother. I . . .'

'What do you have to thank me for? I'm glad I could help,' he smiles.

'Can I give you a lift somewhere?'

'No, don't bother, the depot is just here. Besides, it's already late and you still have to go find a hotel.'

I thank him again as Disha gets astride Kaya.

'You have a wonderful wife, you should take good care of her,' he tells me, his tone indicating he doesn't think I'm doing a very good job.

I simply nod my head and offer a weak smile, my thumb reaching for the ignition button. And just as Kaya is about to ride away, 'May you have a lot of children,' he wishes us.

Kilometer 20769

Depositing Disha in a haveli at the base of daunting Mehrangarh Fort, I mostly avoided her during the two-day stay at Jodhpur. Playing James Bond, I covertly extracted information on my family's daily schedule and passed it on to Disha at the haveli, letting her know what to visit and at what time, making sure we don't cross paths. From Jodhpur, Kaya headed for the district of

Mewar, to Ranakpur and Kumbhalgarh, and still we continued to play a game of hide and seek. The strain began to show, and our brief moments together were emphasized by unhappy silence. Disha remained distant, the brooding taking her places where I didn't want to follow. She never complained, and I didn't ask. Perhaps I should have, but I didn't. It was just one more day, the ride to Udaipur. Then everything was going to be alright.

Kaya gave my folks a wide berth that day, and while they made the pilgrimage to Nathdwara temple, we rode to the fort of Chittorgarh before looping back to Udaipur. Halfway there, we came across a red Honda City bearing Delhi registration plates. The car looked like it had been in an accident involving four trucks, each coming in from a different direction. Alternately, someone had taken a wrecking ball to it. The bonnet was crumpled. All the windows were shattered. None of the lights remained intact. A door hung limply. Three men stood beside the catastrophe, two turbaned peasants and a khaki-clad police constable. Kaya eased up next to them.

'*Bhaiyya, yein kaise huan?*' I ask.

'The car hit a cow,' the constable replies casually.

'What are you saying! Even a stampeding elephant couldn't have accomplished such an impressive result.'

'The cow crushed the bonnet,' he explains with a shake of his head. 'The rest of the damage was caused by angry herders. They attacked the car with sticks, and bare fists.'

'What happened to the people in the car?'

'Oh, they're alright. They've been taken to the police station by the herders to register a complaint.'

'The herders are the one making the complaint?'

'Of course.'

'What happened to the cow?'

'She has a large gash on her leg,' the peasant replies indignantly. 'There, take a look for yourself.' We turn to where he's pointing. In a field on the other side of the road sits the cow, chewing on some succulent grass. If she's in pain, she's doing a damn good job of hiding it, the brave animal.

Night had set in when we entered Udaipur, and I was looking forward to the end of the ride. My folks were returning home the next evening, and I could breathe easy again. Somehow we had managed to pull it off. I was pleased with myself. What ingenuity. What courage. Disha probably deserved some credit as well, and I was going to reward her by planning something special for tomorrow. And what better place than Udaipur, undoubtedly the most beautiful and romantic city in the country, as long as you don't stray from the beautiful and romantic parts. The magical Lake Pichola, flanked on one side by the majestic walls of the City Palace and on the other by the blue hills of Aravalli. And, in the heart of the shimmering waters, the opulent Lake Palace, a white-marble fairytale. Yes, this was just the right place to rekindle our passion.

Unbeknownst to me, I was just then suffering from a bout of premature celebrations. Didn't I mention something about my predisposition for getting caught out? Well, what happened next belongs more in the world of P.G. Wodehouse. In a city of more than a million people spread across an area of sixteen square kilometers, with half a million vehicles plying the streets and nearly as many traffic signals trying to control their flow, in all that space and chaos, from the multitude of red lights to choose from, my cousin's Toyota Qualis pulled up two meters from Kaya.

I couldn't tell if they noticed us, but I squeaked off a sharp warning to Disha. She jumped off in a panic and scurried away, while I desperately tried to take cover behind a van. But it was already too late. My aunt's head popped out of the window and she hollered my name. I faked a look of surprise and waved. Just then the light turned green, forcing them to move ahead. Kaya lost them in the confusion, and squeezing her way to the side of the road, pulled up by the curb.

Here I break out in hysterical, doomed laughter, and only then set out in search of Disha. I find her seated in a bakery, disturbingly calm and nibbling on cream puffs. I start to laugh again, but it dies out when she looks up at me. Her eyes are glazed with tears, but her voice is cold steel.

'Are you pleased, you bastard?' she hisses at me, her face expressionless. 'Now what will your family think of me . . . In the end, you did turn me into a lying tramp. Ha, maybe that's what I really am.'

'What did . . . Angel, I—'

'*Don't!* Don't ever call me that again. I hate that name, and I always have, you condescending piece of shit . . .' I stand still, not wanting to create a scene. 'Just take me to the hotel, okay.'

After dropping Disha off at the hotel, I finally catch up with my family at their guest house, as they are sitting down to dinner. The last supper is a pleasant affair, with the usual inane family banter and the occasional word of advice on road safety. Nobody mentions Disha. Maybe we did get away with it, I begin to hope. After dinner I sit down with my aunt while she watches *Kyunki Saas Bhi Kabhi Bahu Thi*. The following dialogue, though, is not from the soap.

'Who was that girl sitting behind you?'

'What girl???'

'You know what I'm talking about. Let's not pretend otherwise.'

'I don't . . . oh, *that* girl. She's just somebody I gave a lift to.'

'Please don't lie to me.' I hear only disappointment, not anger. 'I deserve more respect than that. We are only here because of you, to show our support for what you are doing. But what exactly is it that you are doing? I thought it's about finding India . . . understanding our culture. You are a grown-up boy, I can't tell you how to live your life. But this much I know, there is nothing *Indian* about roaming the countryside with a girl.'

'I . . . I can't . . . I don't know what you are talking about . . .' Silence. 'I'm going out for a bit,' I say and leave her staring at the television. Oh man, the next few phone calls home are going to involve a lot of crying.

Disha and I sit at the domed kiosk of a rooftop restaurant overlooking the beautiful lake and the glowing Lake Palace. In the background I can hear James Bond, and he's working his charm on a gorgeous blonde dressed in an Indian sari, just as he does every single night on the rooftops of Udaipur. Shot predominantly in Udaipur, the city's palaces, lakes, and streets form the backdrop to 007's *Octopussy*, and all the backpacker haunts subject you to a screening of the movie each evening. My gaze shifts from the television back to Disha's eyes. There is no romance in them.

'. . . so, even now you didn't have the courage to tell the truth,' she says softly.

'I don't understand what you're going on about. It's the first time we've had to hide and lie about our relationship. And you should be the one to talk. Your dad isn't even aware that I exist whereas my family's always known about you.'

'And I loved you for it. It felt nice not having to sneak around like other couples. The fact that you could stand up for us without being a hypocrite, that's what made you different . . . special . . .'

'Ang . . . don't make me out to be something I am not, alright. I'm no Satya Harishchandra okay, I've never been truthful about my weed smoking. The only reason I was open about you was because I thought they'd be able to accept it. I made the error of thinking my folks were cooler than they actually are.'

Silence.

'Reddy . . .'

When was the last time she's called me by my name? I can't remember. I say nothing.

'. . . I wanted to ask you something, and I'm hoping you'll give me an honest answer.' She looks me in the eye, searching.

'If I could stay with you for the rest of the journey . . . do you . . . would you want me to?'

Silence. My eyes drop, and a single word escapes my mouth. 'No.'

'Thank you for not lying. And there's no reason for you to feel upset. It was only a rhetorical question. I've already asked the receptionist to book my return ticket.'

'I'm sorry . . .'

'Don't be. I think I knew the answer before you did, and I also know why. But I'd like to hear it from you anyway.'

'Fuck off!' I snap, suddenly feeling manipulated. 'Do you think this is some sort of a game?'

'No, but it looks like you do.'

'Well, if you must know, you're a damn burden I don't need right . . .' I stop short, realizing I'm letting my emotions do the talking, '. . . you know that's not what I meant. I like having you with me, but it's changed everything about Kaya Dreams. It's gone from being an adventure to a holiday. I've started traveling with a guide book for god's sake! I'm too safe and withdrawn around you. When was the last time I got into any trouble or spent time with other people? How am I supposed to discover anything about the country when I'm busy watching over you? You slow me down and make me cautious. You . . . I feel responsible for you . . . and it's a responsibility I don't want. Not on this journey.'

'Wow,' she smirks, 'now that's what I call brutal honesty.'

'Aw, come—'

'Shhhh,' she cuts me off, 'you've had your say. Now it's my turn. And let me assure you it's not my anger speaking. I've had the time to think about it while you were busy playing the gallant traveler-boyfriend . . .'

In the background James Bond is running his hand up Blondie's thigh.

'. . . it seems like a lifetime ago that this idea of yours was first born, and since then I've been shut out. I saw the gleam in your eyes when you spoke about it, and for you it might have been the fulfillment of a dream, but for me it wasn't. I didn't like the idea of sitting around waiting for you, nor do I like taking such a long time off from my career. Still, I did what any dutiful Indian girl would do. I went along . . .'

James leaps out of bed to take care of the intruders while Blondie covers her boobs.

'. . . When I broke up with you at the start of this journey everybody called me a bitch, your friends and mine. Tell me, why should I feel guilty for not wanting the same as you? You're the hero for putting everything aside to chase a dream. And I'm supposed to put aside everything to chase you. Does that make me a heroine? No, it makes me a loose woman and a burden . . .'

James is riding through the streets of Udaipur in an auto-rickshaw.

'. . . I never asked you to buy that fucking *Lonely Planet*, and I never asked you to protect me. That was just your male ego at work. I came here to share your experience, this passion that you have for the country. Guess what, there's nothing here to share. As far as I can see this journey is about nothing but you.' She stops and takes a sip from her bottle of Maaza.

I say nothing, my gaze turning to the Lake Palace, but seeing nothing.

'I remember when you first decided to do this,' she continues, her tone growing harsher. 'It was all about the joy of traveling and the desire to discover India. Somewhere along the line you seem to be doing it just for the sake of doing it, like an obsession . . .'

James has killed a few more bad guys, except for the one hiding behind the curtain.

'. . . You've lost the plot, love. In your obsession to become a 'better Indian', you're losing the better you. It's sad, but I don't even recognize this person before me.'

Long silence.

James Bond is finishing off the Indian villain. In a couple of minutes he will find himself in the naked embrace of another beautiful woman. *No such luck for me tonight*, I think.

'What now?' I say finally.

'Now nothing. We leave for Mount Abu in two days as intended. From there I return to my life and see where it takes me. And thank you for showing me Rajasthan, it was a real eye opener and inspiration.'

'I was talking about you and me.'

'Nothing there as well. Let's just see what happens. I'm not going to sit around waiting for you. Guess I'm not Indian enough. Oh, and one more thing . . . you know how concerned you are about your Indian identity? There's no cause for worry there. When it comes to women, you're as Indian as a man can get.'

The movie has reached its climax and James is getting his octopussy. Disha gets up from her chair, gives me a smile I can't place, and then walks away. I watch her back disappearing down the stairs.

For us, the road has come to an end.

LEG FOURTEEN

You Can Still Feel Gandhi's Presence Here

KAYA RODE OUT from Abu Station. Disha grew smaller and smaller in the rear-view mirror, until she finally disappeared. There had been no tears, only hollow promises. I felt more alone than ever before. All I had to hold on to was the reassuring rhythm of Kaya's engine and the familiarity of movement. I held on firmly.

The road stretched out before Kaya and me, running west towards Bhuj, resolute and un-judging. We covered six hundred kilometers by the end of the ride, a hundred and fifty more than on any other day. There was no plan, it just happened that way. All I recollect is melting tar and baking mud. No memories of towns crossed or people passed. I didn't stop till we reached land's end. Here – on the secluded western shores of Kachchh, where the sun descends on our nation – the curtain slowly dropped on another day. In the dying light, the skies turned to glowing embers, as did the seas.

Next morning we set off again, through Bhuj, past the rubble of grand palaces, and the recent ruins of an ancient kingdom. On the morning of January 26th, 2001, while the rest of the country celebrated Republic Day, a devastating earthquake rocked Kachchh, claiming 20,000 lives. Built mostly of mud and brick, entire towns were flattened, leaving a million homeless. The power of the earthquake was such that buildings collapsed in 500-kilometer distant Ahmedabad, but then again, this might be more indicative of the excellence of our housing projects. Sitting astride the epicenter, the capital city of Bhuj bore the brunt of the destructive force. Since then, the people have rebuilt their homes, and their lives. The city had healed, but the scars were still visible, evidenced in the cracked walls, the crumbling kiosks, and missing roofs. The empty lots resembled open wounds. A lot of Bhuj's history was lost that day, buried under chunks of ancient masonry. What little survived stood largely unrepaired, neglected, forlorn.

I was in university, two thousand kilometers away, when the event occurred. Two days later a couple of my friends rushed to Bhuj, to inflict their help on the people. I stayed away, suffering as I did from I'm-just-an-ordinary-guy-so-how-can-I-make-a-difference syndrome. So, while my friends witnessed the horrors of rotting corpses, suffering children, and a shortage of rescue workers, I went about the streets with a donation box. If I recollect correctly, my earthquake relief fund yielded a total of 138 rupees, or thereabouts. Congratulating myself on being an involved citizen, I handed over this grand sum to the student body, despite having serious misgivings that any of the money would reach the victims. Rumor had it that the donations contributed to the new motorcycle the head of our student body was riding a few weeks later. Well, I tried, didn't I?

Not since Bihar had we come across a road this cruel. I was living the nightmare all over again, only this time I wasn't prepared for it. 'Gujarat has excellent roads,' my all-knowing father had assured me. 'After Punjab and Haryana, these are the best highways in the country,' his Gujarati friends had boasted. Perhaps this was the fault of the earthquake as well. The road wasn't rotten all the way, but this only made it that much more dangerous. For reasonable stretches it stayed charming and gentle, deceiving me into a sense comfort, and then just as I raised the throttle . . . WHAM! My spine would tear through the back of my neck, take one look at the path, and instantly retreat back in fear. My head, meanwhile, hurt from the glare of the salt plains, from the dust and the exhaust fumes. On reaching Rajkot city, Kaya went straight to the Police Commissioner's Office, but it wasn't to register a complaint against the road for attempted murder.

Upon hearing of my journey, the Commissioner, a classmate of my cousin, has offered to play host while I'm in Gujarat. The meeting with him is brief, at the end of which I'm hauled off to the shower at the luxurious Officer's Guest House. Later, I'm escorted around town by two uniformed police constables, one clean shaven and the other sporting a pencil moustache.

'How do you like our region so far?' Pencil Moustache asks.

'I haven't seen much, this is only my third day in Gujarat,' I reply.

'We don't call this region Gujarat,' Clean Shaven shakes his head. 'For us, this is Saurashtra.'

'What's that?'

'Saurashtra,' he says with prodigious reverence, 'is the land of Lord Krishna and Mahatma Gandhi.'

'This is India's most sacred ground,' Pencil Moustache concurs.

Jawahar Road is busy with traffic, the usual combination of cars honking incessantly and motorcycles retaliating in kind. Little over a century ago, a twelve-year-old boy stood where I'm standing now, and he would have walked across the same street. But today, that boy might not even recognize the bare brick Gothic structure I'm approaching. When he studied here, it was called Albert High School. Now it goes by the name Mahatma Gandhi Pathshala, in his honor.

It is well past school hours. The gates are closed and the campus stands quiet. Resigning myself to coming back tomorrow, I am in the act of turning around when Pencil Moustache sticks his hands through the grill, slides the bolt, pushes the gate open and strides inside. I'm duly impressed by his problem solving skills, for it never occurred to me that I could do that. It's probably knowledge that comes with the uniform. Once inside, they use their professional skills to nab a peon, and the next thing I know I'm talking to the vice-principal of the school, who seems genuinely happy to show me around.

'You must understand, numerous changes have been made to the original structure over the years,' he says in crisp English, leading me down a recently painted corridor, before stopping in front of a latched door. 'This was Bapuji's classroom . . . of course, it would have been different back then.'

He slides the bolt out with a squeak and pushes the door inwards. It opens onto an unremarkable little room – airless, pastel walls, a strip of exposed cement, long green benches, a blackboard with Gujarati scrawling. It's a typical Indian classroom, except for the Gujarati scrawling.

'It still serves as a regular classroom . . . um, I think for fourth standard children.'

'They must feel honored to be in the same classroom,' I smile.

'Are you doing some kind of research on Bapuji?' the vice principal asks, walking me and my escorts to the gate.

'No . . . not really.'

'It's nothing . . . I was only wondering. We don't get too many visitors wanting to see his classroom.'

'They should put up a special memorial to mark the place where Bapu sat,' Clean Shaven suggests when we're back on the street. 'Then maybe more people will start visiting. You can still feel Gandhi's presence here.'

'Uh, yeah,' I nod dutifully.

Tucked away in a small forgotten lane, hidden from view behind an old metal gate, is the house in which the Mahatma's family lived, named 'Kaba Gandhi No Delo' after his father. It's a simple single-level building, the walls stained dark by old rain. Inside, the small rooms wait in darkness, a few old photographs and personal artifacts of the Mahatma emerging from the shadows. The walls narrate his tales and his teachings.

'I saw Bapuji,' the old caretaker says, walking in slow steps beside me. He looks like a relic from the Independence movement, in stark white khadi dhoti and banian, a Gandhi topi crowning his shiny bald pate. With age his back has hunched slightly, but there is no frailty about him. His eyes twinkle from behind the wrinkles. His thoughts are broken, but the voice is strong. 'I was still a boy . . . my father took me . . . I was much younger than you,' he smiles wistfully.

'What was it like? Tell me,' I urge him enthusiastically. 'I've never met anyone who's actually seen Gandhi.'

'Yes . . . few of us survive from those days. It was a public rally . . . we went by bullock cart . . . our entire village was there . . . thousands . . . all in khadi. Bapuji may look small, but when he stepped forward his presence was felt immediately. I will never forget the moment . . . that and the day we got our Independence . . .'

'You are a lucky man. I've never felt part of anything so profound.'

'The times are different. Tell me, how much do you know about Bapuji?'

'Well, I've read a few books . . .'

'Come, I'll show you . . . see this photograph, it was taken during a hunger strike . . .'

I am the only visitor, and I spend an hour in the two small rooms, listening, looking. As I'm leaving, I turn to thank him. 'Talking to you was inspiring.'

'Sheesh! Why do you say that . . . it was my pleasure. We don't get too many visitors . . .' he stops at the door. 'I hope the day doesn't come when people forget him.'

I rejoin my escorts, who are waiting outside. They insist on taking me out for tea, and I insist on taking them out to dinner. All three of us get on Kaya. While the law suggests that riding triples is illegal, who's going to try explaining that to the cops?

Kilometer 22524

Kaya found herself on a promising piece of road as we headed for Jamnagar, which turned out to be an unusually quiet and well-behaved city. The early promise of a comfortable ride, though, didn't last beyond Jamnagar, and for the next hundred kilometers to Dwarka we travelled along poor roads, past super rich industries. For the last hour our path skirted the coast, offering teasing glimpses of shimmering blue as it climbed over the gentle hills that ran along the shore in waves. Visible from a distance, the soaring *gopuram* of Dwarkadhish Temple guided us into this holiest of towns. This was the mythical capital of Lord Krishna's Yadava Kingdom, which, as cursed, on the death of

Krishna, was swept away by the sea. Today all that remains of the city is legend, celebrated by the Dwarkadhish Temple.

Exiting from the southern gate of the temple, a series of steps descend to the confluence, where River Gomti meets the Arabian Sea. I am informed that to bathe here is salvation, which leads me to conclude that it's easier to find salvation in India than a decent pair of socks. Believe me, I've been searching for the socks.

Besides, recent archeological and underwater excavations have revealed that a far rarer miracle than salvation might exist under these waves – the ruins of at least five ancient cities, swallowed by the sea many thousands of years ago, with temples and fortress walls, extending many miles along the coast. Marine archeologist Graham Hancock claims this discovery could completely rewrite what we know about the beginning of civilization. There's a possibility that the legend of Dwarka might actually be true. Now there's a thought that sends a shudder down my spine. We tore down a mosque based on nothing but an Ayodhyic assumption. With actual proof, I fear to imagine what we'll do to the sea.

From the mythical shore Kaya turned south along the coast to the ancient port town of Porbandar. Once a flourishing center for trade, and an entry port for the few black slaves shipped into the country, today it is remembered as the birthplace of the Mahatma. The highway led unerringly to the historic lane, a congestion of wall-to-wall buildings, street carts, grinding traffic, and bustling humanity, all of it coming together in synchronized anarchy. Somehow the cogs keep turning, just like they do all across the country. The two-story skyline was marked by decaying wood, holding on by the last splinters of dignity. Everything was in a state of neglect, except for the two freshly painted memorials, before which Kaya came to a halt.

Since the stopover at Porbandar is meant to be short, I'm hoping to avoid the tedious process of unstrapping my bags and lugging them around the memorials. I'm standing on the side of the crowded street and mulling over my options, when a shrill whistle catches my attention. I follow the sound to a man seated inside the pawn shop before me. He dons a well-worn shirt of orange khadi. A fiery streak of vermilion adorns his forehead. His mouth is equally ablaze from the *paan* he's chewing. He flashes a broken-toothed grin and waves me over.

'Are you trying to visit the temple?' he asks.

'Yes.'

'Just park your bike here and go ahead. Don't worry about your things, I'll watch over them.'

'Are you sure? I don't want to be a bother,' I protest disingenuously, overjoyed at his offer.

'Where's the trouble in this? Do you think it's going to be a strain on my eyes?' he laughs.

'Thanks a lot, brother, you're saving me a lot of trouble.'

Leaving Kaya in front of the shop, I approach the Gandhi House, a well-preserved, 220-year-old building with low-roofed rooms, narrow wooden stairs, and prison cell windows. It is gloomy and bare. A red swastika on the floor indicates the spot where the Mahatma was born. Adjacent to the house stands the

Kirti Mandir. Built in 1950 as a memorial to Gandhi, it climbs to a height of 79 feet and sports 79 candle holders, representing his age. Most significantly, the memorial displays the symbols of all our major religions, a poignant reflection of the Mahatma's strong belief in pluralism.

I'm casually thumbing through the books on Gandhi when it occurs to me that I've left everything I own in the hands of a complete stranger, simply because he told me to. How could I be so gullible, what if he's stolen my last pair of non-disintegrating socks? Damn! I drop the book in my hand and make a frantic scramble for the exit. On reaching the street I spot Kaya standing as I left her, my bags still strapped on.

'What happened, brother?' the shopkeeper asks. 'That was quick.'

'Uh . . . nothing . . . I just wanted to pay homage to Bapu,' I mumble sheepishly. 'I'm satisfied with that.'

'I know how nice that must feel,' he nods knowingly. 'I visit the temple every morning before I open my shop. But tell me this, your bike has an Andhra registration, did you ride down all the way from there?'

'Yes, I'm riding around the country.'

'*Sach*, you have to tell me more. Come inside. What's the hurry? We'll have a cup of tea.'

'Sure, I'm in no hurry.' I step into the dim single-celled little shop and sit down on the cushion he places for me on the floor.

'Just one minute eh, I'll go bring the tea and come,' he says and steps out, leaving the pawn shop to me. There's a small glass shelf before me, mostly empty except for a balance scale and what looks like a couple of tarnished silver rings. In a quick reversal of roles, now he's the fool trusting a complete stranger.

He's back within two minutes, a beat-up thermos in his hand. 'Here you are,' he says, and placing two stainless steel glasses on the counter, pours the muddy contents of the thermos into them. '*Do cup garma garam chai.* Now we can talk in leisure. So what brings you this far from home on a motorcycle?'

'Well, it's a long story . . .' The words don't dry up, nor does the saccharine tea.

'Wah, that's wonderful, and in all this travel have you come across any place that's better than Saurashtra?' he asks with pride. And, not waiting for my reply, he answers his own question, 'Such a thing is not even possible. This is the spiritual center of India, the land of Lord Krishna and Mahatma Gandhi.'

'Yes, I've heard.'

'And we are the sweetest people in the country.'

'That also might be true, so far the people have treated me with great kindness,' I nod in agreement, taken in by his passion.

'Also, Gujarat is not only about tradition and culture, our state even has the fastest growing economy.'

'Really, I wasn't aware of that at all.'

'Yes, it's true, under Narendra Modi we are leading the nation forward. He's brought so much change and welfare to Gujarat, a man of the future.'

'But what about the communal tensions?' I protest. 'Don't you think the riots reflect badly on him?'

'How is any of that Modiji's fault? You shouldn't believe everything the rubbish media people tell you. All he's done is brought back pride in the Hindu nation.'

Suddenly, the tea has lost its sweetness.

Kaya left behind the shores of Porbandar, to ride through a Gujarat that has forsaken Gandhi in all but name. Mohandas 'The Mahatma' 'Father of Our Nation' Gandhi: while the name has the sound of a heavyweight boxer's introduction into the ring, it belongs to a man who said 'when someone slaps you, show them the other cheek' or something to that effect. Gandhi took a concept of nonviolence that existed in our culture through the ages and turned what was seen as an act of docility into a movement so powerful it defied the world's greatest empire. We are almost unique in having earned our Independence without killing for it, to have struggled for our freedom, not warred for it. *Ahimsa* is Gandhi's legacy to us.

But as a young boy I never idolized Gandhi, nor did any of my friends. We were more enamored by all conquering heroes like Alexander the Great, Julius Caesar, and closer to home, Prithviraj Chauhan; men worth emulating in our childhood fantasies. Unlike Cowboys and Indians, where's the fun in playing Gandhis and Britishers? If you're the British, you get to slap the Gandhi. If you're the Gandhi, you have to turn the other cheek and receive a second slap. The rules don't leave much ground for maneuvering. For much of my life he remained Bapu, a frail old man to be revered for bringing us Independence. Gandhism, what's so brave about that? Only today do I understand the valor required to fight terrorism without terrorizing, or the heroism needed to keep our freedoms without suppressing someone else's, and it doesn't seem like we possess either. We are a nation that perpetrates violence in the name of honor, nationalism, and religion; a nation that believes an eye for an eye is justice. In showing the other cheek, Gandhi proved himself to be the bravest man of all.

The Gujarat we were passing through is an exemplary icon of a nation that has liberated itself from the shackles of Gandhian restraint, and eagerly embraced the ideals of a Modi, his antithesis. This state is the epicenter of a violent Hindu awakening, with its leaders using Hindu nationalism to intimidate and suppress a Muslim minority. The 2002 communal riots, which followed the Godhra tragedy, were amongst the most disturbing events of this millennium.* Unforgiving in intensity and savagery, when the madness ended 1,044 people had officially lost their lives; unofficially, the number is closer to 2,000. The score card for this bout of killing reads 790 Muslims and 254 Hindus. How many more were raped, abused, and maimed?

Rather than a spontaneous expression of anger, the violence bore all the makings of a government-sanctioned pogrom – pre-planned, organized, aided by local authorities and goaded by political leaders. Accusations abound of ministers leading the

---

* On February 27th, 2002, a train carrying pilgrims from Ayodhya pulled up at Godhra station, a town in eastern Gujarat. While the train waited to pick up passengers, on the platform an altercation began between local Muslims and Hindutva activists. Nobody seems to know what happened next, except that the train turned into a blazing inferno. Fifty-eight innocent Hindus, including 15 children and 25 women were burned to death. The spectacularly inconsiderate VHP wants to carry their ashes on a parade around the country.

mobs, target lists in hand, and of the police being ordered not to protect the Muslims, with some even actively participating in the murders. More than 1,50,000 people were displaced, mostly Muslim. Ten thousand businesses were destroyed or damaged, the majority Muslim owned. Hundreds of mosques and shrines were destroyed, makeshift Hindu temples sprouting in their place. The message was being spelled out, loud and clear: This was a Hindu Rashtra.

Terrible, yes, but none of this is new to Gujarat. This is a state that's historically prone to communal violence, and there's nothing unprecedented about the horror show of 2002. Take Ahmedabad, for instance. It carries the sobriquet 'Riot City', not because it knows how to the throw a damn good party, but due to its penchant for Hindu – Muslim conflagrations. The riots of 1969 left 512 people dead in the city, in 1980 the number was 300, and in 1992 another 132 died. Baroda has also witnessed its fair share of bloodshed, as has Surat. And every one of these incidents occurred under the aegis of a Congress government, or their coalition.

Nor is any of this new to India, as a recent *Outlook* article poignantly revealed. Since 1967, the 58 major communal riots that have rocked India have been more or less equitably distributed across the country; with 120 lives lost in Jamshedpur, 1,500 in Moradabad, 365 in Hyderabad, 872 in Bombay, 1,161 in Bhagalpur, 150 in Aligarh . . . the list goes on, marking every inch of our map with red dots, and every political party with red smears.[*] Though labeled a communal riot, the single bloodiest incident in the country's history is more a state-sponsored genocide – the ruling Congress party-led massacre of 8,000 Sikhs; 2,733 of whom were hunted down in our illustrious capital. Hindu, Muslim, Sikh – not one of us has spared or been spared. As for the Christians, I guess they are too few to do much killing, but they've filled their share of being killed.

There's little that's unique about 2002, except for the coverage it received. Nellie in '83, Delhi in '84 and Bombay in '92; all have had the characteristics of a pogrom, in one form or another. In Moradabad, the police contributed generously to the death toll, while in Bombay the police were 'Shiv Sainiks at heart'.[†] Where the Gujarat rioters possessed target lists, in Delhi the Congress party distributed voter lists. *S* marks the Sikh. As for Modi's unapologetic stance, does anybody believe that Rajiv Gandhi's 'when a big tree falls, the earth shakes' comment expressed repentant humility? Then why does our current discourse pretend like Modi's Gujarat is an exceptional evil, and why has he become the focus of liberal India's opprobrium?

My fear is that in demonizing him, we're hoping to distance ourselves from these crimes. Rather than face the reality that religious intolerance permeates our social and political makeup,

---

* Even the President has failed to protect us from ourselves, as evinced by the 1,819 killed in Nellie, Assam under his rule.

† Outlook

we feign that Modi is an anomaly in our progressive nation.* Perhaps it stems from a desperate need to believe we are better than Modi's followers, and the more intensely we condemn him, the easier it is to convince ourselves we are morally superior to those who support him. Let's not deceive ourselves. There's nobody out there who doesn't have blood on their hands, especially not you or me. Modi is the outcome of every riot we've let pass without justice, every guilty government we've forgiven – even rewarded through reelection. He's only as evil as we want him to be. As evil as we let him be. As much as I dislike NaMo and his politics, denouncing him will not grant us a better polity unless we use the same yardstick to judge others, including ourselves.

Kirti Mandir in Porbandar is as much a temple as a memorial, and while there, I observed the occasional visitor step inside barefoot, fold their hands, and bow down before Gandhi, a prayer on their lips. Krishna and Gandhi, two omnipresent icons of Gujarat; one, a great god, and the other, much rarer, a truly great man. But where thousands offered prayers to the god, few paid homage to the man, other than lip service. Me? Rather than bow to an imaginary god, I'd bow to a real hero; one who's granted us the greatest boon of all, freedom. Our leaders sacrifice Gandhi's unity to emulate the British policy of divide and rule. We sacrifice Gandhi's *ahimsa* to inflict violence in the name of Krishna and Rama. It was Hindu nationalism that drove Nathuram Godse to

* Recent events in Muzaffarnagar should dissuade anyone but the brain dead from such a notion.

pull the trigger. Unfortunately, his bullets weren't the end for Gandhi.

We are still killing the Mahatma.

Kilometer 23383

Entering Junagadh city, the highway hush was replaced by traffic tantrums, green trees by grey cement, and open spaces by a crush of humanity. Hidden amidst the housing complexes and factories, I discovered traces of an imperial past, best evidenced by the mausoleum of Nawab Mahabat Khan. A grandiose structure with delicate moldings and graceful minarets, the authorities have left it to decay. The garden that once surrounded it has become a trampled playground, and my visit interrupted a game of cricket, with one of the minarets serving as a wicket. Finding the tomb locked, I did what any true Indian would do under similar circumstances – joined the batting team.

In all fairness, the people of Junagadh have little for which to thank the Nawab. During Partition, Mahabat Khanji, the Islamic ruler of Junagadh, chose to integrate with Pakistan, though his kingdom shared no borders with Pakistan and eighty percent of his subjects were Hindu. When the Indian government sent in the army to secure the kingdom for itself, the Nawab promptly fled to Pakistan – but not before taking the time to empty the state treasury. Nor had the Nawab been a particularly enlightened leader during his reign. At the time of his abrupt departure, an incredible eleven percent of the state's income was being spent on the upkeep of the royal dogs, all 800 of them. And this is excluding the wedding of his favorite Alsatian, which cost a whopping twenty-five crores in today's rupees. Hey, the big fat Indian wedding doesn't come cheap, not when it includes wedding finery for all the doggies, a four-horse carriage to take the newlyweds around town, state banquets, firework spectacles, Nautch girls, and a guest list that included the Viceroy of India.* In addition to his kennels, the Nawab is best remembered for the large harem he kept. Unfortunately, compelled to make a quick getaway, taking all his loved ones to Pakistan proved impossible. So he took some of the dogs, and left behind most of the women.

From Junagadh, the road led Kaya past lush grasslands and washed away culverts, past farming villages and cattle herders. The terrain slowly turned rugged, greenery giving way to low rock hills, sparse growth, and stunted trees. There she ran into the barricade at the entrance to Sasan Gir National Park, the last refuge of the Asiatic lion in the entire world. Once upon a time, before humankind discovered the pleasures of a loaded gun, the King of the Jungle roamed the entire north western frontier, his paw prints extending from Bihar to Baghdad. By the beginning of the 20th century they were hunted to the brink of extinction. Incredible as this may sound, the population of the Asiatic lion had dropped to two dozen – yes, *twenty-four* of them – in the entire world. These remnants were herded together into an enclosure on the orders of our inimitable hero, the Nawab of Junagadh. According to his detractors, the man was

* It's hard to tell if the wedding couple was dismayed that the Viceroy failed to show up and bless their union.

no bleeding heart conservationist, instead assembling the lions for the pleasure of shooting them down personally. Thankfully, he had to skip the country before he could, and today those twenty-odd have grown into a population of three hundred, their roars echoing around the hills of Sasan Gir. Regardless of his reasons, the Nawab can be credited for singlehandedly saving the Asiatic lion from extinction.

But there were no lions for us to see, since the entrance was as far as Kaya and I could go. While it is near impossible for Indians to string together a week's vacation, our animals are given a much deserved two-month holiday each year when the parks close for the monsoons. So, with my fingers crossed, I rode around the buffer zone hoping one of the big cats would step out of the forest to greet me. And, despite what you might think, this wasn't all that farfetched an expectation. A couple of years ago, two of the lions strayed out of the reserve and strolled down to the coast near Diu, more than a hundred and fifty kilometers away, through villages and across highways.

I'm assuming they wanted to spend their holiday at the beach.

An hour's ride past Somnath – a temple that's been razed to the ground six times only to defiantly rise again – Kaya breached the barrier of the sea, carrying me over a narrow swampy channel into a different world, the island of Diu, with a history and culture distinct from the mainland. While the rest of the country was bowing to the Brits, the citizens of Diu-Daman and Goa served the Portuguese, until they were finally liberated at the end of a 'one-day invasion' launched by the Indian armed forces in 1961, fourteen years after Independence.

Gujarat is India's lone dry state, imposing a complete ban on liquor, in spite of which every Gujarati determined to get drunk still does so. He simply steps across the state border, much to the joy of this neighboring territory's revenue officers. A similar attempt was made in Andhra Pradesh during the nineties. Then it was discovered that the state was actually getting drunker, with next door Karnataka getting richer. The prohibition was promptly lifted. The Gujarat government unfortunately hasn't learned the lesson, and as luck would have it, I arrived at Diu on an extended weekend. Diu, with its tax exemption on liquor, is a Dionysian paradise, and on this weekend of Janmashtami it looked like every Gujarati not praying to Lord Krishna was intently paying homage to a bottle of distilled pleasure. The little island was bursting at the seams, as wave after wave of revelers washed up on its shores, and pubs aside, every room in every hotel of Diu was taken.

We opted to move on to Palitana. And then to Dasada and Modhera. When Kaya entered Gujarat's capital city two days later, my head hung low from fatigue. But before seeking the comfort of a soft bed, I decided to feel the touch of cold steel. While in Ahmedabad, I intended to stay with some of my dad's friends, the implication being that I had to look presentable. So, with bag and baggage, I sought out a barber saloon.

Only then did I knock on their door.

'It's wonderful what you are doing,' Dr. Shah, my dad's college buddy, comments as a cleaned-up version of me sits down at the dinner table. 'And brave,' he adds.

'Aw, there's nothing brave about riding around the country,' I shrug, dutifully modest.

'Actually, I'm talking about giving up your job. Ha, ha. So, what do you plan to do when you get back? Does this help your advertising career in anyway?'

'Hmm, I don't know if it does.'

'Well, that's okay for now I guess. At least you get to see the country. I've always thought about it too. See, I even bought the *Lonely Planet*. But there's always something more important to do in . . . er, you know how it is . . .'

The grand capital of the Gujarati Sultanate through the medieval ages, Ahmedabad was named after its founder Sultan Ahmed Shah. In British hands, it became the 'Manchester of the East', home to a booming cotton textile industry. In the 20th century, Mahatma Gandhi made this city the center of India's struggle for freedom. In the modern era, Hindu nationalism has turned it into Riot City. Ahmedabad is also where my father spent nine years as a medical student, and Dr. Shah has taken it upon himself to show me around the old alma mater and introduce me to some of their friends who were still around.

'So, are you a doctor as well, like your father?' the anatomy professor asks.

'No, I'm not.'

'What do you do then?'

'Right now I'm just traveling.'

'What kind of a job is that?'

'It's not a job. I'm just riding around the country on a motorcycle.'

'Sounds very interesting . . . but what do you plan to do with your life?'

I get the impression that by the end of this journey my father is going to be the most pitied man in the medical fraternity.

When Kaya finally rode out of Ahmedabad, it was in the company of a new pillion. Captain Hash, my closest friend and inspiration for Kaya Dreams, had just returned from Germany, armed with a blonde-haired, blue-eyed German girlfriend, who needed to remain invisible to his orthodox Muslim parents. So, while he paid a visit to his parents in Srinagar, Heidi had to be, well, pretty much anywhere else. That's where Kaya and I came in, keeping her company over the next two weeks and giving her a taste of India. Needless to say, my mum was now wailing that her son had been swapped at birth.

Fortunately, the road behaved itself, providing Heidi with a gentle initiation into riding around India. Thirty kilometers from Ahmedabad, Akshardham is theology gone hi-tech, an exercise in brainwashing, created by a New Age, media-savvy religious corporation. My lasting memory of Akshardham Temple, though, is not of god, but of the ring of heavily-armed soldiers protecting him, another one of those unsettling shrines that have more guns than priests. A few months after the 2002 riots, two Islamic militants scaled the walls of Akshardham Temple and opened fire on the pilgrims, killing 29 and leaving a further 79 wounded. From what I've observed around the country, religious shrines are a reliable place to meet with an untimely and violent death.

Our journey onwards was interrupted by a troubled detour to Godhra, an unassuming and ordinary town. The railway station was crowded and noisy, the floor and walls stained by splatters of *paan*, gobs of saliva, and rivulets of urine, the tracks were covered in refuse. What few benches existed were already occupied, and most passengers waited on the dusty ground. The air smelled stale. Just as in Deorala, I discovered nothing untoward about the place. It was like any other station, in any other part of the country.

'What are we doing here?' Heidi asked.

'Mulling over the malaise of a nation.'

Leaving Godhra behind, Kaya transported us to Champaner, our last destination in Gujarat. From the forested foothills, a steep foot trail ascends to the summit of Pavagadh, or, if you're distrustful of walking, the only other option is the cable car making its shuddering climb to the top. Just the year before, the cable had snapped, plummeting six visitors to their death. We decide to walk.

Once at the summit, a vertical crag of rock soars from the ground, the famous temple crowning it. And above the temple rests a Sufi tomb. A steady stream of Hindus step out of the temple and unerringly make their way to the *dargah*, where they lower their heads in reverence to a Muslim saint. Perhaps a millennium of shared history and culture may yet survive the political hatred.

In 2004, the historic ruins of Champaner were declared a UNESCO World Heritage Site, recognizing the architecture as 'the perfect symbiosis of Hindu and Muslim traditions'.

LEG FIFTEEN

M.P. Begins . . . The Road Ends

CROSSING THE BORDER, Kaya put the mental tribulations of Gujarat behind her, only to be confronted by the physical trauma of Madhya Pradesh before us. It was a long ride, and the road showed no mercy.

'What the hell is this?' Heidi shuddered as we crashed into another moon crater. 'Why don't you take the expressway?'

'This is the expressway, but don't worry about it too much.'

'Why, does it get better soon?'

'No, you'll just get used to it.'

The punishment ceased to matter as we approached Mandu, a fortress town spectacularly perched atop a flat summit amidst the hills of the Vindhya Range. We were surrounded on three sides by rainforests and rift valleys. Large gateways emerged from the thicket, time portals that transported us to a legendry past of pavilions, tombs, baths, and mosques. The 15th century pleasure capital of the Ghauri Dynasty, Mandu was once Shadiabad, the

'City of Joy', envied for its wealth and contentment. The kings were famed for their endorsement of the arts and pursuit of pleasure. The people were remembered for their grace and generosity. It is said that any new settler was presented a gold coin by each resident of the city to show that all were equal.

Kaya rolled to a halt.

The city of joy is now the city of ruins. Gone the glory and grandeur. Gone the gold for this meager population to pass around. Gone the palaces, replaced by single-celled homes of earth and plaster. What remains though is the character of the past, and where the walls are tarnished with time the people of Mandu shine bright.

'Have a cup of tea before you go sightseeing,' the owner of a clothes store invites us into his tiny shop. 'I'll tell you all about Mandu's history.'

We garner three other invitations to tea by mid-morning, and three different histories to go with them. While the stories read like fabrications of a wishful imagination, the telling is genuine, as are the tellers. And what attracts us to them is the image of Kaya and Heidi taking on the roads of M.P. Where the rest of the world makes polite conversation by discussing the weather, the citizenry of Mandu reveal an unusual preoccupation with roads.

'What! You plan to travel around our state by road?' the cloth merchant gasps. 'Yes, yes, I understand you've completed twenty-five thousand kilometers, but this is Madhya Pradesh.'

'Even the gods fear our roads . . .' another man announces proudly. 'You children don't know what you are getting into.'

'Ah! So that's what a road looks like,' a third smiles mischievously, looking through my photographs. 'What a wonderful thing!'

When not discussing roads they extol the greatness of Mandu, without giving us leave to see any of it. Mandu is one of the largest fortress towns of India, they tell me, its circumference 23 kilometers, 34 kilometers, 45 kilometers or any other number in between, depending on who I choose to believe. One old man assures me it is 100 kilometers, but then, he also claims to have seen the naked ghost of Queen Roopmati. Squealing children greet every step of our slow progress through the town, and voices call to us from every doorway, inviting us in. Within the dimly lit confines of these homes, I find myself sipping more tea and photographing three generations of Manduans huddled around Heidi.

At the domed mausoleum of Darya Khan, we are held up by the eager gatekeeper for a long chat. 'Would you like to smoke some ganja?' he asks suddenly, interrupting what up to that point has been a normal conversation about roads. Heidi, unaware of our dopey culture and my propensity to attract its followers, seems a little shocked. I offer her a sheepish grin and a shrug of the shoulders.

'Thanks, brother, but I think not,' I say unconvincingly.

'Don't get me wrong, I'm not trying to sell you anything. There's not much to do here, so I was just hoping for some company.'

'I'm sorry, but I have to go now, maybe later.'

Having remained abstemious throughout Gujarat, the temptation is compelling, except that Heidi, a health freak, doesn't like the idea of poisoning her body and mind. Wandering around the monuments my mind keeps returning to the squandered opportunity, and unable to fight the guilt anymore I leave Heidi to her own devices at the town center and return to the museum. Sitting beside a broken idol of Shiva, the caretaker and I get stoned in his name.

Boom Shankar!

Boom!

We get along wickedly, and he promises me a special treat. As the day nears its end we are joined by his friend Mahi, a man in his early forties, gaunt, weather-beaten face, large, expressive eyes, long, dark curls parted at the center and glistening with oil. The caretaker closes the museum, and they lead me to a couple of rock-cut caves perched on the edge of a sheer cliff overlooking the valley. A stream flows gently from above the cave, forming a small crystalline pool at its entrance. I sit with my feet immersed in the cool waters, a burning *chillum* changing hands, emulating the sadhus who lived here centuries ago.

'Are you ready for the treat?' my new-found friend asks me.

'You mean there's more?'

I hear no reply, instead a soulful voice fills the space, resonating deep within me, stirring the heart. It belongs to Mahi, a traditional balladeer, who keeps legends alive through folksong. Though I don't understand the words, the emotions expressed transcend languages, carrying me in waves, through romance, valor, and finally, sorrow. Mahi takes me on a translated journey through the hills of Mandu, across the plains of Gujarat, and into the deserts of Rajasthan.

He sings an ode to Rani Roopmati of Mandu, one of the great romances of India. In this kingdom of happiness, Baz Bahadur, a Muslim king, falls in love with Roopmati, a Hindu peasant. Defying culture and tradition he makes her his queen, and on the pavilions of Mandu they play out their love through song and dance. And, like all such tales, it ends in tragedy. Baz Bahadur, albeit a heroic lover, isn't much of a hero, and routed by the Mughal enemy, he flees the field – abandoning the fort and his beloved queen. From the balcony of her delicate palace, Roopmati watches her world crumble, her love betrayed. As the enemy approaches, she surrenders her life by consuming poison.

'We are a dying breed,' Mahi informs me wistfully. 'Nobody cares to listen to our songs anymore, they only want Bollywood music. All the villagers have televisions and tape recorders to keep them entertained. Nor are there any initiatives to promote our traditional art forms.'

'What about you . . . how do you manage?'

'I work in the fields. When the opportunity arises I make a little money singing for tourists or at local functions, but it's not much. I only bother because it is something my family has done for centuries. My father taught me . . . but my sons, they tell me it's a waste of time.' His shoulders sag, his eyes are distant. 'They say it has no future . . . they are right.'

When I part company with them it is with mixed emotions – the joy of being privy to an age-old tradition, and the sorrow that it might be the last time. If I return here a decade later, will I still find a Mahi? As I make my way back to the town, the sun slowly descends behind the hills, its fiery light turning a glowing orange, and then, finally, dying out.

Kilometer 24966

Kaya's journey through M.P. continued along nonexistent roads, sloshing through the mud and kicking up dirt. A fine piece of road would have made little difference anyway, not when Kaya spent most of her time in the runoff beside it. No, her intent wasn't to scare Heidi, but to avoid the trucks cutting across lanes and gunning straight for us. The drivers must believe they are in one of those computer games where you get extra points for crashing into others.

We caught up with the Narmada, and followed its troubled course towards the confluence with the River Kaveri, where the sacred island of Mandhata rises over the churning waters. The river banks were a hive of activity. Giant cranes, swarming trucks, and townships of building material, this was but a tiny part of the Narmada Valley Development Project, which involves the erection of 30 large, 135 medium, and 3,000 small dams across the mighty river. The most ambitious undertaking by Independent India, it has also turned out to be the country's most contentious one.

Since its conception in the fifties, the project has constantly run into trouble, starting with the conflict over the distribution of benefits between the various states. After a decade of deliberation, it finally received the go-ahead in 1979, only to become immediately embroiled in further controversy, with accusations of human rights violations and environmental mismanagement. This period also witnessed the birth of the Narmada Bachao Andolan – perhaps the most influential social movement of our country – which, twenty-five years later, continues to battle against the dams. Meanwhile, following a damning independent review, the World Bank and other international financial organizations withdrew support for the project. Regardless, the government has gone ahead as proposed, for the sake of the three crore Indians to whom the project is expected to provide water and irrigation.

Kaya pulled up by the muddy waters, across the bridge leading to the island of Mandhata.

On the om-shaped island of Mandhata sits the temple of Omkareshwar, its importance manifest by the long line of pilgrims winding through the shop-lined streets to the entrance of the sanctum. One look at the crowd and Heidi decides to wait with Kaya, leaving me to face the crush by myself. Stale air and sweat. Hugging bodies and filth-laden lanes. Wailing children and screaming hawkers. And at the end of a three-hour ordeal, I earn three jostling seconds before the idol. The next instant I find myself standing outside the shrine, carried forward by the crowd's unremitting momentum.

I find my path back across the bridge blocked by a protest march that continues to the streets of the mainland. It's only a small group of villagers, holding up a few banners and shouting slogans, but what they lack in numbers they make up for through sheer passion. Unfortunately, it's not clear to me what they are protesting against.

'Brother, what are you demonstrating against?' I ask, walking over to one of the elders.

'The Omkareshwar Dam,' he replies curtly.

'Why, what is the problem?'

'Why!' he spits. 'That dam has destroyed my life and you ask me what the problem is. Our village is gone. We have lost our farmlands and temples. We are forcibly driven out of our homes like rats, without getting one paisa compensation. Just because we are poor villagers you people think we can be trampled upon. Are we not people of this country? Aren't our needs as important as those of others?'

'But what about the benefits . . . ' my voice trails off, knowing how foolish the words are even as they spill out.

'All of this is for the benefit of others. What will we do with water when we have no farms? We don't even have houses anymore . . .' His voice is breaking. '. . . where am I supposed to go now? I've lived here all my life. This is all I know.' Tears of anger and frustration are poised to spill over, but before they can, he walks away, leaving me to the resentful stares of his companions.

Kaya put the anger behind us and rode towards Indore, but the accusations followed me. 'What do you want to hear about?' another man had growled at me. 'How we were thrown out of our homes? Have you seen how we live now?'

Dams, once the imposing symbol of man's engineering invincibility and his conquest of the earth, have, over the last couple of decades, tumbled from grace. Today viewed as almost medieval in nature, the world over dam building faces intense opposition from activists – 'dam busters' as they are derisively called – on social, economic, and environmental grounds. Despite the damning evidence the damming continues, in the name of farming communities and food security, with the promise of clean energy generation and drinking water supply. Does either side have absolute claim on the truth, or can one side's cons outweigh the other side's pros? I don't know.

But what I do know is this: In our country, while the benefits to the population are uncertain, there is little doubt about the price extracted from some. And what a terrible price it is. Depending on who you choose to believe, since Independence anywhere between two and five crore second-class Indians have had their homes and livelihoods snatched from them, making way for dams and irrigation projects. *Five crore.* Let that number sink in. Now add to that the generation of children born into this vacuum. For we didn't just take their land, but also their livelihood, society, and history. We have stolen from them both their past and their future. Compensating a displaced population on the basis of property is little more than a cruel joke, akin to a father supporting his child's education by paying the price of the paper the degree is printed on. But even this scant succor our government fails to provide, and less than a quarter of all displaced people have been provided their meager reparation.

Fifty years after being evicted, the tribals displaced by Hirakud Dam are still fighting for their dues.

On completion, the Omkareshwar project will submerge 14,000 hectares of valuable land, including nearly 6,000 hectares of intact natural forests. More importantly, it will force an estimated 20,000 villagers off their lands – activists claim the number is closer to 50,000. Judging from past experiences, the protests I witnessed stand feeble chance of stemming the tide. In the past, the Narmada Valley Project hasn't shrugged off from cheating farmers with false promises, forcing them out of their villages at gunpoint, and bulldozing their homes without warning. As an exclamation point on the dam's supremacy over the people, protestors have been fired upon and killed. It's not the dams I fear though, rather the government that protects 'development' over the rights of the people.

Straying off the highway, Kaya took to an uncharted side road. 'Have you seen how we live now?' one of the protesters had said, more an accusation than a question. Seized by a self-absorbed and utterly misguided notion of finding out for myself, we headed towards the town of Kothi.

I won't say I was shocked, because that would imply actually having expectations of our government; nonetheless, the conditions were far worse than I imagined. The 'resettlement village' consisted of a pitiful knot of half-erected hovels, more plastic than brick and concrete. A township had been sacrificed to create a slum. When I think of it, I've seen slums that have a greater sense of pride, permanence, and proprietorship. The 'village' had no sanitation, no running water supply, and – the cruelest irony of all – minimal access to drinking water and electricity. As for their future, these were farmers without land to farm. Everything that's promised us by the dams has been denied to the very persons who've given the most for them. Instead we've made them refugees in their own country: the 'unpeople'. Could anything be more tragic for them? Could anything be more shameful for us?

I tried talking to an unperson at Kothi, a young man sitting in the dirt, outside his plastic world. To my '*namaste bhaiyya*' his response was, 'Are you with the press?' His second guess, perhaps influenced by Heidi's presence, was that we belonged to some NGO. 'Then why do you care . . . can you do anything to make a difference?'

For nearly three decades now an entire spectrum of social organizations have fought to help the tribes and villages, providing a voice for people with no political clout. Cases against the government have been filed, appealed, and filed again, at every stage of the project, and at every judicial level. Much has been done to awaken the public to their plight – actors have spoken about it; writers have written, including Arundhati Roy's powerful and evocative *Greater Common Good*; and filmmakers have filmed, like the documentary *Drowned Out*, which narrates the story of a tribal family's decision to drown in their home rather than evacuate it. The government response to all this has been to raise the height of the dams, and drown out a few more.*

I had nothing to offer him, not a brave face, or even a false smile.

Kilometer 25524

Beyond Indore, Kaya found herself wading towards Bhopal. The rain lashed against us in unrestrained fury. The raindrops struck like bullets. I saw little of the world we passed through, my visibility down to a couple of translucent feet. Kaya's tires slipped in the streams of water cutting across the road. We edged slowly closer to Bhopal, which from a distance resembled the set of a watery disaster movie.

The incessant rains had overwhelmed the city's drainage system. It no longer drained anything, instead flooding large areas of the town with sewage overflow. A toxic combination of filth and shit swept through the streets, in some places the black water rising to knee height. Fortunately, the body count included only motor vehicles. Everywhere we looked, cars lay stricken, men grudgingly pushing them to god-knows-where, while others frantically tried to kick-start their unresponsive bikes. The smarter chaps had simply abandoned their vehicles. Grimacing, people struggled through the water, women with saris hitched up, and men with pants rolled to the knees. Kaya rode on

* Oh yes, they've also introduced a new resettlement and rehabilitation bill, but there is little evidence that it provides adequate redress, and even less reason for the victims to trust it to be properly enforced.

the pavement, keeping a desperate eye out for places where life jackets might come into play. By the time we reached the station area, where most of the hotels are located, the rain had finally let up. It was going to be a while before the water drained out though.

Leaving Heidi with Kaya, I cringe-wade from one hotel to another, but my luck is as dim as the cloud-enveloped sun. Bhopal either has very few hotels, or it is inexplicably India's most visited city. The first few budget hotels I try at are all full. Too tired and dirty to care about the price anymore, I enter one of the plusher-looking establishments, sporting a grand name like Ashoka, or something of the sort.

'What do you want?' the receptionist asks curtly, none too pleased that I'm dripping over her linoleum floor. I'll probably cost her a can of room-freshener as well.

'I was wondering if you have any rooms available.'

'Yes, we do.'

'How much?'

'Two thousand rupees.'

Are you bloody nuts, I want to laugh at her, but my mouth betrays me by saying, 'Thank you very much, I'll take it. I'll be right back.' I skip across the water joyously to where Heidi is waiting, and leaving Kaya on the amphibious pavement, the two of us return to the hotel with our bags.

'Is she with you?' the receptionist asks the instant we step in.

'Well . . . yes'

'Sorry. Indian and foreigner not allowed together.'

'What!' Heidi blurts in surprise. I'm too devastated to react.

'We aren't allowed to have Indian and foreign guest together,' Miss Receptionist restates.

'I don't understand.'

'Sorry,' she shrugs without being so.

Heidi and I try at another hotel on the main road, and this one's full as well. I'm talking to the guy at the reception, checking if he knows about any place where I may find a room.

'Why all this diffi—'

'GET AWAY, YOU BASTARD,' Heidi screams, startling the receptionist and me. I don't get it at first, but the receptionist is already moving. While we are talking, a stranger has edged close to Heidi and made a grab for her ass.

'*GANDU*,' the receptionist shouts, and jumping over the counter gives the molester a hard shove. By now even the bell boy has pounced, giving him a resounding whack on the side of the head.

'I didn't do anything,' the molester protests loudly. Unheeding of his defense, the bell boy drags him by the collar and hurls him out the entrance, tearing his shirt in the process. He hits the street reeling but, regaining his balance, he takes a few staggering steps to the side and then stops.

'What the fuck are you standing around for? I'll break your bones if you show up around here again,' the receptionist spits at him and turns back to us. Heidi and I are standing at the entrance. I haven't said a word the entire time. To be honest, I didn't even realize what was going on till after the event, when Heidi explained it to me in explicit terms.

'Sorry about what happened, madam,' the receptionist apologizes. 'There is bar at the back of the hotel . . . and, you know . . .'

Heidi doesn't say anything. She looks the most composed of us. We leave the hotel and try at another place. After a couple more attempts we find a musty little place in a stinking back lane, the walls stained with seepage. The receptionist appears as rundown as his workplace, but he smiles a lot and is the picture of politeness.

'I only give you separate rooms, ok,' he says.

'Yes, please, that's fine,' I shrug.

'Passport, please,' he asks Heidi, 'I need to make a Xerox.'

'What's this all about? I haven't been asked to show my passport anywhere else.'

'Bhopal police is very strict. All foreigners have to be registered and the C-form handed over at the police station.'

'Is this no foreigner and Indian together also their policy?'

'No, madam, that's not rule. But it's better for everybody . . . less problems this way. A few months ago, a European tourist checked into a hotel here with an Indian youth she'd befriended on her travels. Then in the night this *chootya* friend assaulted and raped her in the hotel room. The police caught the fellow, but they also create lot of trouble for the hotel. Nobody is wanting that kind of problem.'

This sexual assault on a foreigner wasn't an isolated incident. A similar case had rocked Rajasthan recently, and these stories received extensive media coverage much to the nation's discomfiture. Rapes can't be good for the tourist-friendly image of India, now can they? And, apparently, the best way to prevent future embarrassments is to keep foreigners as far away from us as possible.

Kilometer 25746

Kaya didn't roar as much as sputter her way through the next few days, northwards through Sanchi and Chanderi, on to Shivpuri. The rain our steadfast companion, we spent most of the time playing and hide-and-seek. Everywhere was green. Glistening. Lush. Fresh. It should have been rejuvenating, but the same rain also washed away most of the roads. Muddy, bumpy, and potholed, we were subject to a constant physical beating, and it took its toll.

Meanwhile, M.P.'s men were taking a toll on Heidi's mental status. Leering eyes followed her everywhere, sometimes accompanied by a suggestive catcall. It reminded me how different this journey would have been if I were a woman, perhaps not even possible. In setting off by myself, I never felt any fear for my security, but would that hold true for a woman as well? I'd assumed, and assured others, that India was amongst the safest places to travel, but I guess I'd only considered it from a male perspective. How disconnected I was from the concept of sexual harassment only struck home by my reaction, or lack thereof, to what had happened at the hotel. I'd been more shocked that anyone would try such a thing so openly, with so many people around. How did he think he'd get away? Then it occurred to me that he *had* gotten away. A couple of smacks and he was free. It didn't even occur to me, at the time, that we should have turned him over to the police instead of brushing it aside. And why had Heidi not insisted either?

'It's not just that bastard, every other man here makes me feel like an object,' she cried in frustration. 'The only time I feel any sense of private space is when we're on Kaya.'

And so we rode, until our path lay blocked by a group of villagers sitting on the road, their backs turned to us. Slowing down, I edged up behind them, cursing their idiocy, only to discover they were blameless. There was no road ahead for anybody to go anywhere. It might have been there a few hours ago, but not anymore. In all fairness though, I couldn't even fault the road for this development. It was exactly where it had always been. The blame lay with the river, which had risen too high and submerged the culvert. The road reappeared on the far bank, from where it continued on its way, but between us and the other bank flowed a seething mass of chocolate-colored water. We were forced to turn around in search of an alternate route. A few kilometers after, I spotted a bright yellow sign egotistically advertising that this road was part of the network of National Highways being developed under the aegis of 'India Shining'. Apparently, this stretch of non-existent tarmac had cost the taxpayer 43 crores. For now, we were 'India Drowning'.

Kaya kept riding.

At Gwalior, Kaya caught up with Captain Hash, who'd arrived from Kashmir earlier that morning. Ideally, this should have been an adventure that Captain and I undertook together, but circumstances had decided otherwise. So now that he was finally here, even if only for a couple of days, it meant a lot. The onus, though, fell on Kaya, who now had to overcome the worst possible roads with three passengers and a full load of baggage. And she didn't let us down. Handling everything thrown at her with characteristic aplomb, she first got us to Orchha, then to Khajuraho.

We were entering Kama Sutra territory, and having heard such wonderfully lewd and lurid tales, I arrived there with the hope of enriching my life. My great fear was that it would turn out to be nothing but hype, all flaccid and impotent. But Khajuraho doesn't disappoint. The temples are an expression of carnal pleasures unlike anything I've seen, putting the likes of *Penthouse* and *Hustler* to shame; a stone gallery of blow jobs, sixty-nines, doggy styles, threesomes, and everything in between, all in boldly sculpted detail. And then there are the positions that even the most imaginative porn star would fail to conjure up, for instance, two girls holding up a man and lowering him onto a woman performing a hand stand. That one I decided was best left to the realms of fantasy, especially since I'm assuredly incapable of charming three women at once. What wonderfully educative art! All that's required are two coy signs, one saying: 'Parental Advisory – Explicit Sexual Themes', and the other: 'All Acts Performed By Professionals, Please Do Not Try This At Home'.

In explanation of this pornographic profusion on a temple, it is said that the Chadelas were followers of tantric mysticism, which espouses 'sexual pleasure as a step towards attaining nirvana'. They believed that real passion cannot be experienced with a marriage partner and should be sought through adulterous and extravagant intercourse, with the least concern for utility. Put simply, if you were in search of nirvana, your best bet was to sleep with as many people as you can, and in as bizarre ways as possible. If you want my opinion, this method is way more reasonable than all that business of immersing oneself in freezing waters.

Yet, there is little reason for a double take at Khajuraho, for sexuality is such an accepted and integral element of traditional Hindu culture. We pray to phallic objects and follow fertility rituals. Our gods are revealed as master seducers, some of whom have more wives than arms. Bare-breasted women adorn the walls of temples across the country, and at one point in time their halls were the domain of dancers and courtesans. So what's surprising is not Khajuraho, but that the people who gave the world the Kama Sutra are today a nation of prudes, where a bikini-clad actress sends the moral police into a tizzy. Riding away from the monuments, I couldn't help wonder: who stole our sexuality?

Kilometer 26741

Once again, it was just Kaya and me . . . and the pretense of a road.

Captain was travelling in the opposite direction, to Chennai, where he had a new job waiting, and Heidi went with him. Their plan was to find an apartment and settle in before he got caught up with work and she with her yoga classes. They were returning to the daily grind . . . and I envied them. But it shouldn't have been that way. Wasn't I the one living the dream? The days ahead were long, the highways cruel, from Khajuraho to Allahabad, from Allahabad to Pachmarhi. The road might never end, but it was wearing me down.

M.P. hadn't offered much in terms of tarmac throughout our journey, but now it was that much worse, and somewhere between Pachmarhi and Jabalpur it broke my already wavering resolve. The joy and purpose were beaten out of me, leaving only doubt. My arms ached, and every bump sent jolts of agony shrieking through my lower back. With every mile the pain grew stronger, and so did the anger. Unhealthy black rage gripped me, directed at the men responsible for this disaster, at the men who pocket the money instead of improving the roads, at a useless god that I didn't believe in, at myself for being here. Desperate to lash out at someone, something, anything, I took on the road. I hurtled over the bumps, throwing Kaya into every crater, with little attempt to evade them. I was out to hurt myself.

'Do your worst,' I screamed into the wind.

And all the while, I ignored the groan of metal and scrape of plastic. By the time we approached Jabalpur, I'd wrecked Kaya. Her carrier had clean torn off and crashed into the road. I hadn't cared, leaving it and its contents spilled across the highway. The electrical connections were jolted out of sync. The spokes had snapped, and for the third time now, the front disc brake was bent. Most troubling of all was the oil leaking from the engine. In my madness, the only one I'd really hurt was Kaya.

I took her to the mechanic. He spoke of extensive, time-consuming repairs. I told him to fix anything he could by closing time – the rim, the wiring, the loose nuts – deciding to have the rest looked at later. Her wounds were grave, and though I didn't see it just then, some would never fully heal. Self-pity turned to self-loathing. This was Kaya Dreams because she was the soul of the journey. She was my strength. She was the Ka to my Karma. And this was how I repaid her. I had reached the lowest point on my journey.

That's what I thought.

A new dawn. The same hollow sensation. I felt no enthusiasm on waking, only dread. The heart had gone out of the ride. I didn't want to face another one of those roads. I didn't want to stay either. I forced myself to get on Kaya. I forced myself to keep riding. Before starting I did something I hadn't in years. I prayed. For an easy day, a kind road.

It wasn't to be.

Amarkantak lay two hundred and fifty kilometers from Jabalpur, but at the end of a six-hour ride I hadn't yet reached my destination. I didn't even know how much further to reach it. There were no roads, and no road signs. The journey offered not a moment's respite, only a continuous battering of the body, and the mind. The pain mounted steadily, and the frustration. I reacted as I had the day before – by raising the accelerator in rage. I needed to hurt myself. It would be an excuse for giving up.

I hit a crater, and I hit it hard. My arms already weak, the impact pried my grip loose.

Kaya crashed to the ground, and I rolled to the side of the road.

I hear the crash and the scrape of metal, but I don't look. Gingerly getting back on my feet, I see she's lying stricken in the dirt, a pool of petrol collected around her body. I don't pick her up, instead removing my helmet and hurling it at the ground. The visor shatters. I drop down beside Kaya and break down completely.

Flood gates open, the pent-up anguish pours forth in tears, they stream down my grimy face, leaving a trail of failure. I cry like I haven't cried before, gasping for air between sobs. I fling a fistful of gravel at the emptiness. I scream like a caged animal, raw and guttural. In return, my screams are met by silence. The silence is shattering.

The road has defeated me. It has shattered my will . . . smothered my passion. But I know it isn't just the road. A few months ago I'd have taken this on as a challenge and laughed at it, but not now. It's a long time before I lift myself up, and then put Kaya back on her tires. With Amarkantak being the only town in the vicinity, I have little choice but to carry on.

The road passed under me through a blur of tears, the last fifty kilometers taking another three harrowing hours. I remember nothing of it. I was hurting, as was Kaya. The dream had run its course and had soured into a nightmare. The sun had set on us when we rode into Amarkantak. The world appeared grey; as gloomy as my thoughts. It was time for me to go home.

Kaya groaned to a halt beside a telephone booth.

I make the call that weighs heavily on my mind. My stomach tightens in knots as the phone rings on the other end. I play out the conversation in my head.

'Hello,' my father answers the phone.

'Uh . . . hi, dad.'

'Hey, where are you calling from?'

. . . the phone is still ringing . . .

'A . . . Amarkantak, dad . . . dad . . .' I hesitate.

'What is it, what's wrong?'

'I . . . dad, I don't think I can do this anymore. I'm worn out and I want to come home.'

'I don't understand . . .'

'What part don't you understand? I want to quit. QUIT. There, now do you get it?'

. . . the phone continues to ring . . .

'Go on. Why don't you say something?' I scream.

'What do you want me say? This is your journey, you make the decisions . . . but how are you going to explain it to the sponsors?'

'Screw the sponsors. What about you? Do you think I can't sense your disappointment? My son, the quitter. You must have expected it. Tell me how I've failed, again, how I've never seen a single thing through in my entire life, how . . .'

. . . the phone stops ringing. I hear a click as someone picks it up from the cradle. It's mum. I tell her where I am, pretending like it's any other daily status report. But she's Supermom. She senses something's wrong.

'Is everything alright?' she asks. 'You don't sound too good.'

'I'm just tired, ma . . . uh, is dad around?'

'No, he's still at the hospital. I think he's performing a surgery today. Why, is there anything you need?'

'No, nothing of the sort. Thought I'd say hi, that's all.'

'Are you sure nothing is the matter?'

'Don't worry, ma, like I said, I'm feeling tired. I'll call tomorrow okay . . . bye . . .'

Amarkantak is the source of the holy Narmada, where it begins life as a gentle spring, growing into a mighty river as it flows across the peninsula, before emptying into the Arabian Sea. The birthplace is marked by a sacred tank, surrounded by glowing white shrines, their spires rippling in the green water. I sit by the tank, my feet immersed in the water. My thoughts are on the road ahead. They fill me with dread. Gut-wrenching distress. To get to my next destination I'd have to return halfway along the purgatory I just came through.

I can't do it. I simply can't ride anymore.

Amarkantak is too small a place to warrant a transport company, but I manage to locate a man with a mini-truck for hire.

'Where do you need to go?' he asks.

'I need to transport my motorcycle to Nagpur.'

'My truck is leaving for Raipur tomorrow. After that we can go to Nagpur, or you can get down at Raipur and take a train.'

'But Raipur is in the opposite direction, it will be an additional two hundred kilometers at least,' I argue.

'Yes, I know that. Even if I were driving only to Nagpur, I'd still take the Raipur highway. It's madness to take the route you're talking about when there's an alternate.'

'Are you telling me there's a good road ahead?'

'No, I'm saying there's a better road ahead. And I'll be taking it at about six tomorrow morning. Turn up before that and we'll load your vehicle.'

'Thank you. I'll be here.'

I return to my guest house. The tears haven't run dry. I try to understand what's happening here. I've lost control over my emotions, my sanity. I think of Captain; he's got his master's degree, he's found a career, and he's going to take home a good pay check. His parents are proud he's settling down and securing a future. He's doing the Indian thing. Perhaps he hadn't given up on the dream. He'd simply realized that it wasn't meant to be anything more. I had put all that behind me to what purpose. What had I learned so far that I couldn't have by picking up a book or magazine? What if there was nothing to be discovered? What difference did it make? I saw much I didn't like, but I changed nothing. I witnessed many protests, but never joined in any. I spoke to several victims, but helped none. Was I anything more than an armchair critic, except for not sitting in an armchair? I didn't feel any different from the person I was all those miles ago.

The confusion and despair isn't like anything I've experienced in years, not since I returned home from university to tell my parents I was dropping out. Locked inside a dingy, smelly bathroom of a squalid little guest house, in a small town in the middle of nowhere, I'm staring at a broken man in the mirror. What a crappy place to give up on yourself. The thought leads to hysterical laughter, which degenerates into a fresh bout of weeping.

I fall asleep on the dirty tiles.

Kilometer 28380

At 5 a.m. I step out of my room into sleepy darkness. Groping around the unlit hallway I make my way to the reception, and leaning over the counter, I drop off the keys, with the rent tucked under them. Without making a sound, I steal out into the night, rolling Kaya out of the compound. I stroke her tank and whisper a promise never to let her down. It takes a couple of kicks for her engine to splutter alive.

Then Kaya rode out of Amarkantak.

Five kilometers into the ride we entered Chhattisgarh, and instantly the road improved. As we crossed the border I looked over my shoulder, a final glance, a relieved farewell.

A border sign proudly proclaimed: 'Madhya Pradesh Begins.'

Under it someone had painted: 'The Road Ends'.

But I was still riding.

LEG SIXTEEN

I'd Like to Do What You're Doing

CROSSING THE THRESHOLD into Maharashtra there was a marked improvement in the road, but it didn't help Kaya, whose condition only continued to worsen. The engine oil I'd changed at Jabalpur had already turned into a thick black sludge. A harsh knocking sound interrupted the once lovely purr of her engine. The timing was off and she overheated within minutes of riding. Oil stains and soot covered the once lustrous engine shell. The front end wobble had increased sharply, and she pulled violently to the left. Her body was all rattle and squeak.

She pulled up at a highway mechanic on the approaches to Nagpur.

'This bike is in pretty bad shape. What happened to it?' the mechanic asks.

'She's been through a lot,' I sigh.

'It looks like you'll have to open up the engine. I think the pistons are worn out. You need to take it to a proper Bajaj Service Station. You'll find one in Nagpur, but a better option would be Pune or Bombay.'

'Do you think I can ride her to Bombay without making matters worse?'

'Uh . . . you shouldn't have a problem as long as you are careful. Don't ride too fast though, and make sure you stop often so that the engine can cool down. Your other option is to put it on a train to Bombay.'

Kaya took the road. I might have lost faith in myself, but I didn't doubt her, knowing she had more heart than I did. Our immediate intention was getting to Bombay – avoiding any rides that weren't absolutely necessary – yet, as we approached Ajanta I was compelled to take a short detour and drop in at the town of Buldhana, to keep a vague promise made to an unknown person. Since hearing of my journey, Mr. Mayur of Buldhana had been in regular contact with my mum, following my journey and waiting to meet me. He had invoked a promise from my mother that I would visit him when I was passing through Maharashtra, and while I hadn't given it much thought, at the last moment I made a call from Amravati to let him know I was in the vicinity.

'Aha, I've been making so many plans for your visit. You must come to Buldhana and meet me and my friends,' he'd insisted excitedly. 'I am also an adventurer like you.'

It sounded like a pointlessly boring exercise, and I felt little enthusiasm for meeting him or his friends, but I didn't know how to refuse. Riding into the backwater town, I didn't know what to expect. To be honest, I had no expectations at all. I thought I'd drop in, say hello, have a quick cup of tea, and then be on my way. After all, what wisdom did I have to share with them, other than 'don't go to M.P.'.

While Kaya received another oil transfusion at Buldhana's local mechanic, I stepped into the P.C.O. to let Mayur know where I was waiting for him. Within minutes a positively gushing man in his late thirties has my hands enveloped in his, and for a moment I'm worried he's not going to let go. Profusely thanking me for sparing the time, my host – dressed in smart black trousers and white pin-striped shirt, tinted shades resting on his bulbous nose – leads me to his apartment and introduces me to his wife with unconcealed pride.

'This is the young boy I told you about,' he informs her, 'the one who's touring all around the country on his motorcycle . . . alone that too.'

'Sit down, son, you must be tired,' she smiles kindly, betraying none of her husband's fervor. 'I'll bring some snacks and tea.'

'We don't have much time, woman,' Mayur protests. 'I have to take him to the club.'

'You also. If you're in such a hurry, then why did you even bother bringing him here? At least let him rest for some time. Also, he's a guest. How can I let him leave on an empty stomach?'

'Okay,' he surrenders, 'but don't serve too much. I've organized lunch at the club.'

Unheeding, she's already turned her back on us and is making her way towards what I presume is the kitchen. While we are waiting for the snacks to arrive, Mayur calls me over to a small glass shelf, and from the gleam in his eyes – not to mention the eagerness in his voice – I am instantly aware that this is why he's brought me here, to his house. The shelf is a trophy display, filled with medals and certificates awarded to Mayur in various cycling disciplines. Unlocking the cabinet, he reaches inside to delicately withdraw a certificate and holds it out to me.

'I was awarded this by the Olympic committee,' he says, his happiness shining through. 'I cycled across twelve countries, from India to Egypt, as part of a promotional event.'

Suddenly, it all makes sense, why he cares about my journey so much, why he wants to meet me, why he wants to show his support. We are both adventurers, he'd said, believing us to be similar in our shared passion. I am humbled that he thinks my aimless wandering can compare to his Olympian achievement. And all this time, in coming here, I'd assumed I was doing him a favor, blind to the reality that he's the one doing me a service.

At the club I'm greeted with loud cheers and frenzied handshakes by five of Mayur's friends, all in their late thirties and early forties. Two of them are cyclists like him. Also present are two members from the local press and a photographer. It's an animated meeting, and their enthusiasm is infectious. I face a barrage of questions. Fortunately, I don't have to answer any. They are like kids, all of them speaking at once, narrating their own adventures. They reveal a love for the road, and on hearing of my Manali – Leh journey they swear to take it on soon, except on bicycles.

They joke. They laugh.

As for me, I'm overjoyed to be a part of this. What I thought would take up a few minutes of my precious time has gone on for hours. And I don't want it to end. The sun hangs low in the sky when we finally step out into the driveway of the club.

'One minute, please,' Mayur says as we approach Kaya. 'There is one more thing we would like to do.'

'You've already done so much . . .' I protest.

A boy approaches us, carrying a big basket, a cluster of plastic covers slung on his arm. I hold onto bursting emotions as each of the six men removes a garland of marigolds from the basket and drapes it over Kaya. Then they turn their attention to me, each of them handing me a box of sweets, and draping a shawl over my shoulders in felicitation. I can think of no greater display of respect in our country. My uncle has been felicitated, but then again he's a Supreme Court Chief Justice. My father's been felicitated, but then again he's a neurosurgeon of repute. Amitabh Bachchan is felicitated, every other day, but, well, he's a superhero. It's an honor I don't deserve, and the gesture begins to overwhelm me. Please get a grip, I tell myself, or it's going to be a disappointing descent from imagined hero to burbling idiot.

The six men escorted Kaya out of town; a mini-convoy of scooters, mopeds, and motorcycles. Blaring horns. Triumphant fist-pumping. Random yelling. Traffic came to a standstill as the unassuming town gaped at the foolishness. Once on the highway, they surrounded me, wished me luck, and with quick waves peeled away to return to their homes. Of the more than eight thousand photographs I have from my travels, only one of them has me in it, showing a garlanded Kaya and me standing amongst six beaming men. And in that one image I'm reminded of all that I might not have experienced.

While we were at his home, I'd spoken to Mayur about his own experience, wanting to know what he'd learned from it, and how it had changed him as a person. His answer had taken me by surprise. He said he'd never really asked himself those questions. He did it simply because he enjoyed it. For him it had been an opportunity to get out of a shell and do something exciting, something different. Even if only for a short while. Once he'd completed his cycling days, he simply returned to the life he'd left behind. The experience exists as something for him to look back on with pride.

'Would you do the same all over again if you could?' I'd asked.

'I'd do a lot more of it,' he'd replied. 'I'd like to do what you're doing.'

Kilometer 29279

Being forced to slow down changed everything. From the very start, the slower I traveled the more I saw, the more I experienced. But at some point I'd started to chase the destinations instead of enjoying the journey. I'd stopped loving the experience. I'd stopped experiencing the love. It had devolved into a race for the finish line, in hope of some imagined glory. Now the finish line didn't matter. I wasn't even sure I'd get there anymore. I had to take it one day at a time. Once again, each day had become special.

For the first time in a long time, I felt a sense of peace.

We were riding towards Nasik, through sapping heat and draining humidity. Vineyards lined the road, rows and rows of Cabernet and Shiraz, these warm plains of Maharashtra now the premier wine region of a country cultivating an appreciation for fermented grapes. Around thirty kilometers from the city, Kaya stopped to let her engine cool down.

A cyclist passes us by. He comes to a halt a few meters ahead, turns the cycle around and pushes it to where we stand. The cycle is an Atlas, and I'll be damned if they come in models. It's like every Atlas I've had the misfortune of pedaling – no gears, no style, heavy, durable, very cheap. The boy is about sixteen years old, hair parted in the middle and neatly patted down, the first signs of facial hair on his dark, gleaming skin. He wears a thin towel around his neck. Despite the heat and the fact that he's riding a cycle, he looks fresh and eager.

'*Namaste bhaiyya*,' he greets me, 'my name is Vishal. From your luggage I can tell you are on tour. Where are you coming from?'

'Today, from Aurangabad.'

'And where all are you going?'

I explain succinctly.

'Wow! I wish I could do something like that. I also love traveling. Just now I'm returning from a trip to Shirdi.'

'That's more than a hundred and fifty kilometers of cycling.' I'm duly impressed. 'When did you start?'

'Yesterday morning, but I stopped for the night to meet my father. He works on the wine farms. I live with my mother in Nasik.'

'So, you enjoy cycling around.'

'Yes. Every time I get the chance, I go somewhere on my cycle.'

'Then you are quite an adventurer yourself.'

'Nooo!' he blushes, 'it's nothing like what you're doing. Where are you going next, *bhaiyya*?'

'Like you, I'm also on my way to Nasik.'

'*Arre*, wonderful, then you must let me show you around my town.'

'Oh . . . uh, there's no need for you to bother.'

'But I'd really like to. Please, I'm sure you can tell me a lot about traveling.'

'Well, if that's what you want then . . . yeah, fine.'

'Wonderful. You go ahead and I'll catch up with you in Nasik. I can meet you at the entrance to the Sundarnarayan Temple at noon sharp. You ask anybody in town, they'll tell you where the temple is.'

By the time I check into a hotel at Nasik, the sun is at the zenith and my energy levels are at a nadir. For a moment I consider not making our rendezvous, but the thought of leaving Vishal waiting convinces me otherwise. He's already standing at the temple entrance when I get there, and not only has he cycled back to town, he's also found the time to take a shower and change into a pair of crisp, clean clothes. I look like a total bum beside him, but he doesn't seem to notice, or care, and true to his word, for the rest of the day he acts as my guide, taking me on a walking tour of the city. Our entire conversation is in Hindi, and despite repeated requests to call me by name, he only refers to me in the respectful form of *bhaiyya*. Throughout, his enthusiasm is unrestrained.

'*Bhaiyya*, will you come to my house for dinner?' he asks eagerly, at the end of the evening.

'I . . . uh . . . I would love to,' I hesitate, in all honesty not even slightly keen on the idea, 'but really, I don't want you to go to any more trouble on my behalf,' I say, trying to excuse myself.

'It's no trouble at all. I want you to meet my mother. Please *bhaiyya*, it will make her happy . . . I'd really like it.'

'Okay, but I'm coming only to see your mother. I won't stay for dinner.'

'Wonderful *bhaiyya*, you will love her food!'

Vishal leads me to the outskirts of the city, through unlit by-lanes and claustrophobic streets. A hidden turn takes us onto a bumpy dirt path, with puddles of thick sewage. The night is squeezed in by flimsy, ramshackle cubicles patched together with crumbly plaster. A few sturdier buildings are scattered around, highlighting the nothingness of the former. I don't like this place. It's the kind of place stupid travelers are always wandering into in movies, only to never be heard from again. I'm very aware of the camera slung over my shoulder, which he's been particularly interested in all evening. What if he's trying to rob me?

We stop near the very edge of the 'colony', beyond which lies only darkness . . . and the smell of human waste. I have entered a slum of Nasik.

'This is my house,' Vishal points to a box-like structure hiding in the shadows, the paint on the walls long since washed away. Two makeshift steps lead to a rickety green door, damp and half-eaten, barely hanging on to the hinges. The door opens, revealing a thin and tired looking woman dressed in a light brown sari with red borders. She wears a big smile on her face, and her eyes shine in the dim light.

'Meet my mother,' he says, 'Ma, this is my brother.'

'*Namaste maaji.*'

'*Namaste beta*. Come in, come in.'

The house is a single room that would give a shipping container a superiority complex. The walls are sooty and the plaster peeling. A large wooden trunk with mattresses piled on it acts as the bed. It takes up one entire side of the room. The opposite side is the cooking area, leaving a few feet of space to move about. The cooking area consists of a shelf with methodically arranged steel containers and utensils, a pot of water, and a kerosene stove on the floor. Beside the stove and water pot stands a shrine, a small stool with the idols of Rama and Sita.

Vishal and I sit down on the multifunctional cot/couch/trunk. Ma hunkers down on the floor, looking up at us. There are two girls, flowers in their hair, draped in crisp saris; the younger stands by the corner, the other is crouched next to the stool/ shrine.

'This is my younger daughter Meena, and the elder one is Uma,' Ma introduces.

'*Namaste,*' I nod my head dutifully, a false smile hiding my uneasiness. As soon as the introductions are done the girls leave the house and go over to their uncle's place next door.

'I'll make some tea for you. Dinner will still take a few minutes.'

'Please mother, I've only come here to meet you. I don't want to trouble you.'

'You call me mother, and then you talk about troubling me. What kind of a mother will I be if I don't even feed you? You tell me about yourself . . .'

Still crouched near the floor Ma starts the kerosene stove. She is coughing. There is no milk in the house she informs Vishal, asking him to run over to the uncle's place and bring some over.

'*Maaji*, I really don't need tea. I'm not too fond of it anyway.'

'Nonsense, you will love my tea. Run along Vishal, and come back fast.'

'You have a fine son there,' I say when he's gone, and then go silent, not sure what to talk to her about. What I'm most aware of is my uneasiness in these surroundings, too distracted by the poverty and distrustful of their motives.

'Yes, Vishal is a piece of my heart, a lovely boy. Studies very well . . . always helpful. Always wants to do something or the other . . .'

'That's so true, he's full of energy.'

'He never gives me any trouble. My real worry is about Uma, we need to get her married soon. She's seventeen years already. I should have started looking by now, but where . . . you know Vishal's father works in the fields . . . a decent man, but he drinks too much, and most of the money he earns goes away on liquor,' she sighs. 'I'm not too well, but I'm forced to work as a maid in people's houses. Without money it will be impossible to get her married, and how ever hard I try we still have very little saved up.'

The direction this conversation has taken only increases my discomfort, confirming my doubts. I am convinced that at some point they are going to ask me to help them out with a loan or something of the sort. 'Yes, weddings are so expensive nowadays,' I nod lamely. 'My cousin got married recently and it caused much stress to—'

My platitudes are interrupted by Vishal's return, carrying in his hand a steel tumbler three-fourths filled with milk, which he hands over to his mother. The tea is served, and the conversation turns to travel and what Vishal wants to do with his life. There is no further mention of money, and in a short time dinner is ready.

'You just eat my mum's food and see. Mmmm, delicious,' Vishal says. 'What about your mother?'

'Uh . . . she's a great cook as well.'

'One day I'll ride down to Hyderabad on a motorcycle, will you invite me over?'

'Of course, and I'll ask her to prepare a special banquet for you.'

'We have only simple food, *beta*,' Ma says.

'Please don't worry about me. I'm not too picky about what I eat,' I assure her, taking the plate she holds out to me. The food is plain, dry chapatti, mixed vegetables, and chilly pickle. And it's delicious. Yet I find it impossible to relax and enjoy the meal. I don't fully understand why I feel the way I do. I've seen some basic, meager living all over India. I've experienced their hospitality before, and have been more than happy to accept it. Why is this so different? Could it be because this was the first such encounter in an urban setting? There is no rationality in thinking that rural India is more selfless or safe, still it's what my subconscious seems to believe. It is how my prejudices lean. After dinner I sit and talk for a while, all the time looking for an opening to make my exit. Even as I worry I'm hating myself for the way I feel; the doubt and guilt collide. They have been nothing but friendly – why can't I open up for a second?

'*Chalo, bhaiyya*, you look tired,' Vishal says finally. 'I'll show you to the main road.'

'Yes, it's getting late,' I agree, relieved to be done. 'Thank you for everything, *maaji*.'

'Thanks for what? I didn't do anything special.'

'It was very special for me.'

'You will not forget us, will you?'

'How can I?'

'You are a good boy, take care of yourself,' she hugs me.

I follow Vishal's cycle in silence, lost in my own thoughts, till he stops at the main street. 'Just follow this road and you will reach the temple. From there you know the way to the hotel, yes?'

'Yes, I am sure I can find my way back. Um . . . bye then.'

'*Bhaiyya*, can you do me a favor?'

Here it comes, I think. Perhaps I wasn't so wrong after all to be on my guard. 'Sure, what can I do for you?' I ask.

'See . . . I was wondering if you will come to my college tomorrow. I would like to introduce you to my teachers and some classmates.'

'What?' I'm startled by the request. Does this kid really think I'm someone special?

'My history teacher would love to meet you. He's always talking about all the monuments in India and the places he's been to.'

'Actually, I intend to leave for Bombay early in the morning. You see . . . I . . .' I mutter, trying to wriggle out of it, when it suddenly occurs to me that I'm being a complete jerk. 'You know what, I'd love to come.' Oddly enough, this time I mean it.

'Really? Thank you very much, *bhaiyya*. We'll meet again at the Sundarnarayan Temple at nine in the morning.'

'I'll be there.'

'Good night, *bhaiyya*.'

'Vishal, is there anything else I can do for you? Anything you need?'

'No, *bhaiyya*. Why?'

'Uh . . . just wondering . . .'

He is waiting for me the next morning, bright and eager as ever. He greets everybody at the college compound. And he takes great pride in showing me off to every single one of them.

'My brother has come from Hyderabad on a motorcycle,' he announces. 'He's going around the entire country. You want to see his bike? It's standing with the watchman. But don't touch anything, okay?'

All I can do is offer them sheepish grins.

His teacher is a sharp man, a lover of Indian history, who thinks highly of Vishal, and before I realize what's happening I've been cornered into giving a talk in his next class. Speaking isn't my forte, especially not impromptu, and most definitely not in Hindi, but I gamely step before a hushed audience. Over the next fifteen minutes I butcher the *matra bhasha*, but the words spill out, rambling, incoherent, yet they flow eagerly, with purpose. Because for the first time I spoke not about myself and what I hoped to accomplish. Lying awake in bed last night I'd had a lot of time to think long and hard about these things.

'A journey like this will undoubtedly change you,' I tell them, 'but then change will happen regardless. It's not even about the places I've seen. All that matters is that I would have never met all the people I did if I'd stayed at home. But we don't really have to travel across the country to find them. They are all around us, if only we open our eyes and our minds. What the traveling did is take me out of my bubble and force me into contact with them. Between all the touted wanderings, which are mostly meaningless, I occasionally, and unintentionally, run into people like Vishal, and without my recognizing it just then, the journey becomes meaningful. Though you're all sitting here listening to me, he's the one who's the real hero.'

The class stands up and applauds passionately when I finish. I'd like to think the ovation is for Vishal.

Kilometer 29805

Kaya was on her last leg to Bombay, just two hundred kilometers more to the much needed attention of a mechanic. She'd just spent two hundred days on the road, and covered a distance of thirty thousand kilometers. Regardless of what came next, we'd done pretty well.

While getting to Bombay is one thing, getting into Bombay is an epic in itself, with the last twenty kilometers taking longer than the two hundred before them. But that's only a foretaste of things to come. Officially this is a metropolitan of 2 crore people, and then there's the population that doesn't exist – on the streets, in the slums, floating, disappearing, nameless, faceless, millions of them. So it's only natural that in a city of such epic populations, the most difficult commodity to find is space. Nothing is more valuable in Bombay; the space to breathe, the space to think, the space to weep without being heard, and most significantly, the space to live. Housing is so precious, if you have a bathroom to your name, ideally you'd split it into five parts and rent each one out as a studio apartment. As for where to then conduct your daily ablutions, well, there's always the road. There are probably people in Bombay who own a Mercedes simply because it's more spacious than an apartment, and a lot more affordable.

The greatest excitement when traveling through Bombay is not visiting its nightclubs or getting a role in Bollywood, but to find a reasonably unaffordable place to stay. Don't waste your breath looking for cheap – you're more likely to discover WMDs in Iraq or life on Mars. My *hotel* was squeezed onto the terrace of an old building, which had inexplicably survived the monsoon. The room had no windows, no ventilation, and if I were so arrogant as to stretch my hands, I'd have punched a hole through the plywood walls. Coffins generally come with more space and better wood. The manager was a grouchy sob who thought I was being unreasonably high-maintenance for wanting some light in my coffin. Though he was kind enough to warn me that he wasn't responsible for thieves. In the end, I settle for the overpriced rathole, which even the rats have evacuated in disgust, sharing my space with bedbugs and the previous occupant's sweat.

Having settled me in, Kaya went straight to the Bajaj Service Centre even before they had raised the shutters. Hearing her story, the manager promised to prioritize the work and provide the best treatment. The service engineer returned from a test ride with a grave expression. The diagnosis was bad. They had to rebore the engine, and change the timing mechanism and piston rings. In human terms, this was an open heart surgery.

'You must be brave,' the mechanic whispered, putting his hand on my shoulder reassuringly. 'I'll do the best I can. The rest is up to fate.'

It's the residual Bollywood effect.

Without Kaya, my wanderings around Bombay were at the mercy of its suburban railway system, the lifeline of this overgrown city. The 'Locals' are the most mind-boggling transport system known to humankind – if any alien species possesses something similar, we can comfortably conclude that they are a primitive life form indeed – and holds the world record for passenger traffic, transporting more than sixty lakh commuters each day. *Sixty lakh!* That translates to over two billion commuters annually, about a quarter of the world's population. The Bombay trains see more people in a day than most nations see in a lifetime.

During rush hour, the number of passengers exceeds the legal capacity by three times. If, for some perverse reason, you want to know what a canned sardine feels like, the Locals are your ticket to finding out. The scary bit is that they even have a suitably officious name for the phenomenon: Super Dense Crush Load. Those who can't find a place in the train hang out of it, from open doorways and window bars. For the daring heroes there's always the roof, and these are electric trains we're talking about.

People don't get on, or off, the Locals, instead you just stand there and get swept along by the surge of humanity. If you're unlucky, you end up at the wrong station. If you're really unlucky, you end up under the train. Death is common on the railway lines of Bombay, even without terrorist assistance. Every year, more than three thousand people die on, beside, or under the Locals. If this happened in the developed world, they'd have declared a national emergency and overhauled the system. Here the trains go on, as do life and death, and a whole lot of craziness. People live on the train, and make a living off of it. It brings lovers together, and makes friends of strangers. Under its silent gaze, men have been stabbed and women raped, the passengers looking on as mute as the train. The last time I traveled by Local was with a girlfriend. When we got off the train, she suddenly went into hysterics. There was fresh semen dribbling down her pants. It's remarkable where the culprit found the space to get an erection.

This time I was alone, and thankful for the space to move my thoughts around if nothing else. After a few stops I even found the space to wriggle my fingers. When we're talking about millions of people, it goes without saying that at least a few of them have serious issues. But in all these teeming millions, to end up standing next to one is simply bad karma. While I took pleasure in moving my fingers, the unkempt man next to me used his moving fingers for a pleasurable purpose. He busily crushed a bright white paste between his fingers and palm. Once impressed with its consistency, he proceeded to lick his hands clean. Whatever he was on, it must have been pretty potent. First he started mumbling. Then he violently smacked his forehead with the palm of his hand. I'm not sure what unnerved me more; Mr. Crazy punishing himself, or all the others, blind to what was happening.

In an attempt to ignore the craziness, I looked out of the moving train. In retrospect, that wasn't a good idea either. I found myself staring at a line of bared buttocks, and lots of human shit. For wholly unfathomable reasons, the favorite open-air squatting place is about two inches from a hurtling train. People casually walked up to the tracks and hunkered down with their backs to the lines, chatting and sharing a cigarette while going about their duties. A few squat so near to the tracks, I'm assuming they want the train to wipe their bums clean as it races by. Some of the train-related deaths most probably involve people who've misjudged their posture.

The attempted distraction didn't work, especially not when Mr. Crazy started to violently throw up. There are a lot of things you can disregard in life, but not somebody else's puke dribbling down your back. Fortunately, I was standing a couple of inches to the side, but the man in front of me took a direct hit. There was no anger and no recriminations. The puked-on gave the puker a look of disgust, not that it made the slightest difference. The puker had gone back to punishing himself. The victim calmly removed his handkerchief and held it out to me. At first I didn't understand, and when I realized that what he wanted was for me to help wipe the vomit off, my stomach performed an acrobatic lurch. I would have drawn back in horror, but there was no place for such theatrics. Instead, I shrank into my clothes, hoping to disappear. The look the puked-on gave me was far worse than anything he'd reserved for the puker. One of the other passengers took the kerchief from him and calmly wiped his back clean. The soiled kerchief was then passed on to another passenger who threw it out the window. A brief smile of acknowledgement passed between them, after which each retreated into his own space and thought. It was a daily act of heroism and my cowardice made me the villain.

I've never liked Bombay, or its politics, which pretends that pride can be derived from mangling a historically evocative name. Regardless, I have to acknowledge that this is also a city of exceptional bravery. It is a city full of heroes, with no reference to the idiots flexing their muscles on screen. Less than a year after my 'horrendous experience' on the train, the Locals were hit by seven explosions, resulting in 209 dead and another 700 injured. Obviously, none of our reel heroes were at any of the sites, nor did they come to anyone's rescue later. That bit of heroism was left to the real people. The blasts struck a few minutes past six. Four hours later, the trains were running again. The next day Bombay returned to work as usual. By train.

There's no place for the meek in this city.

Kilometer 30064

I started my final day in Bombay by mourning the death of a stranger, a nameless corpse.

Turning up at the historic Crawford Market early in the morning, I found a body sprawled across the pavement, naked except for a flimsy rag wrapped around his waist. A drunk, I thought, but a second glance proved otherwise, for in it I saw an emaciated body, face sunken in and skin sallow. I saw the eyes, wide open and vacant, the absolute stillness, the half-open mouth. I saw the flies that hovered around his lips, and the ants trailing down his fingers. The death did not bother me as much as the ignobility of it. Feet rushed past the body without a stutter, maybe a side step or a quickening of pace. It was an obstacle, nothing more. Around it, the trucks continued to be unloaded, men opened the stalls, and women picked up groceries. The body was invisible. In a world that's short on time for the living, it's probably hard to spare any for the dead.

I stepped into the small cafe, in front of which the body lay, and spoke to the owner. He cursed the beggar for not finding somewhere else to die, before informing me he'd already called the municipal corporation and was waiting for the body to be cleared away. I sat down at the cafe and ordered a tea. My eyes stayed on the body, looking at it between passing legs. Who was this man, who'd found an anonymous death in an impersonal city?

No matter how often I visit Bombay, after two days I'm invariably defeated by the abjectness of its poverty and suffering. We are a nation of beggars, but nowhere else are they as wretched; lepers with decaying flesh, diseased children with broken bodies, men with missing legs, and women with grotesque deformities. I hand over the change in my pocket to an armless boy, guilty for the coins I have, guilty for the hand with which I give them. We are a nation of inequality, but nowhere else is it defined in such stark contrast. A chain of high-rise luxury apartments stare down at sewage-swamped slums. Below the giant billboard advertising surgical weight reduction, a shriveled-up hag scavenges the garbage for a half-eaten banana. In front of the Armani storefront sit children in unbranded nakedness. Unlike Hyderabad or

Bangalore, here there's no escaping this reality till it desensitizes you. Bombay forces even its heroes to be heartless.

The body still lay on the pavement, three hours after I'd sat down at the cafe. I asked the owner why nothing was done about it yet. He shrugged his shoulders, spewing curses at the police and the municipal corporation. It's probably still too early for them. Then he cursed the dead man again. I needed to get out of here.

By early evening Kaya was making her way out of the city. At a Marine Drive traffic signal, a bunch of half-naked children gathered around us, cupped hands extended, wailing incoherently. Snotty, grime-covered, ragged . . . beautiful. Pulling over to the side, I rummaged through my backpack to extract the shawls that I'd been honored with in Bundhela, and handed them over to the kids.

I hope Mayur and friends approve.

LEG SEVENTEEN

Life is a Beach

KAYA SHONE AS SHE made her way across Maharashtra. Fresh, rejuvenated. Her engine still needed to be run in, slow and steady over the next two thousand kilometers. She sounded different now. Gone the raw growl which set my pulse racing. More mellow, her beat was clean and regular. But the soul hadn't changed. She rode with passion.

Crossing the border into Goa, I was simply returning to my favorite hangout. Through four years of university I spent more time on the sands of Goa than in any classroom. Only four hours and forty-two rupees by train between a lecture on fluid mechanics and a rave on the beach, I made the effort to get there every weekend, but rather annoyingly, the university decided to stay closed every Saturday – Sunday that I showed up, preventing me from getting a decent education. Kaya cruised. She knew this road, smooth, gentle curves, the murky seas and frothy breakers, never near, but never far away. I recognized the old lighthouse, the bent over palm tree, the misshapen rock. Red earth rolled by. A bottle-green river flowed beside us, wide, calm. Slender brown boats fished the waters, rowed by long poles. Colors! They define Goa.

Four hundred and fifty years of Portuguese influence has left Goans with alarming names like D'Silva, D'Souza, and D'Costa, and a laidback disposition that is foreign to the rest of the nation. The men are boisterous fellows dressed in bright singlets and even louder shorts. The women, when not in their spacious nightgowns, are partial to floral dresses that went out of style with the Inquisition. A fair number of Goans continue to speak Portuguese, looking back on their pre-Indian days with nostalgia and complaining about their forced liberation – though with the Conquistadors currently sporting a negative growth rate, I'm willing to bet that tune has changed. Especially considering that Goa is India's richest state per capita.

Goa also happens to be India's smallest state, the runt who for the most part is forgotten by the big boys, except of course when they are looking to have a good time. The diminutive nature of Goa is such that, despite being as populous as some countries, most visitors refer to the state as if it were a smallish city. You'll never hear someone going to Bombay or Hampi saying they're going to Maharashtra or Karnataka, no, they'll tend to be a lot more specific. But you could be going for a weekend to Anjuna or a month to Palolem, regardless, no one ever mentions where in Goa they're going to – nope, we're just going to Goa. As far as the world is considered, Goa is just one big vacation.

Unlike any other tourist destination in the country, Goa wears two distinct faces – one an international white, the other a domestic brown – and the two rarely smile at each other. Annually, Goa sees more visitors than it has citizens, and of the twenty lakh plus passersby, nearly a quarter are foreigners. Most of the white folk descend on Goa's beaches to sun and sin in the company of other white folk. Meanwhile, a large number of brown people come here to see the white people. Tragically for all the *desis* whose sole purpose is meeting *goras*, Goa attracts the kind of foreigner who comes to India hoping to never come in contact with any Indians.

It's such an irony really, because Goa is where we go to be as un-Indian as possible, where we pretend real hard to be 'liberal'. Other than the white skin, Goa's premier attraction is the opportunity to leave our taboos behind, breaking off the shackles of orthodoxy, and running away from the morality police – who as individuals are of as much value as a used condom, and as a mob can cause more damage than the AIDS epidemic. Goa is where Indian women wear bikinis. Where Indian men ogle women in bikinis. And where the two can embrace in public. Goa is where the dutiful daughter-in-law can sip her Bacardi with conspicuous abandon and the teetotaler son turns into a coke-snorting fiend.

Much, of course, has changed since my first visits to these beaches in the nineties, when I felt, and was treated, like a second-class citizen in comparison to the *firangs*. Gone are the days when the homestays and cottages in Anjuna were unofficially 'white only' and our presence was seen as 'bad for business' – especially not with today's Indian disposing his income far more liberally than any backpacking European. In some places the two worlds have collided and colluded, and in others each has created its own disparate imprint. A long, long walk along the coast of North Goa transports you from scene to scene, and we're not talking vistas here.

Vagator plays host to the hard drugs and the hardest raves, electronic beats thumping at high decibels. This is the white-dominated land of New Age junkies. Beyond it, Anjuna is the modified, stratified, and much bastardized version of hippydom – ganja power, bare-naked bodies, and unwashed dreadlocks, rustic restaurants under palm trees and soft trance wafting through smoke-rich air. Across the headland, Baga is home to the yuppie Indian from Bombay and Bangalore and Hyderabad, fattened wallets desperately seeking to shed weight. The beaches are lined with trendy cafes and boutique hotels, backed by discotheques and handicraft stores. At night the crowds drive up in fancy cars, step out in designer clothes, and groove to hip-hop. Further down the coast, at Calangute, a seething mass of middle-class Indian families let the waves lap at their ankles – it's hard to go too far into the water when you're burdened down by multiple layers of clothing. Men in neat pants and full-sleeve shirts stand with shoes in hand, watching over the picnic bags. Fully-dressed women shriek excitedly at the approaching waves, the youngest kids huddled protectively between their legs. Meanwhile, the adolescent sons are pretending to enjoy themselves, all the while thinking of ways to find the mythical nudist beaches.

In retrospect, for all the time I spent on these shores, I can recollect few moments of genuine pleasure, having spent most of it trying to be someone I wasn't. Goa always made me feel incredibly lonely, where I first began to wonder about identity and why I fit in nowhere. Regardless of which side of the divide I hung out on, it never played out the way I imagined. I always remained an outsider. It was a clash of values and wants, an opposition between heart and mind, a conflict of pride and prejudice. Walking along the sands of Baga, it occurred to me that three-fourths into my journey towards Indianness, I still didn't feel like I belonged on any side. What comforted me was that I no longer felt the need to belong.

Kaya cruised out of North Goa, heading south to, well, South Goa, stopping along the way at Old Goa. Within the confines of these historic ruins stands the black granite Basilica Bom Jesus, an unlikely building to find one of the greatest miracles of Christendom, the body of St. Francis Xavier, which simply refuses to decompose.

In 1552, the Spanish Jesuit Francis Xavier passed away on the small island of Sancian near Malacca. With no ships available for the immediate transport of the body to Christian soil, it was sealed with lime in a coffin and buried. When exhumed a few months later, the body was found to be intact. Hailing it a miracle, one of the sailors cut a piece of the flesh as a relic, and blood flowed from the cut, as if from a living being. The body was then taken to Malacca and buried there, only to be exhumed nine months later and transported to Goa, still un-decomposed. When these stories reached the ears of the Pope, he promptly had the tomb reopened, Xavier's right arm cut off and sent to him to verify the facts. The satisfied Pope recognized the miracle, and Xavier was declared a saint. While the Saint's saintliness protected his body from natural decomposition, it has failed to save his body from continuous human mutilation. Over the years bits and pieces of the miraculous body keep disappearing. He's lost an arm, a leg, an ear, and almost all his toes. In a most recent episode of disturbing proportions, a super-devout woman, pretending to pay obeisance, bit off the saint's toe and tried to smuggle it out in her mouth. Fortunately, I was saved from any such temptation by the fact that the silver casket is only open to the public – with the body put on display – once every ten years, and I happened to be a year too late, or nine years too early. Though, the rate at which his body parts are disappearing, I doubt there will be much to display by 2014.

Before long Kaya was on the shores of South Goa. Beaches. Sun. Sand. Palms. Foreigners. What's the difference? For one, it's more south. Also, it's more beautiful and tranquil. This is where travelers come to recuperate from the excesses of its northern counterpart. The sense of serenity is highlighted by the coco-shacks, basic single rooms made of wood and cane that stand on stilts. Each night, with the high tide, waves ride up the beach to wash under your room, leaving you suspended in a shimmering black void.

It was my last night at Palolem Beach when just before sunset a commotion broke out on the northern end. I saw people rush out of cottages and run to the edge of the sea. Two youths stood in the shallows, waving frantically. Their screams were driven by panic. Then a hush descended on the beach. The faces around were mainly white and they wore worried looks. 'Somebody may have drowned'; the word spread across the beach like a tidal wave. Nervous glances were cast in search of friends and acquaintances. Within minutes the picture became clearer. It was an Indian tourist who'd been swept out to sea. The immediate sense of relief that swept through the crowd was so palpable, I could have drowned in it. The tension dissipated, to be replaced by simple curiosity. It wasn't a big deal anymore, since the dead person didn't belong to the international traveler community. A short while later, fishermen retrieved the body and brought it back to the shore. I walked over to where the drowned boy's friends gathered around his body, shocked, inconsolable. He couldn't have been more than twenty years old. He'd gone swimming in his jeans and T-shirt.

By this time life had returned to normalcy. The shacks were rustling up food and the sunbathers were washing off their lotions. Laughter carried in the air, as did the first notes of a live band. This is Goa, and in Goa, life is a beach.

LEG EIGHTEEN

They Care More for Monkeys than for Humans

KAYA WAS STOPPED at the Karnataka border checkpost to be searched – for every enterprising visitor tries to smuggle a few bottles of tax-free liquor out of Goa – but was then waved past without examination when the cops heard about her dreams. We were greeted by clouds of clayey dust. The road turned evil. We fought it patiently. Carefully. Still, we took a beating. Kaya kept riding, through the bedlam of Belgaum to the ruins of Bijapur.

Bijapur had so many impressive tombs you'd think the people here did more dying than living. The grandest of these deathly monuments is the sixteenth-century Gol Gumbaz, a big box crowned by a very big dome, which, with an internal diameter of 38 meters, is the second largest dome ever built, just losing out to St. Peter's Basilica in Rome. Besides obesity, the tomb is remarkable for its acoustics, with the softest word carrying across the cavernous chamber and echoing as many as ten times. Whatever Mohammed Adil Shah had hoped to listen to by being interred with a state-of-the-art sound system, I'm sure it's not Ramu, Sunita, and Iqbal repeatedly yelling out their own names. Every time a crowd of tourists bursts in, clapping, hooting and screaming, the ensuing effect is akin to a grand piano dropping on your head, while someone plays a terrible rendition of Beethoven. And what's with this narcissistic obsession we have with our names that we insist on shouting them at every echo point and scribbling them on every monument? Do we really require constant reminding of who we are?

Beyond the tombs of Bijapur, Kaya followed an unpaved road through unnamed settlements to dusty Aihole village, in the rural wilderness of northern Karnataka. Spread out along the river Malaprabha, surrounded by rocky hills, it formed the 'cradle of Hindu architecture'. While Christianity took hold in Europe, and Prophet Mohammed promulgated Islam to the Arab world, in India a Hindu revolution took place in the form of temple design, littering the landscape with 125 temples. The A.S.I. – while doing a sparingly commendable job of the restorations – seems to find nomenclature a rather monumental problem. With no signboards anywhere, it's impossible to tell what you're looking at, when it was built, or even why, so I simply wandered around pretending to know what I was doing.

Approaching Badami, the landscape turned other worldly. Soil turned to rust. Rough-hewn hills, a similar red, loomed beside us, eroded into a fantasy vision. Large boulders balanced precariously atop each other. In time they will topple. The trees appeared extraterrestrial as well – leafless; long, twisted branches reaching over the road like skeletal fingers.

Flanked by rugged, red sandstone outcrops, the mossy green Agastya Lake is the heart of the erstwhile capital of the Chalukya dynasty. Cut into the vertical cliffs are four grand cave temples, with columned halls, larger-than-life sculptures, and intricate friezes. A series of wobbly, uneven stone steps wind their way to the fortified summit of the cliffs, through a narrow gully in the rock. Indiana Jones-style – whip excluded – I drag myself up boulders and leap over yawning gaps to the craggy edges.

The ruins of sculpted temples and once-mighty bastions grow out of each splinter rock. Fractured elephant heads stare at me through sightless eyes. Toppled spires stand amidst their own rubble. Nothing stirs atop the hill but me . . . but not for long. The ruins are not abandoned, and as the sun begins to descend, the inheritors of these ruins return to their homes. They run up the slopes with nonchalant grace, playfully leaping across the gaps, dancing on the teetering spires and dangling from the ledges, all the while scratching their hairy bums. It's so effortless, they'd put Indy to shame. Captivated by their antics, I don't realize they're surrounding me in a pincer movement until it's too late. Their intentions don't look too honorable either.

'I come in peace,' I tell them.

No reply.

'Hanuman is a great god,' I say, trying a different approach. 'I honor him. Really, I do.'

Still no reply. They close in on me. The nearest monkey stretches out his/her – I'm too preoccupied with claws and fangs to identify requisite body part – paw in an unmistakable gesture. He/she wants the satchel on my shoulder.

'No good trade,' I protest. 'No for eat, only for read. I go now ok . . .'

'Khwaaaaw!' he/she growls. I don't speak the language, but the message is clear, roughly translating to: 'your bag or your eyeballs'. The bloody extortionists!

I consider running, then, recollecting the acrobatics they've displayed in getting up the hill, I accept the futility of any escape attempt. Holding on to my camera, I surrender the daypack without a fight. I've learned from experience not to trifle with the Hanuman Monkey. Ignoring my pleading, they rummage through my bag and find a pack of cookies that I've forgotten about.

'I didn't remember, I swear. I wasn't trying to cheat . . .' They don't care to listen, so I just shut up.

Next they pull out Gregory Robert's *Shantaram* from the bag and tear a few pages out of the book. Toilet paper, I presume. Finding nothing else of value in it, they discard my bag for me to pick up. Having no qualms about witnesses, or being identified, they generously pose for a few photographs after the robbery. We hang out together for a while, sitting in a row along the rock edge, feet and tails dangling, watching the sun disappear. They aren't bad chaps really, I conclude, just misguided.

It could have been the beginning of a beautiful friendship. Unfortunately, I need to get off this crag before the light fades completely. A small archaeological museum stands at the foot of the hill, and despite being past closing hour, the curator lets me in.

'Did you have any problem with the monkeys?' he asks.

'Uh, nothing troubling . . . I've had a fair number of run-ins with them before.'

'Yes, they aren't really harmful, but they'll snatch anything they can lay their hands on. The real problem, though, is the litter they are creating, especially plastic bottles. Our Badami monkeys seem to have developed a taste for mineral water, and they have become experts at unscrewing caps. Almost every visitor who goes up complains that his water or coke bottle has been stolen. Every couple of months we have to go and clean up the mess these monkeys make.'

'Well, I guess they're only imitating us.'

'Ha, ha, I never thought about it like that. Let me tell you about this funny thing that happened two years ago,' he grins. 'Some excitable chaps from the municipal corporation decided that they had to put an end to this monkey infestation, and so they went up the hill intending to capture the monkeys and relocate them. Ha, ha. That evening we had to go rescue the municipal fellows from the monkeys.'

Obviously, they had never read their Ramayana.

Kilometer 32358

Kaya made her way south towards Hampi, along a road that's always been bumpy. The hilly landscape is strewn with boulders, as if they rained down from the sky. The heat is harsh, soaking into the granite expanse. There are monkeys everywhere, roaming these barren hills. After all, this is their kingdom, Kishkindha, the mighty capital of the monkeys, as described by our hallucinogen-induced mythology. Every rock here is associated with stories from the Ramayana, and Lord Hanuman, the most fabulous monkey on earth, was born on the Anjaneya Hill overlooking Hampi.

I found myself troubled as Kaya eased out of Hampi, back onto an unfriendly highway. A dark stain had started spreading across her engine. The oil was seeping through again, viscous, gangrenous. Her engine sizzled, heat rising from it like a fever. The cancer was back . . . for good. I caressed her tank. She kept riding.

Once in Shimoga district, all traces of asphalt disappeared. The traffic was gone as well. We had the road to ourselves, to do as we wished. My only wish was to get off it as soon as possible. The rocks were replaced by trees, hard stone by lush fields. The clouds opened up. I lifted my face to the sky and let the water stream down. I prayed for it to keep Kaya's engine cool. The rain stayed with us all the way up the sweeping hills of the Western Ghats till she halted at Jog Falls.

The Sharavathi River rushes across a rocky plateau and plunges 253 meters straight down, making it the highest waterfall in India. At the summit, the river splits into four separate streams, each one thundering down as an individual with its own identity and character. The furthest is called Raja for its majesty and dignity, the second one is the noisy Roarer, while Rocket emerges from a narrow gap with great velocity, and Rani flows with the swaying grace of a lady. Or that's what the tourist brochure imagines. But I see nothing that churns or roars, or displays any signs of majesty. The words that come to mind are slobber, splutter, scrape, and splatter. Miserly streams drip down the wrinkled cliff, like strands of hair on an elephant's side. My shower comes with more force than Rocket. In fact, I can't tell where this incessant drizzle ends and the waterfalls begin.

I'm wondering if I've come to the wrong place, despite the large signboards, rows of shops, and the teeming crowds insisting that I haven't. College students, families, young couples, and tour groups, they've all turned up in substantial numbers. And they appear to be having a grand time. Loud and excitable, most of them are displaying a customary enthusiasm for decorating the landscape. Standing atop the cliff overlooking the falls, their greatest joy is in seeing how far the garbage they are throwing will carry. Watching the juice cartons and coke cans hurtling down the cliff, I'm confident that – regardless of Jog's global status as a waterfall – it is surely the world's largest trash can.

'Where's all the water?' I ask a store keeper. 'With so much rain, shouldn't the river be in spate?'

'Ah yes, but the river is blocked by the Linganamakki Dam upstream. They only open the gates if the reservoir is full . . . or during the holidays when there are a lot of tourists.'

'But today is Sunday, and look at the number of people here.'

'Huh! It must be the wrong Sunday then,' he shrugs.

The crowds disappear before nightfall and a pleasurable calm descends. Taking permission from the tourist officer, I pitch my tent beside a railing overlooking the falls. In the embrace of solitude, the silvery threads dance through the veil of darkness.

Daybreak is murky but without rain. The lack of water provides the opportunity to climb down to the crater at the bottom. I follow the steep path that winds down the cliff face, and all along the trail I discover undeniable evidence of Jog Falls' popularity. Wills Navy Cut cigarette boxes, Uncle Chipps baggies, Frooti and Appy tetrapacks, Kit Kat wrappers, paper plates, mineral water packets, shards of broken beer bottles, and Rajesh's undying love for Sonal emblazoned on a rock. Strange fucking ways we have of expressing our fondness for a place. I don't understand the mindset of the authorities either. The costs of cleaning up this mess on a regular basis can't be that crippling, yet they seem to be waiting for nature to do its best. Unable to ignore it, I spend the better part of the morning collecting the larger and more offensive looking trash . . . well, at least the stuff that doesn't look dangerous to touch. I carry the heavy pile back to the top, where I discover that there aren't any garbage bins. Naturally, I walk over to the administrative office and leave them a present at the doorstep, feeling terrible for not gift wrapping it.

That good deed completed, Kaya followed the course of the Sharavathi River as it flowed down the slopes, through a thick green curtain of leaves, meandering through the haze-covered valley. Descending to the bottom, she stopped for a rest.

I watch the dark waters flow beside me.

'Have you drunk the Sharavathi water?' a middle-aged man in white lungi asks me in Kannada. His peppered moustache rises in a smile to reveal cracked yellow teeth. 'It is the purest water in India.'

'Is it really?'

'Yes, really. Anybody who has tried it will tell you . . . it's better than drinking coconut water. You want to try . . .' he nods eagerly, leading me to a spot where a thin stream has been channeled from the river. Getting down on my knees, I scoop the shimmering flow into my mouth. It is cold, and sweet.

'That's really nice . . . very refreshing,' I acknowledge.

'I told you. Here we say that the Sharavathi tastes as sweet as a kind word.'

Kilometer 33175

Kaya descended from the hills, rolling to the blue edges of our western shores. She traced the Konkan Coast along NH17, the most pleasurable road in India, extending all the way to land's end at the southern tip of the country. The inspiration for all that I'm doing now dates back to the years spent in this region. It was on this road that my passion for biking was born. It was here that I first succumbed to wanderlust.

The road ran flat; delicate curves hugging the coast. Thin streams rushed to join the sea, under the shadow of lanky coconut palms. Fields of golden harvest swayed in the wind, coconut palms standing over them like giraffes. Frothy waves washed onto the shore, lapping at the feet of swaying coconut fronds. Traditional

Konkani houses, mud brick and red tiles, hid behind coconut groves. It was a world of coconuts. There's little remarkable about the Aussie claim that they have more sheep than people – not when they barely have any people to begin with. But when I tell you that the Konkan coast has more coconut trees than India has people, you should be duly impressed, for that's more than a billion coconut trees we're talking about.

Kaya spent the entire day riding through a curtain of rain as we slowly drew closer to my ex-university at Manipal. It was a familiar homecoming. A single word can describe my time at Manipal: wet. It poured for around eight months a year – the monsoons, pre-monsoons, retreating monsoons, post-retreating monsoons, pre-winter showers, post-winter storms. During summer it turned into a sauna; instead of rain, we had sweat pouring off us. In Manipal, being wet was the normal state of existence.

One after the other, Kaya rode past the colleges – Kasturba Medical College, Manipal Institute of Communication, the School of Hotel Administration – until she stood before Manipal Institute of Technology, the engineering college at which I spent three great years of my life. It could have been four, but I dropped out, suspecting that another year of that much fun would kill me. Leaving Kaya near Tiger Circle, I walk down to Dollops, my erstwhile favorite restaurant.

'Sir, how are you?' Rajesh, the waiter, grins in recognition, handing me the menu.

'I'm doing quite well,' I grin like the Cheshire Cat, ecstatic that he remembers me, 'and how have you been doing, my friend?'

'It's been a very long time, sir.'

'Yes, five years. It's nice to be back after such a long time.'

'You've changed fully, sir. What happened to your red and blue hair?'

'Ah,' I smile, embarrassed at the memory. 'I've become old now . . .'

'You've removed all your earrings, and the eyebrow piercing also . . . what sir, it used to look very nice.'

'Oh well. I still have my tattoos.'

'Everything changes, sir,' he sighs ruefully, 'even Manipal is different now.'

Indeed, Manipal has changed, irrevocably so. Other than the wetness, I find nothing familiar. Having carried my memories here, none of them fit the picture anymore. The memories have become lies. I don't recognize the large neon sign perched above the main building, nor the walls enclosing the campus, nor the gleaming new buildings. The shacks where we satiated our midnight munchies have disappeared. My motorcycle service center is gone. The illegal DVD theatres are no more. My first-year hostel, a certified mad house, is now in the hands of the girls. My second-year hostel is occupied by MBA students. I walk tentatively towards my third-year hostel, recollecting its dark passageways imbued with the sweet scent of Mary Jane. Finally, something that still looks unchanged. I sniff the air, and it still smells the same, too. Taking the stairs to the third floor, I amble over to Room 322, and knock on the door of what was once my junkie pad. It is flung open to reveal a tall, broad-shouldered boy, sporting a goatee and long, shaggy hair. His bleary eyes are probably trying to focus on the green fairy hovering somewhere behind my shoulder.

'Wha . . . ye,' he mumbles.

'Hey, I'm Amit . . . I hope I'm not disturbing you or anything but . . . you see, this used to be my room a few years ago and well, I'm visiting Manipal and I thought I'd check to see what's become of it.'

'Oh! Yeah, come on in, man,' he invites me, stepping back from the door. 'The room's a mess though.'

'That's just the way I remember it . . .'

A computer on the cement desk, clothes and discs scattered on the floor, not a trace of any books, and underwear hanging next to a 200 watt bulb to keep them dry – as vital as breathing, unless you have a fascination for cultivating different types of fungi around your nether regions. The posters are different though, gone the Pink Floyd and Jim Morrison, replaced by Linkin Park, and something troubling called Slipknot.

'I didn't wake you up, did I?'

'No man, been up all night . . . kind of.'

'Stoned?' I nod sagely.

'Pretty much,' he grins.

'How's the weed nowadays? Oh, and I never got your name.'

'The name's Gaurav, and the weed's alright . . . but the acid's better.'

'Acid, really,' I squawk, 'when I was here we only did weed . . . there were a few guys on cough syrup and stuff, otherwise it was all green.'

'No man, Manipal is totally happening now,' he says, not hiding the sympathy he feels for me. 'Whatever you want is available, ecstasy, LSD . . . man, you can even get high grade coke.'

'I guess . . .' I say, trying to hide my displeasure at this new development.

'Are you here for a bit . . . we're throwing an awesome party this weekend. You must come, man, it will be wild.'

'Sounds like fun . . . but I'm only here for the day.'

'Hey that's cool, man,' he nods. 'How about a joint then?'

I can't say no to the offer. It's against the ethics.

The Manipal that Kaya rode out from wasn't the one that characterized me, or my generation. The university that had once seamlessly merged into the town was now a walled-in entity, separating the student from the community. Most of the local shacks were traded in for preppy cafes, immaculately impersonal, all gleaming glass and sterile steel. Cell phones, ATMs, traffic lights, credit cards, and shopping centers blighted the landscape. The most ominous change though, something that troubled me since riding into town, was the near complete absence of motorcycles. 'Nobody has motorcycles anymore, man,' Gaurav told me. 'The university has banned them from campus.' It was the cruelest cut of all, for two-wheelers defined our lives at Manipal, and less than a decade ago we bragged of having the highest density of motorcycles in the country. Without our motorcycles, we might never have discovered our passion for the outdoors. We could never have explored the forests of Agumbe or the sands of Turtle Bay. Our seniors would never have led us to hidden waterfalls, nor we our juniors. And I would never be me.

Slipping out of town, I was overcome by a profound sense of sadness. My Manipal had been stolen from me.

Kilometer 33857

From Manipal, Kaya headed inland across the forested hills of Agumbe, the 'King Cobra Capital', one of the wettest regions of the world. Piercing through hill and valley shrouded by fog Kaya reached Kudremukh National Park. Chains of gently rolling hills blanketed by a montage of natural grassland. Tropical greens. A crisscrossing network of creeks and rivers. Home to one hundred and fifty species of birds and a number of endangered animals – including the lion-tailed macaque, Asiatic wild dog, Malabar civet, and tiger – it is amongst a handful of biodiversity hotspots in the world earmarked as critical for conservation.

Despite being of such ecological import, rather incongruously, the national park shares its space with the Kudremukh Iron Ore Company Limited (KIOCL), and the three decades of intensive opencast mining have had a shattering impact. Situated in the wettest region of the country, the opencast mining has led to the erosion of millions of tons of loose soil, polluting the rivers and forest with iron-laden silt. More critically, the dynamiting, road-laying, and pipeline-building have led to devastating habitat fragmentation, the single biggest threat to the region's biodiversity. Since first being declared a national park, some of the unique flora has already disappeared, while many animals have seen a decrease in numbers. In 2001, the NGO Wildlife First filed an appeal with the Supreme Court to have the mines closed and the lands incorporated into the national park. After a protracted, and often bitter, battle, on October 30th, 2002, the Supreme Court ruled against the iron ore company, ordering it to close down the mines. As expected, the ruling was appealed, and the case returned to the courts for three years of further deliberation.

Less than three weeks before Kaya rode into Kudremukh, the Supreme Court had upheld its decision. And from 31st December, 2005, all mining activities were to cease and the mines shut down.

The rain kept falling. A clear stream flowed over a pebbly bed. On the grassy knoll beside it, I pitched a damp tent and settled in for a night in the wild.

I unzip my tent to a misty dawn. The cold rolls in, an unwelcome guest. Packing up my gear, I return to Kudremukh town for a cup of hot tea and a hopefully warm breakfast. At the little tea stall by the side of the road, I walk in on three young men conducting a heated debate, who – after being momentary interrupted by my appearance – return to their energetic deliberation. Asking the owner for a cup of tea, I sit down on a bench looking out at the road and tune them out.

'I guess you're here to visit the park,' the owner asks, nodding towards my backpack as he places a piping cup of chai on the table.

'Yes, I plan to spend a couple of days hiking there.'

'It's very beautiful, especially at this time of the year when everything is green.'

'I know, I've been here a couple of times before.'

'Oh, when was the last time you were here?'

'Early 2002. And before that in 1999, and in 1992 we came here on a class trip.'

'One minute,' one of the arguing youngsters calls out to me, 'can I ask you something? You've been here so many times,' he continues without waiting for my permission, 'can you tell me, is there any difference since you first came?'

'I don't know . . . I can't really say. The roads are better now, and the town seems to be bigger, but even—'

'No, no, that's not what I'm talking about. I'm asking you about the park. Do you see any difference in the park?'

'Well, I guess not really. The trails are better I think, but that could just be my own imagination.'

'So, it's as nice as before,' he asks pointedly, his tone reflecting anger and triumph, the eyes gleaming.

'Yes,' I nod, beginning to feel like I'm missing something here.

'Then why should our mines be closed?' he snaps. 'Why are you people telling lies that the mines have damaged the park?'

'Let it be,' the tea stall owner interrupts. 'Why are you taking it out on this poor boy?'

'No, that's okay,' I assure him, then addressing the young man, 'I am only a visitor, not an expert. To my inexperienced eye everything seems fine, but there are people who have studied these matters and believe that the mines are endangering the wildlife, which is why they want them shut down.'

'So, you think they're right in doing so?'

'Yes, I think it's important to protect the park.'

'But then you are not thinking about us,' the owner says. 'What happens to the people of this town? My tea stall runs on locals, not tourists. My son was a security guard at the mines, and he will lose his job.'

'Ha, there's no point in explaining to these people,' the young man says dismissively. 'They care more for monkeys than for humans.'

Beyond Kudremukh, Kaya's path was stricken with potholes and peppered with bumps. The hills rolled before us in waves. The road surged with them. From time to time, a village broke through the wilderness, reminders that the biggest issue of our times is the conflict between nature and natural resources and, more disconcertingly, between wildlife and people. Across the country, every conservation attempt, and every national park, is required to perform a balancing act between protecting the wildlife of a region and the livelihood of the local population. And so too in Kudremukh. With the intention of including the national park under Project Tiger, the eviction of villagers is currently underway.

Over the last three decades of the 20th century, India witnessed a ten-fold growth in the size of its wildlife reserves; a victory for conservation, but at the expense of the lives of those who called these areas home. During this time, tiger reserves alone have officially displaced nearly 3,000 families – rest assured that any figure prefixed with the term 'official' is a lie, so the true figure is probably a lot higher – and the last ten years have only seen an increasing growth in evictions. As usual, those affected are the poor and disenfranchised, the tribal populations. The Gonds are being removed from Tadoba Reserve to be replaced by tourists. The Baigas have now made way for the tigers of Achanakmar, having previously done so for the tigers of Kanha. The Sahariyas left their homes in Kuno Wildlife Sanctuary to make space for the lions from overcrowded Gir – and fifteen years later, the lions have yet to move in.

Conservation of our ecology and wildlife is not an option but an imperative, the failure of which diminishes your life and mine, and that of every other person out there. Why then, when the benefits of conservation are universal, do we impose the costs on a few, the few who have so little to begin with and are, ironically, the ones who cause the least damage? You and I, hundreds of miles from the nearest wilderness, devour more of nature and her resources, just so that we can remain discontent with our hedonistic lifestyles. On the other hand, these tribes have for centuries coexisted with the forests in which they live.

Instead of addressing the big problems, we pretend to be striving forward by picking on the little guys.* The Baigas are gone, but Vedanta remains, sucking bauxite from a far larger area.

---

* The closure of the Kudremukh mines is an exception, and a significant event in conservation where wildlife managed to trump big-money. But even in this case, where does the onus fall? The worst hit are the blue-collar workers, the little guys, unless they are provided proper safety nets.

More forests continue to be submerged by dams than ever walked by the Sahariyas. Emptied of humans, tigers still die at the hands of poachers in these forests, to satisfy the perverse demands of the middle class – in this instance, probably Chinese.* Our roads and railways, our insatiable need for timber and minerals, our demand for water – all cause greater disturbance to wildlife than the Gonds ever did. Oh, and let's not forget the impact of tourism. Personally, I'm crazy enough about nature to propose protecting it at the expense of man. Only, that the expense should be borne by all man, not just the vulnerable few.

The asphalt we are following runs along a raised embankment, flanked by channels of stagnant water beyond which lurks the forest. A large deer sits motionless in the water, submerged below the curve of its back. It's an unusually exposed position to find the animal in, one that will make a great shot, if only the animal doesn't bolt. I get my camera out.

Click. Click. Looking for a better angle, I inch along the road, careful not to startle the animal by making any sudden movements. That's when I notice the man sitting beside a bush watching me. I ignore him. Click. When I get within a few feet of her, the deer grows visibly tense, but she doesn't make a dash for the woods. The animal trembles as her body rises up a fraction, and then she collapses back into the water. I lower my camera, the excitement replaced by an inkling of uneasiness. The deer lifts

---

* In Orissa, I saw beaches lined with thousands of dead turtles — thirty thousand die every year – and so far government intervention to protect the turtles has only hurt the artisanal fishermen, leaving untouched the big trawlers that are responsible for the slaughter.

her head and looks at me through large, expressive black eyes. In them I see pain, fear, helplessness.

'It is injured and cannot walk,' the farmer calls out. He's hunkered down a few feet from where I am, pulling deeply on a *beedi*. Exhaling a thin stream of smoke he continues, 'It was hit by a truck late last evening and its legs are crushed. Probably its back is broken as well.'

'You mean she's been lying in the water like this since yesterday and nobody has done anything about it?'

'This sort of thing keeps happening. I'm sure someone in the forest department knows by now. Beyond that, what can we do?'

'Trying to help would be a good start,' I snap at him.

'Why don't you do that then?' he snaps back.

'Of course I will.' I take a purposeful step forward. And then I stop, my own helplessness grinding me to a halt. What can I do? I have no answers, but there has to be something. Leaving him there, I ride back to the last village we had passed, hoping to find some assistance. I pull up outside a small store with a public telephone and approach the men standing at the entrance.

'Yes, we know what has happened,' one of them informs me. 'The animals are sacred to us . . . but, there's nothing we can do for it.'

'Come on, there has to be something you could have tried. Does anybody have the number for Blue Cross?'

'What is that?'

I thumb through the telephone directory but find no number in it. I call enquiry, get a number, but nobody answers it. Useless bloody organizations, I curse, never around when you need them. 'Where is the nearest veterinary hospital around here?'

'Chikmagalur has one,' someone replies, 'but it's only for domestic animals. I doubt they will help. You'll probably have to take it all the way to Mysore or Bangalore. How do you intend to do that?'

'Can't somebody arrange for a truck or a tractor?'

No one says a word. Instead, they stare at me, a mixture of hostility and amusement. Then somebody sniggers. 'What, are you going to go along with the tractor, and pay for the expenses?'

'If that's what it takes . . .' I retort angrily.

'How do you expect to get the deer onto the truck? Do you think it will simply get into your arms?'

'Uh . . . I don't know.'

'Where are you going to take the animal? And what are you going to do if you can't find help, bring it all the way back to die here?'

'I . . . I don't know.' I don't know what to do, and it's there for all to see.

'Then, what is it that you know?' they laugh. 'You city people think you can control everything. There's nothing you can do, so stop wasting your time . . . and ours.'

Defeated, I return to where the animal lay. Nothing has changed. I don't say a word to the man. My silence speaks for itself. Unable to stand by and watch, I slide down the embankment into the water and step towards the deer. There is no instinctive connection between me and the animal. This isn't a movie. The injured creature doesn't sit with doleful eyes while the hero comforts it. No miracles. Instead the deer panics. She shudders, and thrashes about pitifully with her neck. Her mouth opens to let out a bark. The sound drills through my heart. I stagger back against the embankment. The struggle has drained the deer's last reserves of energy. Her head hangs limply as her chest heaves. I start to tear up, and decide it's better to leave than sit here and do nothing but beat myself up about it.

Kaya rescued me from there, leaving the Nilgai to become just another road kill, slowly, agonizingly. Like always, she tried to carry me away from my troubles, running. But those eyes haunted me. They followed me for a long, long time. And it took me even longer to own up to why I tormented myself over the incident. I wasn't upset because I'd failed to save the deer, but because I'd failed to do anything. What consumed me was not sorrow but guilt. It is easier to forget sadness because there's always someone or something to blame, but guilt, guilt cannot be shifted.

What had I done for the deer, besides accusing others of doing nothing? I cursed the locals, I cursed Blue Cross, I even cursed the telephone company, all the while trying to push the task onto someone else because I didn't have the will, or the capability, to go through the trouble. What made my farce truly despicable was that the entire time I was in the village trying to get help, secretly all I hoped for was that the animal would die before I got back. That way I could have given myself a pat on the back without having to actually take on any responsibility. I'd been given the opportunity to do something real, but I didn't.

All I did was pretend. I put on an act to make myself feel better, to show that I care. I couldn't escape the fact. In the dark recess of my mind the eyes of the deer had changed, instead of pain I saw accusation in them, same as the displaced man at Kothi. I was the hypocrite, worse than the man who doesn't care. At least their stand is honest. Me, I was amongst those who think, hey, I'm better than everybody else because at least I'm weeping about it. I had the chance to do something real, but I didn't, because that takes self-sacrifice. Once again, I'd discovered who I really was, and it hurt.

We ran all the way to Bangalore.

Bangalore – the metropolis of my childhood, where I grew up and (according to my father) grew rotten – is the epicenter of the urbanization earthquake, and appropriately it's resulted in the total destruction of the city. In the pre-information technology world, this was the 'Garden City', and while the parks still abound, they are mostly car parks and IT parks. B'lore used to be the city of a hundred lakes, but now it's the city of a hundred disappearing lakes, with most of them being filled in and reclaimed. Come on, what good are lakes when you can't build stuff on them? And with the fastest growing land value in the country, water bodies are an unreasonably extravagant use of real estate. Even the sky is slowly disappearing over B'lore, for every time I looked up I found a flyover passing overhead, or a building looming above me. There was a nightmarish quality to it all.

I remember a time when people drove in the city simply for the pleasure of it, whereas today it's an activity that feeds the burgeoning demand for psychiatrists. A large part of the anxiety stems from the fact that Bangaloreans have no idea where a particular road might take them. Just because it took you to one place yesterday, doesn't mean it has to take you to the same place today. In all probability, it won't. The tourist and the local are both equally lost in B'lore, and it's not that Bangaloreans don't know their roads – the difficulty is in knowing if the road is coming or going. The municipality seems to take perverse pleasure in the overnight designation of key roads as one-ways, and then shuffling them around as frequently as possible to make sure we don't get complacent. After all, the key feature of development is to simplify life to the point where the simplest thing becomes too complex to handle.

We continued to run.

Kilometer 34407

Kaya followed the permanently-under-construction highway to Mysore, and further into the jungles of Bandipur. More rain. Giant trees rose over the undergrowth, a tangle of creepers dangling from them like webs. Ahead of us, the Nilgiri peaks climbed to meet the clouds. The road got narrower as it neared Shirur Ghat, the steepest climb in the country, covered in thirty-six vertigo-inducing, blind switchbacks.

The slopes were covered in forest, and the trees glistened with moisture. Sparkling streams cascaded down the hills and raged white as they cut through the valley. Around hairpin number twenty the clouds swept in, swallowing everything around me, including the road. A steady wind blew over the hills, and every few minutes the clouds parted, providing me with a few minutes of sight. It was a maddeningly slow ascent to the top.

The clouds, heavy with moisture, and the wind were sharp as a barb. My teeth started a steady percussion. My knuckles, frozen white to the handle bar. My nose went numb, the skin on my forehead turned taut. Just before I reached my destination, the fog thinned out. Then the rain came again – an unpleasant entry into Ootacamund, the filthiest hill station in the country. Even on a good day Ooty doesn't do much to cheer a person up. Under present circumstances, it's capable of driving you off a hairpin.

Ooty stayed hidden when Kaya set out the next morning. A heavy mist hung over the hills and the grey clouds threatened rain. While looking for a place to stay the previous evening, I'd given a lift to Yoganand, a young MBA student. On hearing about my journey he'd insisted on showing me around, and I'd promised to meet him near the race course entrance at eight. He showed up two minutes behind me, and after a rejuvenating cup of hot chocolate, we spent the day riding the Nilgiri hills.

'Welcome to plastic-free Ooty', 'Say no to plastic', 'Use only paper bags', the signs greet you all over town. The shopkeepers will proudly tell you 'we don't use plastic' as they hand you a paper bag. Big deal, everything in that paper bag is wrapped in plastic. Besides, Ooty has always been ugly as sin. The real tragedy was the garbage traveling beyond the town and onto the beautiful slopes. A few kilometers out of Ooty we stumbled upon a clearing in the forest, the town's dumping yard. Tons and tons of garbage piled high – most of it plastic – spilling onto the road and scattered amidst the surrounding woods. A lot of it had been washed away by rain, and the plastic was now spread over the road in a thick squishy layer. The stench of rot churned the stomach.

A garbage truck had arrived just ahead of us. With no space left in the clearing, and no possible way for the truck to climb over the garbage pile, they casually dumped the rubbish on the road. From the immensity of things, this wasn't the first time they'd done this either.

'What are you doing?' I yell to the man raking the last dregs from the back of the truck.

'Getting rid of the waste,' he smiles politely.

'You can't do that here!'

'Where else? This is the municipal dumping ground.'

'But this . . . this is a forest.'

'I don't know all that. I only do what they tell me.'

'Have you informed your employers about the situation . . . that the *dumping ground* is overflowing?'

'A long time ago. They said they will look into it.'

'Just look at what you're doing. The garbage is all over the road and it's spreading everywhere,' I cry in exasperation.

'There's no need to worry,' he replies reassuringly, 'nobody lives here.'

Kaya rode on, squelching through the plastic field.

Yoganand was an excellent companion, showing me places that I could have only found by getting lost. At the end of a pleasant day, we were heading uphill from Coonoor, when a white Ambassador taxi came sweeping out of a blind curve and hurtled straight at us. In trying to overtake a truck on the bend he crossed into our oncoming lane, leaving me with no space. Forced to swerve off the road, I went scraping into the cliff face before coming to a heart-stopping halt. Leaning against the cliff, I waited for my breath to return. Then the shock gave way to rage. Turning Kaya around, I chased after him, riding like a reckless madman. Within minutes we had caught up with the car, and to attract the driver's attention, I hit him with a barrage of honking. All I wanted was to confront and abuse him. When the honking failed, I rode up beside his window and started shouting at him to pull over. Seeing that he had no intention of complying, I thumped the car with my left hand. Finally, he slowed to a stop on the side of the road, and Kaya pulled up behind him.

'What the fuck is your problem?' he screamed, sticking his head out of the window.

'Who taught you to drive, you bastard, you nearly killed us there,' I screamed back, stepping up to window.

'Nothing happened, no, so what are you crying about?'

'Nothing happened because I made sure that nothing happened.'

'Yeah, yeah.'

'The least you can do is apologize, you bastard.'

'I'm not going to apologize. What are you going to do about it?'

'Come with me to the police station, we'll discuss it there.'

'Hey, get lost you idiot.'

He waved me aside with his hand, and started to move even as I held on to the window. I stood there screaming as he drove away when, from the corner of my eye, I noticed something whiz past me. If was followed by a loud crash as the rear glass of the car shattered. I turned around to see Yoganand staring at the car, a strange expression on his face, halfway between joy and stupidity. The mild-mannered psycho had hurled a stone at the car. Behind me the taxi came to a screeching halt and that shook me from my shocked stupor. We were on Kaya even as the car door opened, and turning around, she raced away in the opposite direction.

It was a full speed, panic-stricken ride back to Ooty, constantly looking back to see if the taxi was following us. If we got caught, we would pay, and it wouldn't be just with money. Until that moment Yoganand had been soft-spoken and easy-going. Suddenly, he was hurling stones and smashing windows. Did he suffer from some Jekyll and Hyde disorder or what? Honestly, he'd scared the courage out of me. Yoganand didn't say a word through the mad dash back, and neither did I, not knowing how to react to what had just happened. Our parting when we reached Ooty was awkward. What was I supposed to say to him? Perhaps sensing my uneasiness, he mumbled something about having to run along, and with a quick handshake he walked away. I felt a twinge of sadness. He'd shown me nothing but kindness, and I hadn't even thanked him properly. I wanted to call him back and say it was alright. I didn't.

Kaya slunk out of Ooty under the cover of darkness, like a wanted criminal, concerned that the driver might be on the lookout for me. Barely a few minutes into the ride I was soaked to the bone as the rain pattered down. At this rate, I might end up developing gills.

LEG NINETEEN

We Were Better Off as Slaves

IF WE WERE TO BELIEVE the marketing gurus, Kaya was entering 'God's Own Country'. Back on NH17, we followed the Konkan coast into Kerala state, which, according to the tourism industry, has replaced Kashmir as paradise on earth. It's not that Kerala is necessarily prettier, but tourists do prefer a paradise where there aren't any guns pointing at them. Riding along the familiar coconut trees, I had the nagging sensation that something wasn't quite normal. And then it dawned on me that in all of India I hadn't once come across such nonstop civilization.

While I knew that Kerala is one of the most densely populated states in the country, what I wasn't aware of was that all those people live along the highway. There seemed to be zero degree of separation between townships, as the cluster of buildings forming one town was connected to the next one by an umbilical cord of individual homes. I only made this remarkable observation because I desperately needed a place to pull over. Having consumed some brown sludge for dinner the night before, probably more alive than dead, I now suffered from hyperactive bowel movements. My first upset stomach on the trip, and it couldn't have come at a more inconvenient place. Elsewhere in the country I'd have pulled up by the side of road and walked into a field or stepped behind a bush. In Kerala, all the bushes grew behind someone's walls.

Once off the coastal highway though, the roads were as isolated as anywhere else. In fact, the rugged hills of Wayanad used to be the most inaccessible regions of Kerala, covered entirely in forest. As we climbed the steep road up the slopes, I noticed that much of the forest has been cleared for cultivation. But other than the neat rows of cash crops, few signs of urbanization interrupted the landscape, which is still home to a million strong tribal population. We didn't pass a single town, or anything that remotely resembled one, until Mananthavady, where I now faced the technicality of seeking out a village called Thalappuzha, and within it one Mr. Thomas, the estate manager of Fringe Ford, a wilderness property owned by my friend, Hamhead. I'd spoken to Thomas on the phone the previous evening, who'd assured me I only had to mention his name for people to point out his house.

'Thomas of Little Life Nursery,' I asked confidently at a local shop, only to be confronted by amazement, followed by a garbled discussion by the shopkeeper and his wife, and ending in laughter. My confidence took another beating at the adjoining store. I rode further from the town till I encountered a man walking on the road. 'Thomas? Little Life Nursery?' I smiled hopefully. He shrugged, and I continued my search, repeating the process a third and fourth time. On the fifth attempt, the man I approached hopped onto Kaya without a reply. He shuffled around a bit, and once comfortably seated behind me, he stretched his hand out and pointed ahead. 'Thomas house?' I asked, just to make sure we were on the same page. He nodded and pointed as before. A few kilometers later, as we approached a white house, he tapped me on the back and said, 'Shtope, shtope.'

'This Thomas house?' I say, pulling up in front of the gate.

'No, Thomas hose hab gilometer bag.'

'Half a kilometer back?'

'Yase,' he smiles innocently, 'dhees my hose.'

Backtracking half a kilometer, Kaya found herself in front of a large, walled compound with a small fading sign, which announced 'Little Life Nursery'. She pulled up outside the gate.

Thomas is waiting for me, seated in a cane chair on the porch of the house, sipping coffee. A short man, no more than five feet tall, he sports a thick black moustache, a few strands of grey betraying his otherwise youthful appearance. A toothy white grin augments his thick, dark lips. He wears black, thick-rimmed spectacles that make him look like a chemistry teacher. His eyes wear the red, glazed look of someone who's just experimented with dubious substances.

'Welcome, welcome. You have no problem in finding the house,' he greets me enthusiastically.

'Not at all. It's like you said . . . all I had to do was ask.'

'Yes, yes, everybody knows my nursery. Come, come, you relax now, have some coffee and snacks, then we go to the estate.'

His wife serves me coffee and banana chips, both homegrown in Thomas's nursery. Later, he takes me on a tour of the place, calling each plant by its botanical name and describing its characteristics, like a proud father introducing his children to a guest. Little of what he is saying registers in my mind, which is preoccupied with keeping a straight face, a tricky matter when words like euonymus, melastomataceae, and lagerstroemia are rolling off a Malayali tongue.

'How do you know so much about plants, Thomas?' I ask, duly impressed.

'I studied the botany in Ernakulam,' he replies. 'I worked in the city for a few years as agriculture consultant.'

'What made you leave your job and come here?'

'I don't like life in the city. I am happier here . . . all is *shanti*. I have my own nursery, and I work on Hamhead's estate.'

Done with the guided tour and botany lesson, we are sitting on his porch drinking another cup of homegrown coffee when a man in a plain white dhoti and shirt approaches the gate. Without making an attempt to enter, he addresses Thomas from where he stands. His tone is deferential, and the short conversation is carried out across the gap of fifteen meters. It's in Malayalam, and I have no idea what they're talking about.

'He is *adivasi*,' Thomas tells me after the man is gone. 'They are not to enter houses belonging to the other castes. I don't care about it, but that's just how things are. Some *adivasi* still live in the forest like the old style . . . but not many, most land is now private, for farming, and most of the *adivasi* are farmers. This man, he Paniya tribe, means worker tribe . . . his ancestors were all slaves. They belonged to the land, and those who owned the land also owned the men and their families living on it.'

'When did the slavery stop?'

'I do not know surely. Maybe forty years, maybe less. Now they all have own small farms. You want, I am going to *adivasi* village in two days, and I take you with me. Now we go to estate, okay.'

Thomas gets up and disappears into the house. He returns a few minutes later, rolling a shiny, black, 1972 model, 350cc Royal Enfield. With all the space available to him, he's chosen to park his motorcycle inside the house, and judging from the way he's caressing it, probably in the bedroom. He pushes the Enfield to the gate and wipes some imaginary dust off it. Getting onto the bike, he makes the sign of the cross and brings his finger to his lips. He pumps the starter to build up pressure, and with one smooth kick the engine roars to life.

Kaya followed the dust trail of the Enfield. Without Thomas I could have spent a month searching and still not found the estate. Hey, it's difficult getting to the middle of nowhere when there's no road leading to it. For a few kilometers we rode along what can tentatively be described as a path. Then we turned into the forest. Narrow tire tracks cut a trail through wild grass. Headlight beams revealed the trees in ghostly shadows. Occasionally the branches reached out to brush against me. Under the soft glow of a full moon I made out the outline of hills, rising from the black depths. The valley appeared bottomless. Crossing a temporary log bridge, Kaya arrived at the old homestead.

A small, tarnished plaque on the inside door frame reads 'Thomson Cottage, 1914'. This is the innermost privately owned property in Wayanad, beyond which extends the largest tracts of jungle in the country, the Nilgiri Biosphere. The surrounding hillside belongs to the Wayanad Wildlife Sanctuary. To the east spread Bandipur and Mudumalai National Parks, and on the north is Nagarhole Reserve. While most private lands have become coffee, rubber, and cardamom plantations, Hamhead has left his estate untouched, guaranteeing himself one billion karma points and a shortcut to salvation. 'Elephants, gaur, and tigers still stray onto the property,' Thomas points out.

The full moon only highlights the remoteness of my surroundings, the sense of being far away. Alone. Sitting outside the cottage, I light a joint that the multitalented Thomas has deftly rolled. 'Ganja from my own nursery,' he informs me, a twinkle in his eyes. 'I grow for personal consumption.' The flickering light of the match is a small speck in the vast ocean of darkness, a lone star in the open skies, shining bright for a fraction before dying out. A stream gurgles nearby, and the crackle of crickets fills the void.

Besides coffee, spices, and whatever else they grow, Kerala's premium crop is marijuana. To visit Kerala and not make a score is like going to Germany and not drinking a beer, and Thomas took it upon himself to see that I didn't commit such an unforgivable crime. After a day spent on the jungle trails, he took Kaya on a thirty-kilometer ride, along a beat-up road surrounded by more forest, interrupted by a few small paddy fields and the occasional house. I noticed bamboo and straw *machaans* high up in the trees, overlooking the fields, like houses that tiny tree people would live in. Curious, I asked Thomas about them. 'They are for farmers,' he replied causally. 'Someone sleeps there at night to shoo away the elephants from field.'

Shoo elephants???

Kaya's ride ended in front of a small brick building in the middle of nowhere.

A smiley woman answers our knock on the door. We step into a room, bare except for a simple wood table, which is aged and scarred. The walls are unadorned, save for years of stains that have taken on artistic patterns. Light streams in through wide open windows. Leaving us in the waiting room, she disappears into the back, returning a minute later accompanied by a smiley man. Thomas greets him with comfortable familiarity. They exchange a few words. The man laughs and turns towards me with a big grin.

'What did you say to them?' I ask Thomas.

'I tell them you are ganja expert, come all the way from Hyderabad to taste the quality of our ganja.'

'Well . . . I hope it's good,' I smile at the man.

The couple disappears into the back room again. When they come out, the woman is holding a white plastic weighing scale in her hand, while the man is lugging a fifty-kilogram rice sack. They place both items on the table.

'So, how many kilograms do you want?' Thomas asks me.

'*KILOGRAMS!* Uh . . . kilograms, I don't want . . . um, how much is it per kilogram?'

'Eight hundred rupees.'

I'm too stunned to react at first. First, shooing elephants and now this. 'One kilogram of weed for eight hundred rupees?' I manage finally. 'Is this for real, Thomas?'

'Sure. He farms his own weed. It is cheap here.'

'One kilogram, please,' I say proudly. 'One kilogram,' I repeat, loving the sound of it. I can't believe I'm buying one kilogram of the stuff for eight hundred rupees. This is better than hitting the jackpot. I watch the lady reach into the sack and pile giant bud after giant bud onto the weighing scale. I've discovered paradise. I start to shake with excitement, which soon turns to disbelief. Who knew so many buds went into making up one kilogram. The pile keeps growing. It's assumed a life of its own, beyond my control. When the needle finally quivers at the 1 kg mark, I let out a sigh of relief. The lady then throws in a few extra buds as a gesture of friendship.

'Thomas, can you ask them to pack it as two separate bundles, please?'

They pack the weed tightly between banana leaves and then wrap it in newspaper, before tying it all up with string. While they are doing this, I interrogate them, with Thomas playing the role of translator.

'Where do you grow the weed?'

'A few kilometers from here . . . inside the forest.'

'Is it your property?'

'It belongs to nobody,' they shrug.

'You mean it is part of the forest sanctuary.'

'I guess so.'

'What about the forest officers?'

'They have bigger troubles, and we have good understanding with them.'

'And the police?'

'We have good understanding with them also. Sometimes, for show, they have raids and burn down the crops. Then we just go to different part of forest and start new field.'

Back at the estate, I hand over one of the weed packets to Thomas saying, 'This is for you. A gift to show how much I appreciate everything you've done for me.'

'No, no, you keep.'

'Please, I want you to have it, I bought it for you. Besides, I don't want to travel with so much weed on me.'

'Thank you,' he says, taking the packet from me. Then reaching into his pocket with his free hand, he extracts a small paper ball and hands it to me. 'I also have gift for you . . . my homegrown ganja,' he grins.

Kilometer 36631

From the hilly interiors of Kerala, Kaya rode past a collage of estates, farm plots, and forest villages, to the coastal town of

Guruvayoor, and then followed the palm-fringed NH17 to Cochin. As promised, on my last evening at Wayanad, Thomas had led Kaya to a small tribal community a few kilometers off the main road to Sultan Battery, from where he wanted to pick up some saplings for his nursery. Single-celled mud huts topped by conical straw roofs, clustered within a dry clearing surrounded by trees. The insides of the hut were dark and plain. A few power cables dangled low over our heads, but they carried no electricity while I was there. Nor was there any water supply at hand either.

The day nearly done, the *adivasis* sat outside their little huts, women sorting grain and the men getting drunk. The women were dressed in saris, mostly white, wrapped around the body as in most regions, except that they wore no blouse underneath. Their hair appeared stringy and rough, almost like coir. The men wore plain shirts over colorful dhotis. The children were scruffy, the youngest with gobs of snot under the nose as if it were part of the traditional makeup. Apart from the dirt their bodies stood bare, mostly skin and bones. Regardless, they displayed the same uninhibited curiosity I'd encountered everywhere else. I smiled. I made faces. I handed out cookies. The kids laughed. The elders treated me with courtesy, as with any guest.

They served me water.

'The village is in mourning, family suicide,' Thomas told me plainly. 'First the parents killed their young son and daughter by poisoning the children, and then they hung themselves. It is common in Kerala,' he shrugged.

'But why?'

'Much loans,' he said with the same equanimity. 'Kerala have many many suicides, the most in India. Everywhere in the state it is big problem. Here, in Wayanad, suicide is mainly farmer and *adivasi*.'

While farmer suicide has been much debated and publicized, I had little real understanding of its severity then, or knowledge that in the twelve months prior to my visit the district of Wayanad alone had witnessed more than 150 farmer suicides. And this is but a small act in the tragedy playing out all across India. In the decade and a half between 1996 and 2010, in excess of 2,50,000 farmers have taken their own lives. That's about 17,000 farmers a year, or 47 per day, or one every half hour. By the time you're done reading this chapter another farmer will be dead.

'The costs of production have gone up by ten times in the last ten years,' Thomas informed me, 'and every small-plot farmer is in debt. If the crop fails even once, or the price drops, it ruins them.'

Depending on which ideological branch you swing from, the blame for this tragedy can be assigned to usurious moneylenders, even more usurious corporates with their genetically modified crops, the WTO and globalization, low yields, or – as the government of Karnataka pointed out – the farmers themselves for their 'bad habits' like drinking; that the National Crime Records Bureau keeps track of the suicides clearly indicates that the government views farmers as the culprits rather than the victims. Regardless of whether there's a single culpable factor, the reality of the situation is that India's current growth pattern is devastating its farmers. Where India might be growing richer, the farmer is relatively poorer.

And this is a country of farmers.

Agriculture employs more than half of India's labor force, with sixty-five percent of the population depending on it for their livelihood. Yet, having steadily declined over the last two decades, agriculture accounts for only eighteen percent of the nation's GDP. This decline has been accompanied by a drop in agricultural wages and a precipitous increase in agricultural inputs. At the same time, subsidies on the exports of commercial crops were withdrawn, while tariffs and quantitative restrictions on imports were removed. What this has done is create a marketplace that is not only volatile, but also reflects artificially lowered prices, pushing the small Indian farmer to the brink.*

'There is no guarantee for the farmer anymore, nothing is in his hands,' frowned Thomas, getting visibly angrier. 'Wayanad's three major cash crops are pepper, coffee, and vanilla. The prices of all of them have crashed in the last couple of years. Coffee used to bring one hundred and forty rupees a kilo, but now it only earns twenty-five. Pepper went from two hundred and fifty rupees to fifty rupees, and vanilla fell from four thousand rupees to one hundred rupees. You tell me, how is that possible, a forty fold change in price. The farmer can't sell directly to the market,

* As in the US subsidization of American cotton farmers to the tune of four billion dollars, thus lowering the price to a point where the rest of the world cannot compete. Cotton growers account for the largest fraction of suicides in India.

and the big corporate monopolies set the price, so how can the farmer protect himself?'

By all accounts trade liberalization is the key to India's phenomenal growth. And in case you haven't heard, growth is good, or god. I don't doubt that liberalization has brought with it huge benefits, but for each of us who's gained something from it, there's someone who's lost a lot more. We must remember that our much-vaunted IT industry employs less than three million people, as opposed to the half a billion people dependant on agriculture. Good policies and reforms are not simply about generating more wealth, but also about protecting those who they might negatively impact.* But where are the safety nets for our farmers? Where are the alternate opportunities available to them?† And how are they meant to survive? In 2008, accompanied by much fanfare, the UPA government implemented the Agriculture Debt Waiver and Debt Relief Scheme to the tune of 600 billion rupees. In 2009, 17,368 farmers committed suicide – a new record – and in 2010, the number stood in excess of 16,000. Who the 600 billion rupees has relieved is a question best left unasked.

'So many farmers have lost their lands or been forced to sell them off,' Thomas had burst out finally. 'I've overheard farmers

---

* Numerous studies substantiate the fact that cheap imports of agricultural produce play a critical role in the pauperization and unemployment of farming communities. These growth policies have also led to the corporatization of agriculture, tipping the balance against small farmers. And although farmer debt is not a new story, the indebted have doubled since the 1990s.

† The last couple of decades have seen a sharp drop in agricultural wages, accompanied by a nearly seven percent decline in agricultural employment, of which only one percent was absorbed into manufacturing and services, the source of India's growth.

curse that they were better off as slaves, at least then they belonged to the land and the owner was duty bound to protect them.'

In what is probably the most profound example of the transformation of agriculture, India is seeing a reversal of its much-revered Land Ceiling Act of the sixties; land that had been redistributed amongst those who tilled the soil is reverting to large landholdings and agribusinesses in the name of economies of scale. India might be growing, but for the small farmer, his life is shrinking.

Kilometer 36712

When Kaya rode out of Cochin, it was in the company of Hans, another one of Captain Hash's German friends. Having watched too many world war flicks and too much German porn, I'd expected him to be a beefy, square-jawed, SS types. Apparently not all Germans look like that, at least not this Hans. He stood an inch shorter than my measly 170 centimeters, and weighed as much as any dedicated junkie. If not for the pale skin and reddish mop crowning his head, he might have passed off for me. The first thing Hans had done when we finally caught up at Fort Cochin was thank me for letting him ride along. Then he'd asked me if I had any weed.

We got on famously.

Over the next three days Kaya slowly inched across the hills of Munnar, sacrificing entire mornings to Lord Indra. Hans and I ventured outside our smoke-saturated room only during lulls in the storm, still managing to get wet every single day. And so it was as I approached Thekkady along washed out roads through ragged hills and scruffy forest. As mentioned, Kerala produces the finest quality cannabis in India, none more legendary than this region's appropriately titled 'Idukki Gold'. Obviously, god's own country has been blessed with god's own weed, and the buds from this region contain spectacularly high levels of THC, without any help from genetic engineering. In an ideal world, ganja would be an integral part of Thekkady's tourist attraction, but seeing how that's not the world we live in, the main tourist draw is Periyar National Park.

Leaving Kaya to a well-deserved rest, Hans and I walk down to the park entrance early in the morning, but by the end of the day we're tired and invariably wet, and I'm in no mood to walk back to the hotel. So when a rickshaw driver approaches us at the exit of the park, we hop on eagerly. The driver is a bright-faced man with a generous paunch, the dhoti hitched up above his knees.

'You want to stay in a cottage, sir?' he says in polished English. 'Very nice and cheap.'

'No, thank you, we already have a room,' I reply.

'Then maybe you want to buy some marijuana,' he asks without further small talk.

'Idukki Gold!'

'Yes sir, the best.'

'Definitely!' Hans declares.

'I have to take you to my house, sir . . . but don't worry, there's no extra charge for the rickshaw.'

He pulls up in front of an elegant cottage, set in a spacious courtyard filled with potted plants and old trees. On crossing the gate I realize there are actually two cottages, a smaller one huddling on the side. 'Please sit down, sir,' he points to the cane chairs in the portico. 'I'll bring the keys to the cottage.' He enters the smaller building and returns a minute later with the keys and a wooden box. 'This is my cottage, sir. I give it for rent to tourists,' he says, taking us on a tour. The cozy little building has two bedrooms, a bathroom, kitchen and dining hall.

'How much do you charge for this place?' I ask.

'With breakfast, two hundred and fifty rupees a night, sir.'

'Man, five euros for this place . . . that's a really nice deal,' Hans says.

We sit down at the dining table, waiting patiently as our host fumbles with the lock on the box. 'I have four different types, sir. Two are ganja and two are hash. This is the best variety of ganja in the country, Neelachadayan and Tappasi,' he explains like a teacher, 'what you call Idukki Gold.'

We are admiring the buds when a woman walks into the room holding a tray in her hands. 'Black coffee,' she says with a smile, and places three cups on the table.

'This is my wife, sir,' he introduces her, and she joins us at the table. This illegal transaction has taken on the air of a social visit. 'You can try out a sample of the weed and see how it is.'

'Are you sure?'

'Yes sir, no problem. I'll also smoke with you.'

'Where does this stuff come from?' I ask, as Hans gets his fingers busy.

'It is grown all over the district. In Galazi, Thaze Bhootar, Chentamala . . . everywhere . . . all are wildlife areas under the forest department.'

'Then how does it work?'

'Big bribes, sir. This is the most profitable plant for the farmers.'

'So, no one bothers them?'

'Until recently they faced no problems at all, but now the police are becoming stricter. This year there were two or three raids . . . In the buffer zone of Silent Valley National Park they destroyed crop worth crores in the market. In Kamabakallu, the Chief Minister personally came down to witness burning of the fields.'

'Man, that must have been one intense high,' Hans sighs wistfully.

'They plan to convert the area into an herbal park. It's all just for show. The farmers simply move deeper into the parks and cut down new sections of forest. The government policies are causing more damage to this region than good.'

'Tell me, how is it that you speak such good English,' I ask.

'I was a teacher in Madurai, Tamil Nadu.'

'Then . . .'

'This is my home. I like it here,' he says evenly.

We try out both strains of weed and it leaves us pleasantly paralyzed. After the warm service he's provided I'd have bought the weed regardless of the price, but even that comes as a pleasant surprise. We buy a bit of everything, and then he drives us back to the hotel where we're staying.

'Next time when you visit Thekkady you must come and stay in my cottage, sir,' he says in parting.

'Man, that dude's amazing,' Hans claims, as we walk up to our room. 'I never imagined that buying weed could be such a relaxing experience.'

I wake up late in the night and rush to the toilet with a stomach that feels like it's turned to liquid, confirming that dinner hasn't gone down too well. Emerging from the bathroom, I find Hans sitting up in bed, hands on waist and grimace on face. If my Indian stomach can't handle the food, I wonder what it's done to his sterile European innards. He ends up spending most of the night on the porcelain throne, and in the morning he's still in no shape to go anywhere. Looks like we're destined to stay in Thekkady one more day.

With nothing better to do, we spend the entire day experimenting with the range of herbal medication we have on us. At around four in the evening, our musings are disturbed by a knock on the door. I open it a crack and put my face to the gap. A bellhop stands on the other side, nervously twiddling his thumbs.

'Yes, what is it,' I ask him.

'Sir . . . uh, there are other people on the floor and uh . . . we . . . er . . . sir, the smell is coming all the way down to the reception. Please, sir, if you don't mind, no more smoking please,' he sounds genuinely apologetic for bothering us.

'Oh . . . yeah sure. I'm really sorry if we've caused any problems.'

I close the door and turn around to face the room. Only then do I notice that the room is foggier than a sauna. Curious, I step out into the corridor. The entire length of it smells like a hot-box. In nearly nine months of traveling I've stayed in over two hundred different hotels, and smoked in most of them. This is the first time anyone's objected to it. Then again, they have every right to be upset if they can smell it at the reception, seeing how it's located two floors below us.

'What do we do?' Hans asks.

'I think we should take our smoke elsewhere.'

'I think I know what you're thinking,' he grins.

Within the hour we have moved into the cottage of the friendliest peddler in India.

Kilometer 37312

Kaya rode on, down the coast towards the beach at Varkala. Overrun by tourists and overwhelmed by tourism, for decades Kovalam was the only beach of any real repute in Kerala, until the discovery, a few years ago, of the undisturbed sands of Varkala. A new paradise was at hand, to be turned into a commercial playground. Today you can drop in on Varkala straight out of the air and land on its helipad. Tour operators are thrilled with business, and tourists are delighted with the luxuries.

Backpackers, meanwhile, are nostalgic for the 'old days' and have begun the hunt for a newer paradise.

Kaya's path ended near the cliff top hotels of Varkala.

'*Cómo estás, quieres habitación*,' a young dreadlocked fellow at the reception asks.

'Pardon me,' Hans stares back blankly.

'*Excusez moi*, I thought you were Spanish.'

'No, I'm German.'

'Ah! *Guten tag*.'

'Naamaastay,' Hans drawls.

The beach at Varkala is a thin crescent of sand at the foot of the cliff, flanked by two projecting headlands. When we step onto it, most of the sand is irrevocably occupied. Serious sun bathers are a lot like hippopotami, extremely territorial, and each of them has marked out their space with brightly colored towels and pale naked bodies. Great ingenuity has gone into getting as naked as possible without exposing anything vital. Bikini tops are rolled into razor-thin censor strips, and the bottoms are pulled so tight they disappear between available crevices. Crowds are a wonderful thing, especially if they are female, beautiful, and naked.

We walk down the short length of the beach to the far end where there are fewer people. Throwing our towels on a rock, we run headlong into the gentle waves. Though the beach is swarmed with people, none are in the water, except Maria, an Italian staying at our hotel. We are in the water for about fifteen minutes when I sense we're being steadily swept out to sea. It doesn't set off any alarm bells though. The shore can't be more than ten meters away.

'Man, we should swim back,' Hans interrupts my thoughts.

'Yeah, my thoughts exactly,' I reply.

Maria and Hans are half a body length ahead of me. Holding my head above the water, I kick out towards them. I don't seem to be going anywhere. Still, I'm not too concerned, but I want to catch up with them. I put my head down and throw in a few powerful strokes. I lift my head up and find myself in the same place. The other two have moved further away from me. This is not good. I try again, more franticly. My arms go slack. I'm fighting for breath. I see Hans turn back to look at me. His face is a mask of worry.

I feel fear for the first time.

A few more desperate strokes and I'm done. Drained. Finished. I don't see the wave come crashing down on me. It pushes me under, swirls me around and spits me out. I gasp for air, and look towards shore. The world is shaking. The second wave sweeps over me. This time I stay under for longer, violently rolling around. The water forces itself into my nose and mouth. My eyes tear open to see a swirling, bubbly green space. It burns. For a second time I resurface.

The third time is supposedly the last. The thought runs clear in my head. So, this is how it's going to end. I don't fight it, no longer having the energy to do so. I look to the shore. A crowd has gathered at the edge. I turn around, in time to see the third wave curling over my head. I see death riding it. No panic, nothing. I purse my lips tight, but the sea rushes into my mouth. How long am I in the darkness? It feels like eternity. There is light again, and air. I swallow hungrily.

Someone is swimming towards me. Keep your mouth shut, I tell myself, you just need to hold on till they get to you. Another wave rolls over me, and even as I thrash around I feel a firm grip on my arm. The sea tears me away from my rescuer. I'm sucked in. My head strikes against a body, and then my flailing hands. I reach for him blindly and find the safe clasp of his hands again. He pulls me up, and I go limp in his arms. If he lets go, I'll sink without a struggle.

'Sppruuutttt . . . huuuuh.'

'Hold shoulder,' a reassuring voice says, 'you be okay.'

I hold on tightly as a second person swims over. With each of them holding onto one arm they start pulling me towards the shore.

'You put legs down,' one of them tells me when we're closer to the beach. That's when I notice for the first time that we are in waist-deep water. I try to push my trailing legs down, but they are swept up by some strong, unseen force. I try again, and fail again. Helpless, I collapse on my rescuer's shoulder.

'Is okay, take easy,' he says calmly.

I see people standing at the edge of the waves, watching anxiously as my rescuers drag me towards them. I flounder on the sand, slightly dazed, but still alive. My eyes closed, I pick up a flurry of voices floating in the wind.

What happened . . . I saw him and shouted . . . This water . . . dangerous al . . . He's Indian . . . Why don't people . . . scare . . . any lifeguards in this . . .

'You good?' my rescuer asks. I look up and nod my head. He steps back, giving me some space. Everybody else disappears along with him.

'Man, are you okay?' a visibly shook-up Hans asks. 'I'm sorry, man . . . I couldn't swim back for you . . . it's the current . . . it was too strong . . . really I—'

'Come on, it's not your fault,' I splutter between gasps, glad to see him. I think about the boy who drowned in Palolem. If not for Hans, I'd be just another dead person, a two-minute curiosity, a stranger in the circle. I feel better knowing someone would have cried over my body if I'd drowned. Then it occurs to me how pathetic the thought is.

'I looked back, but it was too late.'

'Hans, just let it go.'

'Hey, are you alright?' This time it's Maria, the Italian. 'I tri . . . I couldn't . . .'

'Listen, it's nobody's fault . . . and I'm glad you didn't swim back to help me.' Honestly, if foreigners had started to go down as well, the lifeguards would probably have rescued them first. By the time my turn came up, I'd probably be dead. 'Now if you'll just help me up.'

My legs are a little rubbery and my stomach makes a lurch, but my head feels light. Strange how good it feels to stand on my feet. I turn to look at my rescuers, who stand at a discreet distance, talking amongst themselves. They appear to be in their thirties, short and stocky, skin weathered by sun and salt. Men of the sea.

I walk over and thank them for saving my life. 'If you hadn't been . . . are you lifeguards?' I ask, wondering where they'd suddenly emerged from. I've never actually seen a lifeguard in India, and I know we don't have anything like Baywatch or Bondi Rescue.

'We is fisherman, sometimes we are guarding on beach,' he stutters in broken English. 'Varkala hotels and tourism pay us to do guarding, our real work is fishermen.'

'So, there isn't someone here at all times.'

'No, only little time. You lucky we see you. All year many die. Varkala have strong currents inside water.'

'Yes, I guess I am lucky you guys were around,' I smile.

His smile is tentative. When he speaks now his voice is changed, more deferential and hesitant. 'Sir, me no want ask . . . but is only our living. You gives little reward . . . sorry to—'

'Please, come up to our hotel,' I say with a quick smile, trying to ease his discomfort, 'and have lunch with us . . . I'd like to give you something for saving my life. Also, please stop calling me sir.'

'Thank you.' The relief is written clearly on his face. 'Why you not swim in green flags?' he asks as we climb the stairs leading up the cliff face.

'I don't understand.'

'Looking sign,' he says pointing to a sign next to where the stairs begin.

Written in English, Hindi, Malayalam, and – of all languages – German, it says in bold red lettering: 'GEKREUZTE ROTE FAHNE GEFAHPLICHE GEGEND - CROSSED RED FLAG DANGER AREA'. I turn around and look back at where we'd been swimming. Sure enough, it's precisely in the center of two prominent red flags.

As Kaya rode out of Varkala the next day, it occurred to me that my journey could have ended on this shore, except that karma had been on my side. Hans had found the lifeguard's request troubling, but it had come as no surprise to me. I'm not sure what the deal is with lifeguards in the developed world, perhaps they're well paid or recognized for their efforts, and if nothing else, they can always make a hit television series. In India, I seriously doubt being a lifeguard is much of a career, so no, I'd have to be dead before begrudging him a reward for saving my life. The only thing I found irksome was that there is no fixed rate for these sorts of things.

Suddenly, I'd been forced to ask myself a question best left ignored: What was my life worth, and how much should I pay someone for keeping it going? It was disquieting to bring it all down to money, and it gnawed at me all through lunch. Instead of sharing an appreciative meal together, both my rescuer and I were preoccupied with the same question. What would the reward be? It cast a shadow over the table, and I could tell that he was eager for lunch to be over. In the end I gave him all the cash I was carrying on me, amounting to a little over one thousand rupees, thereby paying out the price of a decent toaster for my life. He smiled broadly and left. I never saw him again.

As for my brief tête-à-tête with death, when I found the time to reflect on it what bothered me was how little it had bothered me. Going down that third time I'd been sure it was the end, and I'd accepted my fate without panic, without much of a fight. It still troubles me, not that I'd nearly died, but that I'd nearly died and not cared about it. All great travelers have near-death experiences, which change their perspective on life. This is usually the pivotal point in adventure stories, the profound moment when the protagonist finds the true meaning of life, mortality, and his journey. My thoughts in the water were more like, 'What a stupid way to die on a motorcycling adventure . . .' and 'Oh crap, who's going to take Kaya home?'. Even after further deliberation, nothing remotely insightful entered my head. All I learned from the experience was that I'm a lousy swimmer and a cheapskate.

Kilometer 37446

Kaya headed from one beach to another, this one on the southern end of Kerala, and it was only poetic that our last destination on the Konkan coast bears the name 'coconut grove'. Kovalam in the seventies gave Anjuna stiff competition as the ultimate hippy hideaway, and it was here that Indians were first exposed to the wonderful concept of nude sunbathing. Needless to say, only foreigners did the exposing. Indians indulged in the ogling. Then the politicians and police came down to see what the fuss was all about, and having satisfied their curiosity, they promptly banned it so that no one else could enjoy the sight. The hippies may be a dying tribe, and the nudists an exiled one, but that hasn't put a dent in Kovalam's popularity, so we steeled ourselves for a crush of back-to-front hotels and a throng of ass-to-cheek tourists. Fortunately, my absence of directional sense led Kaya astray to the north beach – the least visited of Kovalam's three beaches – where, a few feet from the shore and hidden behind a coconut grove, we discovered a simple two-room cottage in seclusion. One of the rooms was still vacant, which we promptly occupied.

Later, Hans and I are sprawled on the grass outside, looking up at the stars, when the door of the other room opens. Hearing the shuffle of feet, I turn around and raise my head to see a tall figure in the shadows, the silhouette revealed in the orange light seeping through the half open door.

'Hey man,' Hans calls out to the silhouette.

'Eh, hello,' he replies softly after a moment's hesitation.

'Would you like to join us?'

'Uh . . . no, I'm fine here.'

'It's really nice out here.'

'I . . . uhh . . . I'm alright,' he says, moving towards the table and chair in the portico. His steps are unsure, wobbly, but I don't give it any thought. We continue to lie on the grass, throwing him the occasional question. His name is Andreas and he's comes from Austria.

'Would you like a joint?' I ask, about to light one.

'I'm rolling one myself,' he replies. I scramble over to where he's sitting and hold out the unlit joint to him. He refuses. 'Uh . . . you go ahead and light it. I'll join you later.'

'Fine,' I shrug, deciding he's an asshole.

Meanwhile, Hans has come over as well, and the two of us join Andreas at the table. For the first time I really look at him, revealed under the dim glow of a single flickering candle. His face is gaunt and the cheeks sunken in. Thin stubble darkens his pale skin, hair so light it looks like he has no eyebrows. His deep blue eyes are filled with pain. Then I see his hands, and I know he's not well.

Hans holds out the burning joint for Andreas. He reaches for it with a skeletal hand. It trembles. The shake isn't violent, but the joint quivers between his fingers, held so limply I'm worried it will drop out. Andreas doesn't look at us as he smokes. He passes the joint and turns his attention back to the rolling. I'm transfixed by his hands. The paper is shaking, and most of the weed spills out before he can even start to roll it. He catches me staring.

'I am sick,' he mumbles self-consciously, making me feel like an insensitive jerk. After a moment of awkward silence he gives a weary smile and lights the shapeless joint he's rolled with so much difficulty.

We talk late into the night, but the subject of his illness doesn't come up till the end. 'I suffer from multiple sclerosis,' he volunteers before retiring to bed. 'It's a nerve degenerative disease. My muscles are decaying.' Andreas speaks softly, picking each word with care. He sounds like someone who's spent many hours in contemplation.

Dawn found Hans and me back on the grass.

'*Guten tag*, Andreas. Slept well I hope?' I call out when the Austrian steps out of his room. 'Would you like a smoke?'

'No, thank you,' he smiles. 'I have to go for my treatment now . . . I know a nice place to eat near the clinic, if you want to join me.'

'Sure, do you want to ride down?'

'No, we walk. The exercise is good for me.' He picks up a stick leaning against the wall and we head out on foot. Andreas is twenty-nine. He moves like he's eighty. Hans and I walk on either side of him, slowly. 'Chandy gave me this stick,' he says, referring to the cottage owner. 'He is a very nice man, always watching out for me. When I first moved in he wouldn't rent out the other room, thinking people would disturb me. I had to tell him that it's okay. I don't mind the occasional company.'

'How long have you been here?'

'Almost seven months. I first came to Thiruvanananana . . . whatever. I was there for a month . . . then I found out they have another clinic in Kovalam.' He stops to catch his breath. 'I'm happy I came here. It's a good place to live.' We walk in silence for a while. 'That's my barber,' he points suddenly. 'I can't shave myself anymore. Do you mind waiting? I think I need one.'

'Great, I could do with a shave as well,' I say, running my fingers through my thick beard.

The barber shop is a closet-sized cell with peeling plaster. Water seeps in through the ceiling creating a dark patch. Fungus grows freely on the walls. A wooden chair faces an age-tarnished mirror, and a customer is already seated in it. The shaggy-haired barber flashes Andreas a big smile and indicates for us to wait outside. The bench outside already has two occupants sharing a Malayalam newspaper while waiting their turn. They shuffle to the side making space for Andreas. When the next turn comes up, they shrug their shoulders, smile and gesture that we can go before them, first Andreas and then me. They wait patiently, ever so often throwing us a big grin.

'When I first came here, I would look at the people sitting around idly and think what a waste of precious time, what a waste of life,' Andreas tells us while we're walking to the clinic. 'I thought of all the things I wanted to do with my life . . . but then I realized that even when I was well I hadn't really done any of those things. I had been so caught up in making something of my life . . . I never actually lived it. I used to believe time is money . . . I spent a lot of time making money. Now, the only thing I want is that time.'

'What about the treatment you're undergoing?'

'I think it's helping. They make me exercise and practice meditative breathing. I take homeopathic medicines and have regular massages with special oils. Initially I felt very weak because of the medication, but I've grown much stronger since then. When I first came here I could barely walk,' he says wistfully. 'I am beginning to have hope again, maybe I can fight it.'

'Do you miss home, Andreas?' I ask, sitting around the table later at night.

'Vienna? No, I don't think so . . . I miss my family, but it's better for all of us that I'm far away . . . I'm more relaxed here. I never really thought much about Asia before. To me it was the under-developed Third World, a backward place. Ha, ha, I was more of a party, good lifestyle type of person, never thought of coming here. And now . . . I finally came here for help when my modern country couldn't help me. I tried many doctors in Europe, but nothing worked. All my savings are gone. I get some benefits from Austria, and in India it is sufficient for my treatment and daily expenses.'

'Do you plan to return home sometime?'

'I don't know . . . What about you? How much longer before you go home?'

'Let's see, so, today is the 1st of December, which means I have one more month and four thousand kilometers to complete the journey. I didn't realize it's going to end so soon. I have no idea what I am going to do after that.'

'It's not important what happens after,' Andreas says with utmost seriousness, 'what's important is that you're chasing your dream today. If you'd decided to wait longer, the longer the wait would have lasted. In the end all you'll be left with is regret . . . the regret that all you did with life is wait.'

Kaya had planned to leave early the following morning, but it wasn't till late in the day that we rode out from Kovalam. Whatever the reason, neither Hans nor I wanted to disappear on Andreas without a proper goodbye. So, we accompanied him on his daily trip to the Ayurveda center, and hung around till it was time for his therapy session. I've met so many people on this journey. Some of them I can't even remember. I have most of their addresses, and the photographs of a few of them. Of Andreas, I have nothing. I never took his picture. I never noted down a contact.

Sometimes the future is best left imagined.

LEG TWENTY

Am I Not Normal?

TAMIL NADU WELCOMED Kaya by dripping all over us. We didn't know it, but this was only the calm, a precursor to storm Fanoos, which escorted us through the state. Every time I looked at the satellite imagery of India in *The Hindu*, Tamil Nadu was obliterated by a big white patch. Hans cut them out as souvenirs to take home.

My heart raced faster as we neared Kanyakumari. Kaya's engine rumbled. My hands quivered. We reached land's end. Before me, the last bit of Indian soil dissolved into the Indian Ocean. Kanyakumari, southernmost tip of the Indian peninsula, where east and west coasts meet as an inverted summit to give India her unmistakable shape. Kaya and I had traversed the country, from her snowy crown to her watery feet.

Leaving Hans to watch over Kaya, I leap onto the beach. He doesn't understand my excitement, but then again neither do I. The strength of my emotions is unexpected, and I let myself be swept away by them. It's no surprise that a temple marks the shore, a thin strip of sand separating it from the waves. I run past the pilgrims gathered on the beach and crash into the sea, my clothes still on. They are wet anyway. My long pilgrimage drawing to an end, I can't think of a more appropriate place for a final sanctifying dip. In a country marked by confluences, this is the greatest of them all, the meeting point of three water bodies. The murky green Arabian Sea from the west, the dark and turbulent Bay of Bengal from the east, the aquamarine Indian Ocean from the south, all kissing one shore.

Returning to Kaya, I find Hans in deep conversation with a professionally-dressed middle-aged man. Mr. Senthil Iyer, a physician from Madurai, is explaining the legend of Kanyakumari to Hans, something to do with a virgin, a failed marriage, and a slaughtered demon.

'. . . Kumari Amman is the protector of these shores,' Mr. Iyer says. 'The gleaming nose ring on her idol can be seen from far away. In olden times that light was a guide for ships.'

'Like a lighthouse?'

'Yes. But if they were bad people, the ships crashed into the rocks.'

'Wow!' Hans expresses dutifully.

'The multicolored sand of Kanyakumari is very special,' continues Mr. Iyer. 'It is called monazite, and uranium is extracted from it. This uranium is used to create nuclear energy. It is the manifestation of Shakti, the divine power.' At this point we leave him to his confluence of science fiction and ancient mythology, and head towards our homestay, wondering if we should be concerned about radiation sickness.

Back at the homestay, stepping out of the common bathroom after a refreshing shower, I stumble upon a man strutting around in nothing but black silk briefs. Well, he must be gay, I think, followed immediately by guilt for making such a stereotypical assumption. As I discover at dinner, he's the husband of our hostess, and the father of an adorable baby girl. Following a quiet but sumptuous meal, I climb out on the terrace, accompanied by a joint. The city lights spread before me, leading to the black emptiness of the sea, which dissolves into the sky somewhere in the distance.

'I hope I'm not intruding?' a soft voice calls from behind me. It belongs to George, the man in silk underwear, who's now covered up.

'Not at all. My random thoughts don't mind the break.'

'I'm feeling a bit alone and need someone to talk to,' he sighs. 'I'm terribly unhappy today.'

'What's wrong?' I ask lamely.

'I . . . I miss my boyfriend,' he says slowly, probably weighing my reaction.

'Oh!' I gasp. It's all I can manage, more than slightly stunned. A stranger confessing his homosexuality to you is not a run-of-the-mill experience, especially not in the world I've grown up in.

'I hope I've not made you uncomfortable,' he says, 'I know how most people feel about it.'

'Please, there's no reason for concern. I have gay friends back home,' I assure him, recovering from the initial surprise. 'You just took me by surprise . . . you know, with a wife and child, and . . .' I bite my tongue before I can say anything stupider.

'I can't express my feelings to anyone around here,' he continues, ignoring my nonsensical assumptions. 'They won't understand . . . or worse. It's easier to talk to guests. You are only strangers passing through. You might judge me, but then you will be gone.'

It's difficult for me to know what George must be going through, but I sure understand where his fear and loneliness must come from. It can't be easy to be openly gay in our country, especially not in a small town like Kanyakumari. We are a proudly homophobic nation – one of the few that doesn't have a law against male rape because we can't bring ourselves to accept that such a thing exists – casually brandishing about words like 'unnatural', 'disgusting', and '*namard*'. After all, every Indian knows it's his duty to have an opinion, even if he's pulled it right out his ass. For the most part homosexuality is simply ignored, rarely featuring in public discourse, same as most sexuality. We aren't even ready to screen movies with serious gay and lesbian themes without protest and scandal. The best Bollywood can do is lampoon them. So, for now, the Georges of India are forced to hide, the alternate being daily confrontation with bigotry. At least with a stranger like me, it's less worrying. I'll be gone tomorrow, taking his secret with me.

'I can't even talk to my wife,' he says glumly. 'She refuses to understand.'

'Well . . . it can't be easy for her either . . . I mean . . .'

'But she doesn't even try. Oh, I feel sooo trapped in this marriage.'

'What about friends . . .'

'I'm originally from Goa and that's where my boyfriend lives. We were so happy, but because of the social pressures he suddenly started seeing a girl. Then my family found out that I was gay. My father went into severe depression. My mother blamed me for everything. She said if people found out then nobody would marry my sister. She threatened to commit suicide. So, when they brought me this marriage proposal, I accepted. I thought the move to a new place would make things better. But I can't change how I feel. I still love him so much.'

'How does he feel about all this?'

'Oh, he still loves me as well. He calls sometimes, but now it's too late. I hate my marriage, but I can't get out of it. My wife has control over my life. She has the support of my parents as well. She checks my phone calls, and even beats me if I mention him.'

'I'm . . . I'm sorry . . .' I find it hard to picture his kindly wife as a husband beater, but I know that has more to do with my own prejudices than reality.

'I can't take it anymore. I think I'll go visit him . . . but then what? If only I had the money. Maybe then we could run away to some other city.'

I say nothing.

'Thank you for listening to me . . . it helps.'

Kilometer 37624

Following a failed sunrise the next day, Kaya turned around from land's end and headed north. Rain dampened the spirit. I thought of George.

Our society doesn't provide him the opportunity to lead a fulfilling life, nor does our law. Section 377 of the Indian Penal Code, commonly known as the Anti-Sodomy Law, has subjugated homosexuals by criminalizing their relationship, declaring it illegal to have 'carnal intercourse against the order of nature with any man, woman or animal', punishable by life imprisonment. By their reckoning, 'against the order of nature' includes oral sex and sodomy, regardless of sexual orientation. Having said that, the law courts are clearly against the prosecution of homosexuals, and in the last twenty years we've had no convictions on that ground.

What this law does instead is to steal the homosexual's right to stand up for himself, leaving him open to victimization. Other than blackmailers and hustlers, it is an instrument for the police to oppress, harass, extort money, and most ironically, to extract sexual favors. It is a tool for bigots to wield against their opponents, for example, in Lucknow AIDS workers educating gays were imprisoned for 45 days on charges of 'spreading homosexuality against Indian culture'. In another reported case, gays were forced to undergo medical treatment to 'cure them of the disease'. Finally, it provides unaccepting parents with the threat of lodging a complaint if their children stray sexually.

Unfortunately, a simple change in law will not see an end to the discrimination and humiliation. For that we need a change of mindset. As in George's case, the real source of despair is the family and social circle, the very people meant to provide love and support. It is social fear that gives the blackmailers and chauvinists real power over gays, the threat to expose them to ostracism. If I were gay, my mum's concern wouldn't have been its illegality, no, she's more likely to go: 'But how? Shiva, Shiva, what will people think? You are bringing shame to the family. I won't be able to show my face in society. Listen to me, I'll find you a nice girl and everything will be okay.' It is society that declares the gay an outcast, making him question his own humanity.

'Am I not normal?' George had asked me. 'My wife says everybody calls me a freak. They say that even if it is acceptable in the West, this kind of behavior does not suit our culture.'

What culture are we talking about here? This prejudice and cruelty has little to do with Indian tradition. Manu the Lawgiver had little to say on homosexuality, while Hindu mythology and texts have numerous stories involving divine gayness. And in Khajuraho the temples are replete with sculptures of men on men, including that of a sage performing oral on a king. Even when it comes to Islam, which abhors the notion of sodomy, in India as in much of Persia, the Muslim rulers treated it with indifference. The concept of sexual offenses against the order of nature is essentially a Western creation, and intolerance towards homosexuals, as a moral and cultural issue, only became prevalent with Colonialism. They were the ones to criminalize it in India, replacing tolerance with oppression; the infamous Section 377 is a British statute dating from 1860. Yet, while they repealed it in the UK in 1961, we are still holding on to it.

George spoke of going to a different city. But where could they run? Bombay and Bangalore are known to have a vibrant gay nightlife, including discos and bars for stags. But how many of them are still gay when they step out of the nightclubs? What are they at family gatherings – still gay? Who are they in university the next day – still gay? Who are they when they go to work – still gay? While the occasional fashion designer, journalist, or urbanite might flaunt his sexual preference, the majority wear the appropriate masks, pretending to be somebody else. They can't legalize their love through marriage. They can never hope to adopt a child together. They can't even get a joint bank account.

Despite being an issue of human dignity and rights, not one of the major political parties has taken a strong stance on gay rights, because they know it's of insignificant concern to the electorate. That most people don't care is evident by the lack of social commentary and the complete absence of media coverage of issues related to homosexuality. On June 29th, 2008, more than 100,000 people hit the streets of Sydney – a city of two million – in celebration of gay rights. On the same day, Delhi, Bangalore, Kolkata, Indore, and Pondicherry held gay parades. The collective population of these cities is around forty million, and a combined 2,000 people showed up. Maybe we are starting to come out of the closet, but the door is still only open a crack.

All the world was rain, and we were lost in its wet embrace all the way to Madurai city (which, in 2012, celebrated the country's biggest rainbow festival), honing in on the extraordinary *gopurams* that pierced the grey sky. Spectacular spires define the temples of Tamil Nadu, and Madurai's Meenakshi Temple flaunts four of them, each facing one of the cardinal points and soaring fifty meters over enormous granite gateways. Tapering on their journey heavenwards, the spires are covered in thousands of stucco figures of gods, demons, sages, angels, and other mythical creatures. All of them painted in a glut of mind-numbing, god-awful colors.

While the city's color coordination is of questionable character, Madurai's prominence as a center of culture, philosophy, and theology is indisputable. From the early centuries before Christ, known as the Sangam Age, the city witnessed the composition of India's greatest classical works in poetry and literature, with the Golden Lotus Tank at the Meenakshi temple serving as the focal point of this talent. During the Sangam period, the Tamil world's greatest intellects gathered around this sacred tank to display their works of literature. Apparently, the academy and the critics judged the literary value of the work by throwing it into the holy water. Only the ones that didn't sink were considered worth reading. It was the publisher's way of saying: 'Keep it short and simple, we only appreciate light reading.' Correspondingly, 'This soaks!' or alternately 'You soak!' must have been the most terrible criticism in those times. This probably goes a long way towards explaining why we've produced a lot more sculptors than writers.

Kilometer 37902

The road led Kaya east, towards the coast and the eye of the storm. We cut a wake through the rain and crossed the sea, discovering that Rameswaram is an island only as we crossed the Pamban, the longest sea bridge in India (until 2010, when it was surpassed by the Rajiv Gandhi Sea Link in Bombay), arching over the channel. Running alongside, skimming the water surface is the Pamban Rail Bridge, an engineering marvel when it was built by the British in 1913. We were surrounded by seductive blue waters. Coral reefs shimmered below the shallow sea.

Dropping our bags off at Rameswaram, Kaya continued beyond it to a place of myth and magic, and a sad reality. Dhanushkodi is the navel from which the umbilical cord joining India to Sri Lanka stretches out across the ocean. A conduit of sandbars, limestone shoals, and coral reefs, Adam's Bridge (the internationally preferred name) or Rama's Bridge (the Hindu preferred name) is at the center of a raging debate between creationists and naturalists on the question of its origin. Like Christians who argue that man was created by god and not by natural selection, Hindus claim the bridge was created by god and not by natural sedimentation. Or, to be precise, it was built by Lord Rama – who, by my reckoning, is more controversial than the BCCI – along with his army of monkeys and bears, for their assault on Lanka.

Scientists and modern technology, true to form, have simultaneously helped prove and disprove the legend, leaving us with as many differing motion theories, statistical analyses, and dating studies as there are atolls. Estimates from carbon dating vary between 1,70,00,000 years old, 1,25,000 years old, 5,000 years old (which suits the mythologists just fine), and as little as five hundred years old (which suits nobody, not even the thousand year old corals). The Geological Survey of India conducted 'Project Rameswaram' only to report, inconclusively, that there was little evidence that the bridge was man-made – not much use, since the question was about god and monkeys, not man. Only the judges of Madras High Court are without any doubt; they ruled that the bridge is 'definitely man-made', proving without doubt that the Indian justice system has little to do with evidence.

Ten kilometers into our ride towards Dhanushkodi the road abruptly and irrevocably disappeared beneath the sand dunes. By this point I'd gotten used to vanishing roads, and trusted that it would make a comeback at some point in the distance. But that wasn't to be the case. It's almost as if the road builders, having brought the road to this point, realized there's nowhere really important to take it to – so, promptly dropping their shovels, they returned home for dinner.

Kaya was at a confused and resolute halt.

Leaving Kaya beached, Hans and I set off on foot with no real intention of getting anywhere. The ground, made of sand, shell, and pieces of coral, crunches loudly under our feet. A few minutes into our ambling walk, we hear a new sound – the welcome noise of a struggling engine. It's coming from a tractor slogging across the sand.

'Dhanushkodi, Dhanushkodi,' I scream. The tractor stops and the hairy driver yells back. '*Nooru rubai.*' Hundred rupees – well, that sounds fair enough. We climb onto the open trailer at the back. 'Right! Right!' I thump the sides, and we're on our way. The end of a visible trail doesn't mean the end of the road, or the end of the world.

I start a conversation with the driver, but we get nowhere since neither of us knows what the other is saying. Tamil Nadu has always frustrated my attempts to talk with the locals, but I've never been more aware of how fucked up this is than just now. Having traveled to the furthest ends of the country, the people it's hardest for me to communicate with are the ones closest to home. I hold no particular affection for Hindi, and understand the political arguments against its use as a national language, but that doesn't take away from the fact that we have no tongue to unite us. English is the closest thing to being a universally accepted language in this country, and what an irony that is. We're in a situation where, to protect our cultural identity, we'd rather speak a foreign language than an Indian one. So, the only real communication I have with the driver is at the end of the ride, trying to find out when he's heading back.

'*Yetta mani*, return,' I ask, putting my ten-word Tamil dictionary to good use, while also pointing to my watch and then back towards Rameswaram.

'*Naala*,' he replies, sticking up four fingers in front of his face.

'*Nandri.*'

'Thanks you,' he grins.

Dhanushkodi has the feel of a post-apocalyptic ghost town, melancholic and eerie, the few ruins that grow out of the dunes making the picture all the more haunting – the weathered shell of a church, an arch that was part of the post office, a crumbling station amidst the rubble, a temple buried under sand. Once a thriving fishing village and religious center, connected by both road and rail, all of it disappeared in a flash. On a stormy night in 1964, death swept over the town, riding in on a thirty-foot tidal wave, and when it passed by, nothing remained, except a few shattered survivors. The sea reached ten kilometers inland. Fifteen hundred lives were washed away.

Declared unsafe for living, the town has remained mostly abandoned, but not entirely dead. A temporary fishing village of a few hundred people stands by the shore, a sign of human resilience. Walking along the shore, we come across a solitary man standing on the water's edge and looking out to sea. Dressed in pant and shirt – unlike the fishermen, who are wrapped in lungis – he introduces himself as Shanmugam.

'Are you here on pilgrimage?' I ask.

'Ha, ha, no, I'm here on work.'

'Work?'

'I work for the Fisheries Department. I'm here regarding the Sethusamudram Shipping Canal Project.'

'Uh, what is that?'

'It's a plan to dredge through the atolls and make a shipping channel across the strait. It will save thirty hours on the shipping route to Sri Lanka, but they've run into some difficulties.'

'What kind?'

'All kinds. Lot of people are against the project. The environmentalists are concerned for ecological reasons. The fishermen are unhappy because they are not sure how it will affect their livelihood. The Hindu fanatics are angry because it is destroying god's creation. And the government, ah!' he grins. 'The BJP government, which originally made this plan, is now opposing the project. These fans of Rama were willing to destroy his creation, as long as they made money, but now that they aren't in power and the money will go elsewhere, what do they do . . . they become the saviors of Rama. Every political party has used this issue to gain votes.'

'Which side are you working for?'

'Me? I'm on the side that saves the bridge.'

'Why, do you think the bridge was built by god?'

'I don't know who built it. Nature, god . . . it doesn't matter, it's still a miracle.' He gazes at the sea wistfully. 'I'll be heading to Rameswaram soon and I can give you a ride back,' he offers. 'You should leave before it gets dark. It's not very safe here.'

'Why, what would happen here?'

'This is the entry point for illegal refugees from Sri Lanka . . . also for drugs and weapons.'

While Shanmugam wraps up his work, we wade out to sea. The water is calm and inviting. Little fish dart past our legs. Ten meters out, the water still only comes up to my waist. It's hard to imagine this holds such destructive power. On the drive back, I stare out of the window. The sand rushes by in a blur. Dhanushkodi, lost without a trace, excepting the rubble. Occasionally, a gleam of forgotten railway track runs beside us.

'. . . you know Abdul Kalam . . .' Shanmugam is telling Hans, '. . . the current President of India, he comes from Dhanushkodi . . .'

Kilometer 38129

Kaya returned to the mainland, and traced the semi-submerged coast of Tamil Nadu on her way north to Thanjavur. It rained, and rained. It felt like we were in for another humanity-ending deluge, and instead of riding around on a motorcycle I'd be better served building an ark. The water was sweeping in along the coastal areas. Homes became swimming pools. Fields were flooded and crops destroyed. The region appeared to be sinking. The government claimed to be doing its best. Matter of fact, the government *was* doing what it does best, twiddling its thumbs.

The rain could cause me no annoyance since I began the day's ride wet. Like most Hindu centers, an important part of the Ramanathaswamy Temple ritual is to bathe in the holy water of the *theertham*, or tanks – all twenty-two of them – with each tank bestowing a special blessing. Considering that the waters can absolve you of all sins, make you rich, rid you of curses, tell the future, cure your diseases, give you wisdom, provide you longevity, etcetera, etcetera, if the *theertham* truly works, by the end of the experience you should turn into an immortal god yourself. Having doused myself in water the requisite twenty-two times, I didn't feel any more superior than I otherwise do. I did, however, proclaim myself the most sanctified soul in the world. I've completed the pilgrimage of the four holiest places in India; I've been purified by the Ganga, Yamuna, Saraswati, Narmada; I've visited a few dozen other sin-cleansing sites – Hindu, Muslim, Sikh, Buddhist, Jain, and Christian.

If I don't attain salvation, rest assured the concept doesn't exist.

Salvation or not, there didn't exist much of a road, and what little there was lay mostly submerged under a foot of water. Streams spilled over the culverts, and whenever needed, the locals helped us carry Kaya across the water, accompanied by cheering kids. But when it came to directions, they were of no help. First, there's the language barrier to overcome. Then, there's the matter of coaxing something other than '*nera po*' out of them.

'How do you get to Madurai?'

'*Nera po.*'

'Kumbakonam?'

'*Nera po.*'

'Which way to hell please?'

'*Nera po.*'

For Tamilians, there's apparently only one route between any two points: a straight line. *Nera po*, literally meaning 'go straight', was the standard answer to any directional query and, to emphasize, they'd even raise their hands and point it out. It didn't matter if I was standing on the edge of a cliff or facing the sea. After a number of *nera pos* that led nowhere, we took a few random lefts and rights to reach the desolate ruins of

Gangaikonda Cholapuram, a small town with a big name. In the 12th century this was the capital of the Cholas, the greatest empire of its time in the world. The Byzantines were on the verge of collapse, the future Ottomans had just begun their meteoric rise, and the Qin Dynasty was crumbling under the Mongol onslaught. The Cholas, meanwhile, had developed into the richest empire, and their power took them where no Indian had been before.

For the first time, a Hindu kingdom raised a naval fleet and set out across the seas in conquest. Sri Lanka fell, followed by Burma, Southeast Asia, the islands of Java, Sumatra, and Bali, and finally parts of the Malay Peninsula. Also for the first time, a South Indian king chose to invade the north of the country, leading a victorious army all the way to the Ganges. This was about as natural as a bird migrating north for winter. In the normal course of Indian history, armies have invariably marched in a southerly direction.

Like the military conquests, Hinduism is also a religious concept that swept down from the North, both historically and mythically. The Mahabharata is predominantly an epic of the North. The great kings in the tale are from the North as are the great kingdoms. Rama is the prince of a Northern kingdom, and in Ramayana the South is described as the realm of monkeys and bears – presumably my ancestors. The gods reside in the summits of the Himalayas, and other than a rare vacation or exile down South, it remains their preferred home. The Kumbh Mela, the greatest religious event, is restricted to the northern half of the country. Most importantly, Ganga, the essence of Hinduism, flows exclusively through the North.

So, while Gangaikonda Cholapuram is marked by impressive ruins, its importance is not architectural. The significance is far more profound, for it represents the conquest of the Ganga. It is a symbol of the ascendancy of the South over the North. The very name implies 'the city of the Cholas who captured the Ganga'. For centuries, this region was the center of Hindu culture, and while the rest of the country succumbed to Islam, the temples of Tamil Nadu survived them all. Yet, they couldn't just reject the North. So, they attempted to bring it to the South.

The greatest achievement of any king was to bring the gods to reside in his city, to show his subjects that divinity was on his side. Ample evidence for this can be found in the names given to towns, the designs of temples, and the myths relating to them. Gangaikonda Cholapuram epitomizes this endeavor. After his triumphant march to the Ganga, Rajendra Chola I achieved the improbable. A train of thousands upon thousands of donkeys and bullocks transported large vessels filled with water from the sacred river across the country to this place. The water was then ceremoniously poured into an enormous reservoir created for the purpose.

The Ganga reached the South.

Kaya reached Thanjavur.

Kilometer 38482

Fanoos lashes against Thanjavur city. We are trapped in our hotel room. The Blitz, only instead of fire, it rains water. Streets are abandoned. Buildings shake, windows rattle, and thunder rolls. The pounding is relentless. When the raid ends, people step out from their shelters warily, eyes turned to the skies. They tremble, looking dazed and vacant, victims of shell shock. They know this is only a short break before the next wave of sorties sweep over the city. The streets come alive with a sense of urgency. People scamper, trying to salvage whatever little time is available to them. We do the same.

Kaya follows the washed out roads to the coast town of Pondicherry.

Established in 1673 on the northern shores of Tamil Nadu, Pondicherry was the earliest colony in the Indian Subcontinent and the center of French rule in the country. British India, Portuguese Goa, Dutch Kerala, and French Pondicherry – apparently anybody who owned a boat and knew how to sail it took a nibble at us. During the early days of colonization, the French vied keenly with the English over the possession of India but were soon overwhelmed. By the end of the thrashing, what they were left with was Pondicherry, all of 492 square kilometers, and this they held on to with customary pig-headedness and arrogance – even after the British had departed – only relinquishing Pondicherry in 1954. Grudgingly, I might add. A treaty of cession was signed between the France and India in

1956, but it was ratified by the French Parliament only in 1962, wherein India gained complete sovereignty over the territory.

'Looks like the only land the French ever surrendered without a fight was their own, to the German Blitzkrieg,' I joked to Hans. It didn't go down too well.

Known as La Côte d'Azur de l'Est, the city is a living monument to French culture in India, retaining a distinct French flavor. To this day the police wear berets instead of hats like in the rest of the country. The streets still bear names that I'll never be able to pronounce. Neither can a majority of the populace. They aren't even called streets but Rue this and Rue that. With such wonderful roads, I really don't see what's to rue. It wasn't merely interesting to ride down these foreign *rues* but also a great pleasure, designed as they are along grid patterns, featuring neat sectors and perpendicular lanes. They may not be much good at pitched battles, but when it came to town planning, the French sure had the British beat.

The city was neatly quarantined into two sectors – Ville Blanche 'white town' and Ville Noire 'black town' – and no points for guessing who lived in which half. Running along the seafront, the Ville Blanche still exudes elegance and old-world charm, home to the affluent of Pondicherry. The rues are cobbled and chic, lined by Mediterranean-style mansions and ornamental gardens. The statues staring down are those of Dupleix and Joan of Arc. Monuments consist of the old tribunal Palais du Gouvernement, L'Eglise de Notre Dame des Anges, Le Foyer du Soldat – a hall for French legionnaires – and a graceful war memorial dedicated to the French heroes of the First World War.

When in France, spend as the French do. Kaya stopped for lunch at the Raison de Arte, an appropriately expensive looking place, with ivy replacing the paintwork and a seaward balcony replacing most of the building. It was the kind of establishment where the custard is called a crème brûlée and the steak is something else I'm never going to be able to pronounce. Even if I say it right, I'm still wrong, by dint of my non-French origins.

Regardless, we boldly step in.

'*Bonjour monsieur*,' the smartly clad manager welcomes us.

'*Bonjour*,' I smile back.

'*Ooh, parle-vouz francais*.'

'No, *parle engles, por favor*.'

'Ah, *oui*,' he says. I hear disappointment in his voice. 'Welcome to Raison de Arte.'

'Do a lot of people still speak French here?' Hans asks.

'*Oui*. French is one of the official languages of the region.'

Around thirty thousand people continue to regard French as their mother tongue, and many more understand it. One of the clauses of the Traité de Cession was that French maintains its official status. When the territory was ceded to India, thousands opted for French nationality and moved to France, and more than 10,000 people living in Pondicherry have French passports.

'What about you?' I tease him. 'Which country do you belong to?'

'I am a proper Tamil,' he feigns shock, 'but I also like Pondicherry's French heritage. We still celebrate Bastille Day every 14th of July.'

'Are people aware what it stands for?'

'Everyone knows of the egalitarian revolution.'

The table beside ours is occupied by Julie, a lovely blonde Belgian with mesmerizing blue eyes. She also possesses a gratingly shrill voice, which ensures you don't stay mesmerized. Over the course of a relaxing lunch, we get to know her, and her voice, better.

'I'm staying at Auroville,' she squeaks.

'Man, what a coincidence,' Hans says, 'we are planning to go to the township in the evening. Are you an Aurovilian?'

'I've lived there for eight and a half months now, but I am not a full member. There's a long apprenticeship period before anyone is accepted into the community . . . anyway, I've decided to leave the township, so I guess it doesn't matter.'

'Don't you like it there?'

'I've enjoyed living in Auroville. The community people are friendly. It's beautiful and green and spiritual . . . harmony between human and nature. But . . . I'm disillusioned with the whole future-of-mankind concept.'

'What do you mean?' I ask.

'How much do you know about Auroville?'

'Very little really.'

'Auroville is meant to be an ideal, classless society where everybody is equal . . . but that's just bullshit. Distinctions are visible at every level. It is a dogmatic, class-driven society that has too many rules about not having rules. The members are untrusting of newcomers, and senior members always get things done their way. In a closed society that pretends no such differences exist, it becomes more grating. It is run by a bunch of egotists who are in love with their creation . . . they think they've created a society of equality, and they feel superior to everybody else because they've created this equal society . . . but who do you think does all the menial work around the place?'

I stay quiet, presuming it's a rhetorical question. I presume correctly.

'Cheap local labor, that's who,' she continues after a heavy pause. 'Equality begins here at fifty thousand dollars. That's how much you need if you hope to make a go of it. If you have more than that, you can be more equal. They make a big deal of not using currency, but all they're doing is using credit cards instead. I was shocked to discover that after The Mother passed away, the society was investigated for mismanagement and diversion of funds.'

Auroville calls itself a non-religious organization and claims income tax exemption as a scientific research organization. Suddenly, it was seeking minority status from the Supreme Court on religious grounds.

'Finally what it comes down to is money.'

'You sound like you hate the place,' Hans says.

'But I don't. What really annoys me about Auroville is how much I like the place. It could have been all that it started out to be, and even more, but . . .'

It is a grey and leaky afternoon when we drop in for a tour of the international community: 'an ideal township devoted to an experiment in human unity'. Auroville, the 'City of Dawn', was the vision of Mirra 'The Mother' Alfassa, a devout follower of the philosopher Sri Aurobindo, whose teachings dwelt on new forms of individual and collective societies. Sanctioned by UNESCO, obtaining a land grant and financial assistance from the Government of India, Auroville became a reality on 28th February, 1968, when 5,000 people from 124 countries assembled under a banyan tree in the center of the township. Each carried a handful of their native soil, which was mixed together in a white marble urn shaped like a lotus. So began the ideal. Auroville was meant to be the embryonic center that gave birth to the new human – now we enter the realm of science fiction – a wiser, better, and more advanced intellect, who attained a state of consciousness beyond the mind. Aurobindo called it 'The Supramental'. This was to be a species evolved to the highest rung of creation, as different from humans as humans are from apes.

From where I stand it doesn't appear like they've made much progress. A balding member pants and cusses while pushing his Enfield to the mechanic. A mother drags her unwilling child through the dirt. The cashier at the merchandise boutique needs a calculator to add up the cost of two packets of incense, something that takes me five seconds mentally, and I'm someone who sucks at math. I can't help but feel sorry for them. At least we have the option of saying, 'Hey, we're only human.' They, on the other hand, are 'the chosen ones'. It's hard to be special.

On an earthier plane of thought, the concept was to create the perfect international society. 'Auroville belongs to nobody in particular. Auroville belongs to humanity as a whole,' The Mother had proclaimed. This 'humanity as a whole' was always meant to be a reserved group involving, like Julie said, fifty thousand dollars and membership approvals. Kind of like a country club. For visitors walking in and out of the place, Auroville is no more than a curiosity. And as visitors, we are pointed straight towards the Matrimandir, the inspiration center of Auroville.

Set amidst manicured lawns, the Matrimandir looks like the world's biggest golf ball. One that's gold in color. What's a society without religion doing with a temple? While contending to create a fresh way to look at life, Auroville is a reconstruction of the old order, gold and all. Changing the shape of the building doesn't change what it symbolizes.

In the womb of this giant golf ball/temple/space-station, a large crystal orb rests on a gold base, and a beam of light streams in from the top making the ball emanate a blue light. It was conceived as a symbol of 'the divine's answer to man's inspiration for perfection', which to me sounds uncannily like Bush-speak. By the way, the self-sufficient and non-materialistic Supramental species had the centerpiece of their society designed in Germany by the legendary lens-maker Zeiss at the cost of a cool quarter of a million deutsche marks. Welcome to New Age mysticism and spirituality, where we worship our egos and nothing more.

In the end, Hans and I don't even get to see the orb, and my description of the interiors is plucked from the internet. The state-of-the-art dome is closed for *rain leakage repairs*, a design flaw that's plagued it from start. Perhaps the leaks are symbolic of the holes in the Auroville experiment.

We meet up with Julie along the beach and she leads us to a small fishing community, a cluster of sparse but newly raised houses.

'The houses are part of the Auroville Tsunami Relief and Rehabilitation Program,' Julie points out. 'Since the tsunami, members of Auroville have devoted their energies to help resettle the affected people. They've provided counseling and helped start new cottage industries, including raising funds to buy new nets and boat engines for the fishermen.'

The work still continues.

Close at hand, the debris of the original fishing colony still lingers, a reminder of that fateful morning. At eight in the morning, on 26th December, 2004, while some parts of the world were still celebrating Christmas, the tsunami struck, leading to the biggest natural disaster of our times. Within seconds, ten thousand lives were lost on India's eastern shores, and a million more were homeless. Tamil Nadu was the worst hit. I was holidaying on the west coast when it happened, and didn't even hear about it till the next day. While I lazed on the sands of Om Beach, the members of Auroville had rushed to the scene and set up a relief center, before the government even woke up to the calamity. In those first couple of days, they provided more than two thousand locals with food, water, and shelter.

'Most importantly they gave the people hope,' Julie sighs wistfully.

I can't say I'm impressed by their supramental abilities, but there's little doubt about their humanity.

Kilometer 38841

Kaya swam more than she rode as we entered the temple town of Kancheepuram. During the great Buddhist migration of the 6th century, a monk set out from Kancheepuram for distant China, where he settled down in a little-known monastery to teach the path of Buddha. Troubled by the weak and unhealthy physical condition of the other monks, he began to train them in the art of Varmakkalai, a traditional Tamil style of boxing. Over time, what started off as a daily exercise developed into the most renowned martial arts technique of the world. His name was Bodhidharma, and the monastery is known today as the Shaolin Temple.

I am in the shower at our hotel room in Kancheepuram when I hear a knock on the front door, followed shortly by a stream of excited chatter in a nasal voice I don't recognize. On stepping out of the bathroom, I find a sharply dressed man sitting on the bed, involved in an animated conversation with Hans. His hair is short and afro curly. Clean-shaven, his dark mid-thirties skin shines like polished leather. Seeing me, he stands up and leans across the bed with his hand outstretched.

'Hello, I am Father Kurien,' he says.

'Nice to meet you, Father,' I reply, taking his hand. '. . . uh, is there something we can do for you?'

'Nothing like that, we're having a meeting in the upstairs hall . . . the hotel manager mentioned your friend and I just came by to have a talk.'

'He was telling me about his visit to Italy,' Hans says.

'Yes, I visited the Vatican,' Father K tells me, meanwhile picking up my camera from the bed. 'Are you a photographer?'

'No, it's just a hobby.'

'Very nice camera.' He places it back on the bed and his eyes start roving around the room, until they home in on the weed and rolling paper sitting openly on the corner table. 'What is that?' he asks excitedly.

'That . . . er . . . it's for smoking.' Now I'm concerned. He isn't behaving like any priest I've met.

'It is ganja drug, isn't it?' he says. I turn towards Hans with raised eyebrows. He shrugs his shoulders in confusion. 'What does it do to you?' Father Kurien continues.

'Nothing really.'

'It must have some effect.'

'We don't smoke much . . . and not to get high.' Even as the words leave my mouth I'm sure he's not going to believe the crap that's coming out of it. 'Only at night, to relax after a tiring day.'

'Isn't it bad for your health?' he asks distractedly, and – as if it's the most natural thing for a complete stranger to do – starts poking through Hans's backpack. It's so offhanded I don't know how to react. Is he a cop or something, I begin to doubt. Then again, this sort of behavior isn't unusual in India. We are a wonderfully open and curious people, obtuse when it comes to tact and respecting other's space. 'Does it make you feel sexy?' he asks suddenly.

'Excuse me?'

'Ganja, does it make you . . . you know, get sexy feelings?'

'No . . . it . . . it does the opposite,' I mumble.

'Oh!' he says and plops down on the bed again. 'I saw everywhere in Italy, the white people always having sex and taking drugs. I thought the two are related . . . like Viagra.'

'No, this is not like Viagra.' This guy's no cop or priest. He's a complete whacko.

'Is it true that white people have bigger penis?' he asks turning to Hans.

'I . . . I . . . um . . . no.'

'But you are making better sex, yes?'

And so the conversation goes, for the longest fifteen minutes of the week. Occasionally, he shifts to topics of great import, like how the tsunami has affected the sex lives of people, why it's important for men to hold on to their sperm, and how gays are going against the laws of nature.

'I have to go and look into the arrangements for the meeting,' Father K says finally. 'You must come and join us for a while, it will be interesting,' he insists, stepping out of the room.

'Sure, we'd love to,' I smile and shut the door. 'What the fuck was that all about?' I gasp, turning to Hans.

'How should I know?' Hans defends himself.

'You invited him in.'

'Hah! As if he waited for an invitation. I didn't see you trying to get him out.'

'He was a Catholic priest. I didn't want to offend your religious sentiments. At first I thought you were having a serious discussion.'

'Man, that guy . . . if he's a priest, then I can become the pope.'

'How come you attract all these weirdos?' I accuse.

'It's your country that's full of weirdos,' he retorts.

Hans sparks up a joint and we sit down with our journals, waiting for the rain to let up. An hour has passed when we're disturbed by a knock on the door. We look at each other, and I can see the same thought passing through his mind. Oh no!

'Quick, hide the shit,' I whisper to Hans and step up to the door. 'Who is it?' I ask, knowing the answer quite well.

It's Father K and he isn't alone this time, accompanied by a plain, snub-nosed and square-faced woman in a blue sari. 'This is Dhanalakshmi,' he introduces, stepping past me into the room. 'She is helping me with the meeting.'

'*Vannakam*, please sit down,' I say politely, now that they're already inside the room.

She smiles and sits down beside him on the bed. Hans and I remain standing. We don't have much choice since that's all the furniture our cell-like accommodation has. Is he a pimp? I chide myself for the inappropriate thought, but this guy is confusing me. At least with Hindu priests there's no ambiguity in what they want.

'I was telling Dhanalakshmi about you boys,' Father K says, 'and even she thinks it is a good idea for you to come to the meeting.'

'Really, what's the meeting about Father?'

'You're not listening to me then, I already told you,' he rebukes me. 'I'm helping with an NGO, for education of homosexuals and sex workers.'

'How can we be of help?'

'It will be big boost for us if you come and meet them,' he addresses Hans.

'Why me?' Hans asks in panic.

'They will listen to a white person. Who knows more about sex than you?'

'But I don't know anything about . . . what you are doing.'

'What is there to know? You tell them prostitution and same-sex relationship is wrong. It is a sin against god and they will all get AIDS if they don't stop.'

'But . . .'

'It will mean a lot.'

'We are glad to help,' I butt in. 'When does the meeting begin?'

'In one hour. It's on the third floor.'

'We'll be there.'

'Good, that's settled then,' he says, getting up to leave. Dhanalakshmi smiles. She hasn't said a word the entire time. 'I will come and call you boys,' he nods in parting.

'Sure, sure.'

'Are you mad?' Hans hisses at me when I close the door.

'No, but I think he is.'

'How can he be involved with educating sex workers? He probably does more harm than good. I can't go and say such rubbish . . .'

'Which is why we're leaving right now.'

'It's still raining outside,' Hans grumbles.

'Which would you rather face – him or the storm?'

Sneaking out of the hotel, we step into the heavy downpour.

LEG TWENTY ONE

Will You Never Change?

THREE HOURS AFTER escaping the sewage-drowned streets of Madras, Kaya rolled across the state line separating Tamil Nadu and Andhra Pradesh. I'd convinced myself we would leave the clouds behind on crossing the border, even picturing the clear demarcation between grey and blue. But nature recognizes no borders. And the clouds on the other side looked greyer.

This was it – the last leg. From here I was homeward bound.

Kaya's first stop on this final stretch is the Venkateswara Temple, on the seventh peak of the Tirupati Hills. Attracting around fifty thousand visitors each day, it is the second richest religious institution in the world after the Vatican – unconfirmed reports claim it's moved to the top spot. And it makes perfect sense that Tirupati is so popular. While most of the sacred places I've visited thus far promised a good death, Tirupati offers a good life. Lord Venkateshwara is the granter of boons, for the right price, of course.

Venkateswara is our family deity, and I've visited Tirupati on more occasions than I care to remember. As a child I had no option but to accompany my parents, an event I looked forward to with as much enthusiasm as a visit to the principal's office. How excited can you get over a weekend involving lousy food, jostling crowds, and waking up at a most ungodly hour? Once I turned sixteen though, they gave me a choice. I haven't returned since.

The climb to the summit is steep. Thousands of devotees choose to do it by foot as a symbol of their devotion. The air echoes to the screams of 'Govinda, Goooovinda' as they praise the lord for the struggle. At the top I am greeted by a painfully familiar sight, the long snaking line of pilgrims not rich enough to take the shortcut to salvation. It is cold, and there's rain in the air. That wasn't going to deter them.

'Hey man, why is everybody bald?' Hans asks.

'Shaving the head symbolizes surrendering your ego to god. It is seen as the supreme sacrifice and is rewarded by good fortune.'

Hundreds of expert barbers crouch over wooden platforms outside the shrine and in tonsure halls. Devotees form long queues, waiting for their turn. When the time comes, they quietly take a seat on the platform and bow down their heads. It's a lot like sheep shearing. By the end of the day, a few thousand pilgrims will have donated their hair, making this the greatest congregation of bald pates in the world. As a child I lost my hair to god, for reasons I never understood. Every subsequent visit I made my mum swear it wouldn't happen again. I didn't necessarily trust her though, and only when we began our descent from the hill would I let myself relax.

The shave is a service provided for free by the temple authorities – the least they can do since the hair makes the temple around 300 crores annually. The much sought after hair is auctioned to the highest bidder, usually German pharmaceutical companies and American wigmakers. Recently this humble hair became embroiled in a big scandal when Orthodox Jews discovered where the hair for their wives' wigs was coming from. Rabbis in Israel went on a rant that wearing wigs made from ritually tonsured hair is extremely un-kosher and akin to idol worship. The sales figures have gone up since then. Lots of un-kosher wigs were bought so that they could be burned in protest against buying un-kosher wigs.

Another moneymaking venture at Tirupati is the sale of god-sanctified *laddus*. While the temple generates a few crores from the sales of *laddus,* they squeeze out a couple more crores from the sale of *laddu* covers. Yes, *covers*: the small plastic bags in which we carry home the blessed sweets. And we aren't talking about fancy boxes and artistic gift wrapping here, just a flimsy plastic cover in which to place the fist-sized *laddu*. That's two rupees a bag please – and look! – it even comes with the temple logo.

All this, though, is pocket change compared to the roughly eighteen billion rupees a year generated through donations. That's more than the GDP of some countries. Back in the day, the kings of empires endowed our temples with opulent donations. Today the kings of Bollywood and Big Business do the same. An actor can gain more publicity from making a substantial offering at Tirupati than by performing well in his next role. Thanks to their generosity, the Lord Venkateswara possesses a jewelry collection that makes the Queen of England look like a cheap tart. Obviously, the common man also wants to make his contribution to the wellbeing of god, and his money is as good as anybody's, even if he doesn't have as much. A huge white sack, looking a lot like an oversized punching bag, hangs at the entrance to the sanctum, and it fills up faster than an Irish Pub at happy hour. From loose change to wads of hundred rupee bills, as long as it's money, it's all good. Few banks in the world handle such large sums of money in hard cash, and the temple maintains a team of employees for the express purpose of counting and sorting the money as it pours in.

My poor mother – I've always given her a hard time. And not one to squander an opportunity, I started with the very act of being born. Having entangled myself with the umbilical cord, the doctors were forced to perform an emergency caesarian – this is before caesarians became cool – and it was touch and go for a while. My mother's life was in the balance that day along with mine. Fortunately for my mother, she survived. Unfortunately for her, so did I. Thanks to the grace of god, I lived – a move he must sorely regret now. On recovering, my mother made a visit to the temple and dropped 10,000 rupees into the bag, a large sum of money in 1979, and one that my father could little afford. He's another person who regrets I made it.

For my mom, it was the birth of a child: Please, god, save my baby and I'll give you more money than my husband can afford. The farmer begs: Oh, great Lord, see that my crops are successful this year and I'll make an offering at your shrine. A mother prays: Govinda, make sure my son gets his American visa and I'll donate a diamond ring to you. The business man cuts a deal: Venkateswara, keep the Income Tax Officers off my back and I'll split my ill-gotten wealth you. We've turned god into the king of kickbacks. In Hindu epics, you hear of duty and self-sacrifice, of great penance and unshakable devotion, before anyone received a boon from god. The protagonists never bribed god with money for his help. You don't hear the warrior Arjuna say, 'Shiva, I'll buy you a wonderful Cartier diamond brooch if you hand me your weapons of mass destruction.' Life based on moral codes was the path to god. Not anymore. Today a demand draft will suffice.

I prefer Santa Claus. At least he expects people to be good.

My lasting memories of Tirupati are not of god or his gold-plated roof, but of the devotees queuing up for an audience with the lord, in the thousands. Sometimes these lines extended for miles – the unwell and the crippled, infants and grandparents, men, women, and children – a crush of humanity with one word on their lips: 'Govinda'. They waited through the night – out in the open, cold, and sometimes wet – and then most of the following day, under a searing sun. I admired their resolve. I dreaded having to join them. And I never had to, not once. We were the favored ones – brushing past those in queue, breezing into the corridors of faith – but it wasn't a privilege earned by extra-superior devotion, rather bought by money and influence. Over the years, relief that I didn't have to wait slowly gave way to guilt, to the point where I found myself avoiding the eyes of those we passed by.

We strolled inside and performed our prayers, spending a lot more time in the presence of the deity than the 'general public', who are pushed along after a second's glimpse. When we stepped out a few hours later, I saw the same tired and expectant faces still waiting their turn. And it wasn't just my family. The privileged were in the hundreds, holding on to their 'special tickets'. Apparently, even at god's doorstep all that mattered was money. He was no different from an airline, a few extra bucks for a first-class ticket got you an easy entry and better service.

Hans and I wander around the town for a brief while. There are a lot more hotels and restaurants than I remember. I'm guessing the food isn't as terrible as before. That's about all the change I notice. The drizzle turns into a torrent. The faithful still stand in line. The privileged still scurry past them. I look out at the gold-plated dome of the sanctum. Then we turn around and go back down the hill. I don't have enough faith to stand in line. I have enough faith not to cut the line.

Kilometer 39449

Kaya finally left the rain behind and headed deeper into Andhra. We rumbled through a dry, boulder-strewn landscape. The circle was nearing completion. The odometer edged towards 40,000 as I rode into my hometown, approaching the gates of my ancestral home. This is where my personal history began, at Tadipatri, a crowded and dusty town in the industrial region of Rayalaseema, a land of searing heat and soaring tempers, a place of fragile egos, the maintenance of which involves a lot of moustache twirling. Rayalaseema is best known for spicy food and blood feuds. Instead of Montagues and Capulets, we've got Reddys versus even more Reddys, and the killing is never as glamorous as Baz Luhrmann shootouts. Death is invariably gruesome, involving blunt sickles, crude bombs, and burning tires. Most people can't remember why they hate each other, but if you took away this simple pleasure there really wouldn't be much point to their lives.

My family isn't involved in any silly feuds. We indulge in Rayalaseema's other nefarious activity, politics. And politics in Rayalaseema can be as spectacular as freedom in Iraq. We have a rather peculiar understanding of elections here, where rather than garner support for our party, we think up convoluted schemes to undermine the opposition. This involves anything from the abduction and swapping of ballot boxes, pouring ink into them, scaring voters away and casting their votes for them.

Everybody in town knows our family, and they regard us with great respect. Whether they feel the same way behind closed doors is up for debate. Except that no one is bold enough to debate it. As a child it was family tradition to celebrate Dussehra in Tadipatri, my most memorable holidays, a grand family reunion and the rare opportunity to meet my cousins, the brothers and sisters

I didn't have. Sadly, the politics turned uglier and the violence more personal. First it was death threats, and then random bomb blasts. If it wasn't a would-be-assassin knocking at the door, it was the police. In my twelfth year the Dussehra celebrations had to be called off due to security concerns. The next year was the same, and the year after. Soon there wasn't even any talk about it. Holidays in Tadipatri were relegated to memories in family albums. The violence has died out since, but so has the tradition, and in the last decade I've been here just once.

Despite the years of absence I found my way home unerringly, a heightened sense of excitement as we drew nearer, with Kaya finally stopping in front of the arsenal.

'Hey man, I haven't seen this much security at the Reichstag,' Hans says, staring at the ring of gun-toting men around the house. 'What's in there?'

'My uncle,' I reply reverentially.

And he's waiting for us when we enter the house. As a child my uncle visited me in my nightmares. A hulking man, with thick handlebar moustache and a thundering voice, in my febrile imaginings he bore an uncanny resemblance to the fearsome characters our mythologies are so full of. While no longer afraid of *Rakshasas*, I still tremble on seeing my uncle.

'Hi *mama*,' I squeak.

'Look at how shabby you fellows are. Will you never change?' he roars. 'Go upstairs and have a bath immediately. And please put on clean clothes when you come down, I've invited the press over.'

It feels good to be home.

Stepping into our designated room we find a new set of clothes laid out on the bed, size M shirts and elastic-drawn pants that fit us perfectly. While Hans is in the shower, a maid knocks on the door to inform me that the barber is waiting for us downstairs. My wonderful aunt is making sure I make the right impression. It's all a bit unnecessary. The press wouldn't have noticed me if I'd dressed up in a gorilla suit and beat my chest in their faces. They are too enamored by Hans. My only purpose at the meeting is to act as a translator.

I'd added Tadipatri to the journey for entirely personal reasons, so it comes as a surprise when, after the press meet, my uncle tells me I should visit the 16th century Rama Lingeswara and Venkata Ramana temples. Hah, who knew there's something worth looking at in Tadipatri? As it turns out, the black granite temples are amongst the most exquisitely sculpted monuments I've seen in the country. They stand three kilometers from my house, but in all my earlier visits, not once did anyone mention the temples, nor did I ever visit them.

How typically Gen X – or is it Gen Y that I belong to? – that it's taken me ten months and forty thousand kilometers to discover something that's been sitting in my backyard all along.

Unbelong to Belong

40050 . . . 40060 . . . 40070 . . . Kaya's odometer ticked along as she headed away from Tadipatri, and then we were there. 40,075 kilometers, the length of the equator. We'd done it. Kaya and I had traveled around the world in India. I let out a throat-tearing victory cry. My heart swelled. Joy, relief, pride, satisfaction, all of them having their say, but mainly it was joy – genuine, unbridled joy. I kissed Kaya, hugged Hans, and burst out in another shriek. Then, even as I got back on Kaya, I felt all that positive emotion wash away, leaving me with a sense of emptiness.

I'm not sure what I'd expected. Fireworks, a twenty-one gun salute, a victory parade to celebrate my awesomeness, a gaggle of Victoria's Secret models throwing themselves at me. Perhaps a transformation from troubled pothead to wise sage. At the very least the comfort of knowing I was a better person than the day I set out, all those months ago. But no, none of it played out. I felt no different from the Amit of forty thousand kilometers past. I didn't feel more Indian. All I felt, for a long time, was disappointment, and anger, that I hadn't found what I was looking for. Who stole my India?

The very moment I'd set out to discover 'my India' was the instant the quest was destined to fail. For my India didn't exist. Except in my imagination. And I was the thief who stole it from there by making this journey. It took me a long time to realize that the India I envisioned was of my own making, and in all likelihood no other Indian saw her as I did. India is an idea. Well, considering every Indian has his own idea of what India is, it's more like a billion ideas, explaining why the country suffers a severe case of multiple-personality disorder. And as individual ideas go, she's a beautiful thing – at worst, harmless. But as a collective, the idea is often corrupted to the point where I fear her.

India is the individual old woman who gave me shelter from the storm. India is the collective government that drives the disenfranchised out of their homes. She is the individual mechanic who worked on Kaya for karma points. She is the collective Kar Sevaks who incite hatred over false gods. She is the individual bicyclist who restored my faith. She is the collective priesthood that steals all hope. She is the individual bus conductor who took care of Disha. She is the collective chauvinism that subjugates women. She is the individual Mahatma who taught me pacifism. She is the collective patriotism that condones military excesses. She is the individual fisherman who saved my life. She is the collective greed that hounds the poor to death. She is the individual tanner who shared his *beedi* with me. She is the collective religion that prejudices us.

This journey began as a quest to belong, to earn my Indian stripes, but if nothing else, my travels showed me that we are better humans when we don't view the world through the eyes of a group. Religion, ethnicity, class, and nationality – each one of them in the end act as identities of overt exclusion. Belonging to one is to exclude the other, while being excluded from the other. The truly accepting never question who you are. To the point of exception, all I experienced on the road was kindness, with help invariably at hand whenever I found myself in trouble. That help always came in the form of an individual, not a national agency or a religious institute. And help never asked me if I was Hindu or Indian. On the occasion that identity did come into question, it was never for assistance, but invariably as a tool of exclusion – a temple I couldn't visit, a border I couldn't cross, a place I couldn't enter.

As a rule these social identities inherently demand pride in belonging – proud to be Muslim, proud to be Indian, proud to be Tamil – fostering a sense of superiority over those on the outside, a sense of superiority that entitles the urbanite to brush aside the tribal dweller, the Telugu to suppress the Kashmiri, the Hindu to disenfranchise the Muslim. The way I see it, nothing I've ever done makes me believe that I'm superior to anyone else, nothing I've ever done entitles me to profit at the expense of anyone else. Besides, I've decided I don't need the burden of being special. I prefer to be me, without any labels, and I know now that I don't need to wear a badge of Indianness to belong. I am a part of India. A part of me is India. As for the rest, perhaps I'll find out further down the road.

Afterword

Having finished reading the book, and hopefully enjoying it in the process, you might be wondering if this tale is really real, or is it more like Hollywood's 'based on a true story'. I'm not sure if there exists a precise formula to gauge when a book crosses over from non-fiction to fiction, but having taken certain liberties with the characters and the chronology, I'd grudgingly classify *Who Stole My India?* as a novel, and stack it in the fiction section. Having said that, everything you've read on these pages I've experienced on the road. All the encounters and characters in this book are real, including the most unlikely of them.

Acknowledgments

Left to myself, *Who Stole My India?* would have remained nothing more than an idea, floating about in the dark, smoke-filled recesses of my mind. That it hasn't is to the credit of the wonderful people who make up my life, and I'd like to take this opportunity to thank them. No one has played a more important role in the process than my parents, Sumana and Krishna Reddy, from tolerating my crazy schemes to encouraging the more practical ones like the writing course from Australia. Thanks mum and dad, and sorry for all the disappointments. My lovely, and troublingly patient wife, Alison, who has probably read the book more times than I have, painstakingly correcting my spellings and making sure I've used my apostrophes appropriately. The maps, the formatting, and the design are all her. The other important influence in my life is Hashim, my friend and fellow dreamer. He is the inspiration for Kaya Dreams, my mentor and companion on the road. Thank you, Captain, for always believing in me.

A huge chasm separates wanting to write a book from actually writing one (that you're not embarrassed by), and in my case some very special people helped in bridging that gap. Professor Antony Jach by revealing that the inspiration needs to be accompanied by large dollops of deliberation, Peta Murray by showing me how to tap into the creative reservoir, and Di Morrissey for teaching me the value of even the minutest detail. Gallantry awards for Benjamin de Buen and Xavier Toby for reading the painful early drafts of the manuscript, and whose feedback and criticism shaped the book into its current form. And I haven't forgotten Michael Falk and Samantha. Without all you guys, the original tome that rivalled *War and Peace* — in verbosity only, not beauty — would never have gotten leaner. Cheers mates! My regards to Robert Sessions at Penguin Australia for believing in the potential of *Who Stole My India?*.

Who Stole My India? attempts to take on some pretty weighty issues, and the early drafts of the book were driven by a lot of passion and very little wisdom. That the published version addresses the political and social conflict in a more analytical fashion is thanks to the remarkable professors at Georgetown Public Policy Institute, especially Gillette Hall, Jennifer Tobin, and Andreas Kern. Thank you for knocking some sense into me.

Finally, thank you all for reading.